British Foreign Policy

British Foreign Policy

Tradition, Change and Transformation

Edited by

MICHAEL SMITH
Coventry Polytechnic

STEVE SMITH
University of East Anglia

BRIAN WHITE
North Staffordshire Polytechnic

London
UNWIN HYMAN
Boston   Sydney   Wellington

Published by the Academic Division of
Unwin Hyman Ltd
15/17 Broadwick Street,
London W1V 1FP

Allen & Unwin Inc.,
8 Winchester Place, Winchester, Mass. 01890, USA

Allen & Unwin (Australia) Ltd,
8 Napier Street, North Sydney, NSW 2060, Australia

Allen & Unwin (New Zealand) Ltd in association with the Port
Nicholson Press Ltd,
60 Cambridge Terrace, Wellington, New Zealand

First published in 1988

British Library Cataloguing in Publication Data

British foreign policy: tradition, change and transformation.
1. Great Britain – Foreign relations – 1945-
I. Smith, Michael, *1947, Apr 19.*
II. Smith, Steven M.   III. White, Brian, *1947-*
327.41   DA589.8
ISBN 0–04–327080–8
ISBN 0–04–327081–6 Pbk

Library of Congress Cataloging-in-Publication Data

British foreign policy.
Bibliography: p.
Includes index.
1. Great Britain – Foreign relations – 1945-
2. Great Britain – Foreign relations administration.
I. Smith, Michael, 1947-   .   II. Smith, Steve, 1952-
III. White, Brian.
JX1543.B75 1988   327.41   87–18721
ISBN 0–04–327080–8 (alk. paper)

Typeset in 10 on 12 point Bembo by Nene Phototypesetters Ltd,
Northampton and printed in Great Britain by
Billing & Sons Ltd., London and Worcester

Contents

Notes on Contributors

David Allen Senior Lecturer in Politics, Department of European Studies, Loughborough University. He is the author of a number of articles on European foreign policy-making and the European Community, and edited (with R. Rummel and W. Wessels) *European Political Co-operation* (1982) and (with A. Pijpers) *European Foreign Policy Making and the Arab-Israeli Conflict* (1985).

Michael Clarke Lecturer in Politics at the University of Newcastle upon Tyne. He was educated at the University College of Wales, Aberystwyth and lectured at the University of Manchester before taking up his present post. He has published widely on foreign policy and defence issues.

Christopher Farrands Senior Lecturer in International Relations at Trent Polytechnic. He was educated at the University College of Wales, Aberystwyth and the London School of Economics before taking up his present post. He specializes in West European foreign and foreign economic policy and has published several articles in these areas.

Christopher Hill Lecturer in the Department of International Relations, London School of Economics and Political Science. His doctoral thesis was on British foreign policy between 1938 and 1941 and he has published widely in the general area of foreign policy analysis. His recent publications include the edited book *National Foreign Policies and European Political Cooperation* (1983) and 'Reagan and Thatcher: the sentimental alliance', *World Outlook*, vol. 1, no. 2 (Winter 1986).

Richard Little Senior Lecturer in the Department of Politics, University of Lancaster. He was previously a lecturer at the Open University where he helped to prepare the course on World Politics. His publications include *Intervention: External Involvement in Civil Wars* (1975) and (with R. D. McKinlay) *Global Problems and World Order* (1986).

Tony McGrew Lecturer in Government at the Open University. He previously taught at Liverpool Polytechnic. He has edited (with M. Wilson) *Decision-Making: Approaches and Analysis* (1982) and (with J. Simpson) *The International Nuclear Non-Proliferation System: Challenges and Choices* (1984) and authored (with R. Maidment) *The American Political Process* (1986).

Michael Smith Senior Lecturer in International Relations at Coventry Polytechnic. His special research interests are in foreign policy analysis, British–American and European–American relations. He has written many articles, edited several volumes on United States–European Community relations and was the author of *Western Europe and the United States: the Uncertain Alliance* (1984).

Steve Smith Senior Lecturer in International Relations at the University of East Anglia. He has also taught at the State University of New York at Albany. He has published extensively in the fields of foreign policy analysis and nuclear strategy and is currently completing a study of the major theories of foreign policy behaviour.

Roger Tooze Principal Lecturer in International Relations at North Staffordshire Polytechnic. He has also taught at the London School of Economics and the University of Southern California. He has published widely in the field of international political economy and is currently editing (with J. Maclean) *The International Political Economy of Knowledge and Information*.

John Vogler Principal Lecturer in International Relations at Liverpool Polytechnic. He has published on international theory and technological change and contributed to Open University course material. His current research interest is the International Telecommunications Union with special reference to North–South issues and the management of satellite communications.

Brian White Senior Lecturer in International Relations at North Staffordshire Polytechnic. He has published widely on foreign policy analysis and British foreign and defence policy. He edited (with M. Clarke) *An Introduction to Foreign Policy Analysis* (1981) and is currently completing a study of the British contribution to East–West détente.

Preface

This is the third book produced by a group of British international relations scholars most of whom have met regularly to discuss aspects of foreign policy analysis for more years than they care to remember! The first group product, *An Introduction to Foreign Policy Analysis*, edited by Michael Clarke and Brian White, offered an approach to the foreign policy analysis literature for students new to the subject. This was followed by *Foreign Policy Implementation*, edited by Steve Smith and Michael Clarke, which broke new ground to the extent that it sought to illuminate a hitherto neglected area of foreign policy theory by a series of case studies.

This book on British foreign policy, perhaps the most ambitious to date, has nevertheless followed the established practices of previous efforts. The overall concept of the book was agreed by the group. Contributors then wrote drafts of each chapter which were commented upon extensively by the other contributors at a series of meetings. Final drafts were then submitted to the editors. Given the scope of the project and the number of contributors, editorial functions were divided. Steve Smith was managing editor of the project as a whole, while Michael Smith and Brian White were responsible for the academic content and co-ordination of the chapters. The editors are grateful to the contributors for their hard work and commitment to the project over a long gestation period and to the ESRC and BISA for financial support.

June 1987   Michael Smith
                                                             Steve Smith
                                                             Brian White

Introduction

It could be argued that by the late 1970s a decisive transition had occurred in British foreign policy, by which the old tenets of Britain's role in the international system had been replaced with a new set of realities. Much of the existing literature on British foreign policy dates from the early or mid-1970s and one of its central assumptions is that entry into the European Community, along with the strategic withdrawal from East of Suez, had completed a once-and-for-all adjustment to life as a secondary or regional actor in world affairs. Along with this adjustment, it seemed that policy-makers themselves had brought their images of Britain's appropriate role into line with the facts of the situation: despite the oft-noted 'cognitive lag' between perceptions and changing circumstances, by the end of the 1970s it could legitimately be supposed that a new normality characterized British foreign policy. Notwithstanding the failure of proposals for the fundamental reform of the foreign policy machine – arising from the Berrill Report of 1977 on Britain's overseas representation – it was evident that policy had changed and that the practice of policy-making had changed along with it.

The 1980s have demonstrated that, despite changes in its substance and formation, British foreign policy retains immense analytical and practical significance. Two features in particular bear out this judgement. First, it is apparent that assumptions of a once-and-for-all transformation are questionable: there are strong elements of continuity both in the substance of policy and in the assumptions of policy-makers. Although the Falklands War of 1982 can be seen as an isolated and freakish throwback, it undoubtedly provides evidence of continuing power-political concerns beyond the European theatre in British foreign policy. Such concerns have been underlined by the revitalization of strategic and ideological preoccupations in the context of the 'New Cold War' and the 'Thatcher-Reagan axis'. It is equally apparent, though, that such revivals of old-style foreign policy have taken place in a transformed world. The adjustment of British foreign policy did not end with the 'retreat to Europe' in the early 1970s; in common with other advanced industrial countries, Britain has felt the impact of inter-dependence and transnationalism, creating problems both for policy-makers and the policy process. Although these conditions are at their highest stage in Western Europe, they permeate Britain's relations with other societies on a global scale. The major axes of British involvement with the outside world – East–West, North–South, West–West – are thus arenas of pervasive change and often fundamental dilemmas.

These twin features – of tradition and transformation – lie at the core of the analysis offered in this book. The contributors are not so much concerned to recount the story of British foreign policy during the 1970s and 1980s as to identify broad patterns of continuity and change and to explore their implications for policies and policy-makers. The approach is explicitly analytical since it is part of the purpose of this book to locate the study of British foreign policy in the evolution of foreign policy analysis itself. In this way, it is hoped that both an awareness of the changing pattern of British foreign policy and a sensitivity to the ways in which it can be approached for the purpose of analysis can be communicated to the reader.

In approaching these analytical tasks, the contributions focus on three interrelated components of British foreign policy: settings, themes and arenas. The first of these, settings, encapsulates a focus on broad patterns and influences in the analysis and practice of British foreign policy. Chapter 1 thus reviews the ways in which British foreign policy can be and has been analysed, and locates them within the evolution of foreign policy analysis more gener-ally. Chapter 2 addresses the problems raised by the historical background to British foreign policy, as it constrains and is interpreted by policy-makers. Chapter 3 assesses the relationship between broad social forces, the role of the state and the changing nature of British foreign policy. Finally, Chapter 4 pursues the problems raised by the evolution of the policy process itself and relates it to some of the broader patterns of change identified by earlier chapters.

The second part of the book addresses itself to major underlying themes of foreign policy. More specifically, it is designed to identify tensions arising from the pursuit of sometimes conflicting principles or commitments and to link them to Britain's changing position in the international order. A particular concern is the relationship between the pursuit of national objectives, especially those surrounding national security in the military and the economic spheres, and the imperatives of the international order. In Chapter 5, the analysis centres on defence policy and national security, while in Chapter 6 the emphasis is on economic concerns, although both chapters uncover the linkages and interpenetrations between the two areas.

The third part of the book takes the analysis further, by focusing on the substance of British foreign policy in a variety of arenas. Here, the emphasis is on patterns of behaviour and adjustment to changing circumstances, in the light of the broad themes explored in Parts 1 and 2. Thus, Chapter 7 assesses the changing role of Britain in relation to East–West conflict and the superpowers, stressing considerations of power, influence and diplomacy. Chapter 8 takes a contrasting yet complementary line of attack by analysing Britain's entanglement in Western Europe and evaluating the extent to which British foreign policy has become essentially European or regional in its focus. Chapter 9 examines another major axis of Britain's international involvement, that of North–South relations, with particular reference to the ways in which Britain has become part of a broad northern coalition in debates about the world economic and political order. Chapter 10 takes as its central focus the British position within the advanced industrial arena and assesses the ways in which exposure to interdependence and transnational relations conditions the range of responses and strategies available to policy-makers.

Throughout the book, the contributors are concerned not only to expose the continuities and changes affecting British foreign policy itself, but also to explore the perceptions and responses of policy-makers. This aim is coupled with that of seeing what can be gained from an awareness of changing analytical approaches to foreign policy. Chapter 11 is designed to act both as an overview of the broad findings produced by earlier chapters and as an evaluation of the ways in which theory and practice can be brought into a fruitful relationship. Whilst no claim is made here for a fundamental advance either in the understanding of British foreign policy or of foreign policy analysis itself, it is hoped that the interaction of these two concerns can provide food for thought both for analysts and practitioners and that the juxtaposition of the two strands can enhance the student's appreciation of both perspectives.

PART I

Settings

1 The Analytical Background

Approaches to the Study of British Foreign Policy

STEVE SMITH and MICHAEL SMITH

Attempts to analyse British foreign policy confront two moving and often ill-defined targets. In the first place, the evolution, the nature and the possible future course of British policy have given rise to recurrent debate and the analyst must, therefore, allow for the contestability of much of his or her subject-matter. Secondly, the development of foreign policy analysis as an academic discipline has been influenced by many of the debates about methods and approaches that have accompanied the growth of international studies within the social sciences. The aim of this chapter is to outline some of the approaches that have been taken to the study of British foreign policy and to relate these to changing perspectives in the broader field of foreign policy analysis. Substantive issues in British foreign policy itself will be the concern of later chapters in this book; here, the intention is to establish the context within which any study of those issues in the late 1980s must take place.

The first element in this scene-setting exercise is a review of methods and levels of analysis. In respect of methods, the study of foreign policy has displayed a continuing tension between approaches that could broadly be described as 'historical' and 'scientific' – the former starting from the historical record and deriving from it conclusions about policy, the latter taking a more theoretical and self-consciously systematic line of attack. Such a dichotomy, though, is rather misleading. In fact, it might be more appropriate to think of approaches in foreign policy studies as occupying points on a spectrum. At one end of the spectrum would be those studies that offer little more than a narrative of events, on the assumption that 'the facts speak for themselves'. At the other end would be found the products of 'pure science', with an emphasis on testable hypotheses and on the quantification of evidence. The vast majority of foreign policy studies would fall between these two points, more or less 'historical' or 'scientific' in their orientation (the flavour of such methodological debates in the context of British foreign policy can be found in several academic exchanges: see Barber, 1975, 1978 and White, 1977; Berridge, 1980, 1981, 1982 and Smith, S., 1982; Cable, 1981 and Frankel, 1981).

Diversity of analytical methods in foreign policy studies has gone alongside diversity of levels of analysis. Broadly, it is possible to conceive of three contrasting levels of analysis in most investigations of foreign policy. First, there is what can be termed the 'domestic process' level, which emphasizes the origins of foreign policy in the internal workings of states and societies, both within and outside government. Secondly, there is the level of the 'international setting', with its emphasis on the external environment within which national policies are pursued and on the constraints that arise from it. Finally, there is the level of 'cross-national comparison', which stresses the diversity of national policies but also the similarity of many underlying issues and policy responses. Once again, it is more appropriate to talk of differences of emphasis and of varying combinations of these levels rather than of sharp divisions between them; any rounded analysis of foreign policy is likely to contain a measure of each.

No study of foreign policy in the late 1980s, though, can confine itself simply to issues of analytical procedure or levels of analysis. Although the 'great debates' between adherents of classical or scientific methods, or between scholars stressing the uniqueness and the comparability of national experiences, have played a major part in the evolution of foreign policy studies, they have also been permeated by assumptions about the broader nature of the international scene which have a quasi–ideological tinge. In other words, as became apparent during the 1970s, it is possible for scholars and policy-makers to disagree not only about how and at what level foreign policy should be studied, but also about the nature of the international world in which foreign policy has its place. For the purposes of the argument here, it is possible to identify two schools of thought about the changing nature of the international arena: the 'traditionalist' and the 'transformationalist'. The 'traditionalist' or 'state-centric realist' perspective argues that there is a profound continuity in international affairs and that in the 1980s just as in the 1880s they centre on a competition for power and security between sovereign states. On the other hand, a 'transformationalist' perspective rests on the assumption that much – if not everything – has changed. In this view, states and their concerns are only part of a much broader and more diverse reality which encompasses a host of participants, issues and interactions, affecting and constraining states but often neither controlled nor even strongly influenced by them.

Such differences of 'world view' provide a vital part of the background against which British foreign policy should be assessed at the end of the twentieth century. Both the 'traditionalist' and the 'transformationalist' perspectives carry with them a set of assumptions about the world in which British foreign policy is formulated and implemented, about the content of foreign policy and about its conduct. The remainder of this chapter will address itself first to the analytical approaches that can be identified in the existing studies of British foreign policy and then to the broader issue of 'tradition', versus 'transformation', with the aim of exposing their major implications and interconnections.

The Study of British Foreign Policy

As argued earlier, it is possible to conceive of the methods by which British foreign policy might be studied as points on a spectrum ranging from 'pure history' to 'pure science'. As might be expected, there is a good deal of historical writing which deals with Britain's place in the world and which aims to provide an effective narrative of events. One major category of this writing is biographies or memoirs – a valuable source of insights into specific issues or events, but one with inherent limitations on the extent to which the assessments or conclusions can be given a more general analytical relevance (see, for example, Eden, 1960; Macmillan, 1971, 1972, 1973; Wilson, 1971; Bullock, 1985). More detached treatments can provide a somewhat broader context, and much of the writing on Britain's role in the developing Cold War of the late 1940s and early 1950s presents not only a narrative but also an interpretation that moves some way towards more explicit analysis (Barker, 1983; Young, 1984). The emphasis, though, is still – and for very good reasons – on the thoughts and writings of those who made the decisions, and the value of such studies lies less in analysis than on the extent of the evidence cited and the coherence of the explanation of decision-makers' perceptions and motivations that is offered. The approach, that is to say, is essentially inductive, constructing explanations from evidence and using as evidence the explanations of behaviour offered by those who were involved in decisions or actions.

If the 'history' end of the spectrum is well populated, the same cannot be said of the 'science' end in respect of British foreign policy. Very little work has been done that develops systematic theories or testable hypotheses about the formulation or the conduct of Britain's external relations. One interesting attempt was that of McKinlay and Little (1978), which related the allocation of Britain's bilateral aid to an explicit and formal model of foreign policy criteria. As might be expected, the attractions of such formal or quantitative approaches depend upon the availability of suitable quantitative (or quantifiable) data. Thus aid policy and defence policy, for example, lend themselves to 'hard' quantitative treatment, but the connection with foreign policy in its more general sense is rarely made.

Much of the extant writing about British foreign policy is thus to be found in the middle of the spectrum; it takes the form either of broadly historical or institutional approaches with an awareness of analytical concepts and procedures, or of analytical studies that rely on largely historical evidence rather than 'hard' data. By definition, it is difficult to separate these treatments into hard and fast categories; it is important, however, to illustrate the range and the richness of this material as well as to identify some of its central preoccupations. To take one example, there is a substantial body of writing about British foreign policy before and during the Second World War that not only gathers together considerable amounts of 'conventional' historical evidence but also deploys concepts and criteria deriving from foreign policy analysis in its 'scientific' manifestation (see, for example, Watt, 1965; Steiner, 1969; Williamson, 1969; Thorne, 1972 and 1978; Kennedy, 1981). Similarly, the growing body of literature on British policies in the early postwar period often makes use of the insights to be gained from theories of decision-making or perception (Shlaim, Jones and Sainsbury, 1977; Shlaim, 1983–4).

Quite apart from the linkage between historical materials and ideas of perception or decision-making, it is apparent that many writers use analytical devices to underpin their interpretations of the broad sweep of British foreign policy since 1945. Perhaps the most widely used of such devices is that of power and status: the widely held opinion that British foreign policy since the Second World War is a story of more or less terminal decline has led many commentators to use this notion as a way of organizing historical evidence. In this case, there is a subtle and often complex inter-action between the analytical ideas and the evidence. Whatever the dominant direction of the relationship between concepts and evidence, this constitutes a rich vein of material (see Younger, 1964; Leifer, 1972; Northedge, 1974; Calvocoressi, 1978; Kennedy, 1981).

Finally, in assessing the methods adopted for the study of British foreign policy, it is possible to identify a number of treatments that set themselves an explicitly analytical or even quasi-theoretical course. Here, the concern is with ideas, phenomena and issues of which British foreign policy is taken to be an instructive example. Significantly, many such analyses focus on the changing nature of foreign policy and on the ability of policy-makers to recognize and respond to such change. They start from the assumption that policy-makers in many societies have had to adapt both their perceptions and their actions to new international realities, and they judge British foreign policy in terms of the effectiveness with which it has made this transition. Very often, there is an implicit comparison of the British record with those of analogous societies and an attempt to relate the process of policy-making to the quality of policy produced. These issues will be explored further below, but it is important here to note the extent to which the more overtly analytical studies of British foreign policy provide a basis for evaluation and comparison (see Kaiser and Morgan, 1971; Jones, 1974; Frankel, 1975; Wallace, 1976; Barber, 1976; Hanrieder and Auton, 1980).

From the discussion so far, it is evident that the study of British foreign policy has extended across much of the spectrum between 'history' and 'science', although there is a major concentration of studies in what might be called the 'middle ground'. What, though, of the second analytical issue raised at the beginning of this chapter: the different levels at which analysis can be conducted? Three analytically distinct levels were identified, each with its distinctive implications for the questions asked and the evidence considered important in relation to British foreign policy. First, there is the 'domestic process' level; second, the level of 'international setting'; finally, the level of 'cross-national comparison'. A comprehensive account or analysis of foreign policy in any country will take account of all of these levels, not only individually but also in terms of the linkages and interactions between them.

The starting point of a 'domestic process' approach to British foreign policy is the assumption that foreign policy is the external output of the domestic policy-making process. Such an assumption has implications not only for the analyst's definition of the salient policy arena, but also for notions of the likely or appropriate policy-making process. To put it in a rather different way, the 'domestic process' approach sees all the important stimuli and demands facing the policy-makers as originating in the national political, economic and social systems. The international arena is thus essentially the arena in which policy is implemented, not the source of policy itself. In consequence, the central elements of the policy-making process are those political, constitutional and organizational factors within Britain itself that shape the policy output. Much work on the policy-making or administrative process in Britain either relegates international factors to a decidedly inferior status or effectively ignores them altogether (for example, Brown, 1971; Smith 1976). Whilst this can in some cases be explained as a natural consequence of the substantive issues on which the studies are focused, it is striking that relatively few works on British politics include explicit treatment of foreign policy issues, even though many of the processes and issues they present have important international origins or implications.

This having been said, it should be stressed that the formulation and administration of foreign policy itself have formed a persistent focus of studies dealing with British foreign policy (Richards, 1967; Waltz, 1967; Vital, 1968; Boardman and Groom, 1973; Barber, 1976; Wallace, 1976). Two features of these treatments are striking and significant and convey some of the importance of the level of analysis problem to the study of British foreign policy. First, the emphasis on domestic contexts and processes predisposes a number of such analyses towards highlighting the extent of choice that policy-makers have available to them in the foreign policy arena. It is natural given such an orientation to assume that the national leadership exercises authority over what goes on in foreign policy and how it goes on. Second, there is a concomitant emphasis on the determining role played by domestic debate, either at the elite or at the popular level. Foreign policy, it appears, is made at home and implemented abroad.

The more sophisticated of the 'domestic process' approaches, such as those by Wallace and Barber, show that it is not enough simply to describe or assess the domestic input into policy-making. It becomes clear in such accounts that the structure and operation of the domestic process itself is often a reflection of international forces. Perceptions of Britain's changing position in the international arena and of the impact of novel issues generated by international interactions, have constituted powerful inputs into the domestic debate about the making and the substance of foreign policy since at least the mid-1960s. Not only this, but the ways in which the domestic process has changed to accommodate participants and pressures from a variety of international sources demonstrate the increasing limitations of a crude 'domestic process' approach to the analysis of British foreign policy (for a general treatment of this issue, see Smith, 1986; Clarke, 1986).

In counterpoint to the 'domestic process' approach of some writing about British foreign policy, there has persisted a distinct tendency among other analyses to emphasize the international setting as a source of pressures and constraints. As noted earlier, the assumption that Britain's foreign policy problems can be explained primarily in terms of declining international status has been a powerful influence on much writing in the area (see Leifer, 1972; Northedge, 1974; Kennedy, 1981). There is much evidence to show that perceptions of decline and of the limits this places on independent action have been a determining factor in much of British foreign policy since 1945. In contrast to the 'domestic process' focus, this line of argument downgrades the effect of domestic debate or governmental structure, implying that successive leaderships have had little choice but to work within the straitjacket of objective international factors.

As with the 'domestic process' approach, though, the power of an 'international setting' analysis is not sufficient in itself to account for the course of British foreign policy. Several treatments that place a strong emphasis on the international setting are careful to point out that the linkages between international and domestic factors are potent and persistent (see Jones, 1974; Frankel, 1975). An interesting development of this line of argument is provided by a number of writers from a broadly marxist background, who have discerned a very strong connection between Britain's position in the world economy and the development of British domestic capitalism (Aaronovitch *et al.* 1981; Coates, 1984; Gamble, 1985). In common with other countries in the 'developed West', Britain has experienced the political and economic impact of the growth of a capitalist world economy. Whilst this is a rather different argument from that put forward by the mainstream of writing on British foreign policy, it none the less reinforces the point that the coexistence and intermeshing of levels of action and analysis are important to an understanding of British foreign policy.

Arguments such as those outlined above have led a number of analysts to stress analogies and comparisons between British foreign policy and the policies of other countries. The assumption is that an examination of the ways in which societies confront and cope with foreign policy problems can reveal significant patterns and regularities. One of the key areas in which such comparisons have been carried out for British foreign policy is that of the linkage already discussed – between domestic and international issues. The dual imperatives of domestic and international constraints and demands are faced not only by Britain but also by other societies in Western Europe especially; in addition, Britain is not the only country in the period since the Second World War to have experienced a significant loss of international status. The comparative studies that have resulted from recognition of these factors have generally succeeded in demonstrating the ways in which Britain's position has strong parallels with those of other countries (see Kaiser and Morgan, 1971; Morgan, 1976; Wallace, 1978a; Hanrieder and Auton, 1980). They have also demonstrated two other central features of the British foreign policy problem, which are explored in the rest of this chapter. First, in common with other countries such as France and the Federal Republic of Germany, Britain is an 'old state in new circumstances' (Wallace, 1978a). Second, the British response to change in its domestic and international situation may be comparable to those of other countries, but this does not mean that British foreign policy is unaffected by the distinctive combination of domestic and international forces outlined in this chapter.

Changing Perspectives on Foreign Policy

It is apparent from the discussion so far that British foreign policy can be – and has been – analysed through a variety of methods and at a number of levels. However, it was suggested at the beginning of the chapter that the nature of foreign policy itself, and thus of foreign policy analysis, has been the focus of debate and controversy. The emergence of competing perspectives on the study of foreign policy has created a dialogue between the forces of 'tradition' and 'transformation' which reflects on and interacts with developments in the 'real world' of policy. In relation to British foreign policy, it is clearly important to establish the ways in which the context, the content and the conduct of policy can be viewed from competing, but not necessarily mutually exclusive, perspectives.

For centuries, it appeared that foreign affairs and foreign policy could be relatively easily defined. The context was established by the structure and operation of a state-centred international system; the content of policy was mainly though not exclusively military and diplomatic, concerned with the 'high politics' of war, peace and international order; the conduct of policy was entrusted to elites at the highest levels of government, with public involvement and interest sporadic at best. Fundamental to this definition was a view of the international system in which states acted as closed units and in which they interacted with each other in isolation from the direct concerns of national populations. The view was well expressed in the notion of the 'balance of power', which was thought to have operated from the formation of the states-system in the seventeenth century until the early part of the twentieth. The operation of the balance meant that the governments of states were involved in complex patterns of negotiation, alliance construction or warfare, in which ideology took second place to national interests. The structure of the international arena thus made it logical to assume that each state had a set of interests that were impervious to ideology or other broader values. Lack of any government above states meant that each state was effectively judge in its own cause; thus foreign policy was seen as the preserve of a professional elite, dedicated to advancing the interests of the state through diplomacy or, if necessary, through the use of force. This is not to say that economic goals, for example, were ignored – only that foreign policy, because of the quasi-anarchical structure of the international arena, could be portrayed as something above everyday political or economic dealings, concerning itself with the diplomatic resolution of conflicts, the management of alliances, or the fighting of wars.

Such a view was underpinned both by the relatively small number of states in the international system – concentrated in Europe – and by the absence of democratic processes within national societies. The central premisses of what has been called 'state-centric realism' grew out of a world in which the dominance of national governments and their pursuit of security was taken as read. For realists such as Hans Morgenthau (1973), this meant that foreign policy was essentially determined by the interaction of the states-system with the self-centred nature both of governments and of policy-makers. Decision-makers were assumed to be rational and dedicated to the maximization of power; this enabled realist thinkers not only to explain what states were doing but also to prescribe what they should be doing. As the study of international relations developed, these state-centric assumptions pervaded the literature, to such effect that even the 'great debates' between classical and scientific analysts during the 1960s took place within the dominant realist perspective. Foreign policy continued to be seen as the actions of independent national units within a system of such units, and the key to an analysis of policy was thus an understanding of a given unit's location in the international power structure. This provided the basis for an assessment not only of a state's interests but also of its capacity to achieve them.

Much of traditional international relations analysis thus conceives of foreign policy as the rational behaviour of a national unit within a system of power relations. Specifically, such traditional views reflect three central assumptions: first, that nation-states are the dominant actors in international relations; second, that there is a sharp distinction between domestic and international politics; third, that international relations is a struggle for power and peace (Vasquez, 1979). Although some aspects of the content and conduct of foreign policy are indeed a reflection of such considerations, it is important that this should not automatically be accepted as a universally valid perspective on either international politics or foreign policy. The 'state-centric realist' approach to 'the politics of power and security' is powerful but not unchallengeable (Smith, Little and Shackleton, 1981). In the last two decades, analysts of international politics and foreign policy have questioned the utility of each of the traditional assumptions, arguing that both the international system and the nature of foreign policy have been transformed (Morse, 1970, 1976). States, it appears, are no longer the only significant actors in international dealings; the distinction between domestic and international politics has become blurred; and the struggle for power and peace has been displaced at least partly by concern for economic and social matters. Foreign policy itself thus exists not within a slightly amended version of the traditional context, but within a world transformed by the rise of transnational (non-state) actors and the impact of 'complex inter-dependence' (Keohane and Nye, 1972, 1977).

Such changes in the conception of international politics as an arena for foreign policy led inevitably to new conceptions of the content of policy. No longer was foreign policy to be seen and analysed as the diplomatic and military activity of discrete national units in the interstate system. Rather, it should be seen in terms of government attempts to control and manage a wide range of economic and other issues in a setting where states were joined and challenged by other actors and where the boundaries between domestic and international politics were distinctly fuzzy. The notion that states have rational sets of national interests had to be replaced by the recognition that foreign policy now dealt with a constantly changing agenda – an agenda influenced by a broad range of non-state groupings and domestic forces. States (and governments) could not validly be presented as hermetically sealed units and foreign policy could not be detached from the domestic political arena. Interdependence and transnationalism implied that political and economic groupings within societies did not necess-arily see national governments as a primary focus for their loyalties or their activities – rather, they might see non-state actors such as multinational corporations (MNCs) both as the base for and the targets of their operations.

From a 'transformationalist' perspective, therefore, the context and the content of foreign policy had undergone fundamental change. This had major implications for the conduct of policy, since the linkage of domestic and foreign concerns and the participation of new actors meant that the external relations of many societies on many issues need not pass through channels controlled by national governments. The ways in which foreign policy was made and executed thus needed reassessment, not only by academic analysts but also by the policy-makers themselves. By the mid-1970s it was almost the conventional wisdom that foreign policy, especially in the advanced industrial countries (AICs), could not fruitfully be studied on the basis that the state was an autonomous, sovereign unit in the international arena. Traditional theories of the ways in which states behaved and of the ways in which policy was made seemed simplistic, unable to account for the new policy agenda or for the complex interaction of domestic and external forces. The increasing number and variety of states in the international system during the 1950s and 1960s would have forced even the most traditional theorists of foreign policy to reassess their position, but the apostles of transformation argued powerfully that expansion and diversity were not a sufficient explanation of the profound and irreversible processes at work.

It is important to note, though, that the 'transformationalist revolution' in thinking about foreign policy has itself been open to challenge during the late 1970s and the 1980s. By 1980, the argument for a once-and-for-all transformation seemed well-established, especially among American writers (Morse, 1976; Mansbach, Ferguson and Lampert, 1976; Rosenau, 1979; Mansbach and Vasquez, 1981). Almost at the same time, though, events in the real world posed a challenge to the new orthodoxy. The outbreak of the 'new cold war' between the USA and the USSR seemed to bring the state back on to centrestage in world politics, whilst the revival of military and political tensions either relegated economic and social issues to a subordinate position or infused them with a strong strategic content. It appeared that the context and the content of foreign policy still contained potent elements of the traditional, and this was borne out by the attitudes of political leaderships in both the USA and Western Europe – precisely the areas in which the idea of transformation had seemed most relevant.

In the late 1980s it is apparent that the claims of 'transformationalists' were overstated and that the 1970s did not see the completion of a once-and-for-all revolution in the nature of international politics and foreign policy. The international relations literature faithfully reflected the situation by spawning a school of 'neo-realist' thought (Waltz, 1979; Keohane, 1986), but it was apparent even in their writings that a full reinstatement of undiluted traditionalism would be neither possible nor appropriate. The situation is neither one in which the assumptions of 'state-centric realism' are wholly acceptable, nor one in which the assumptions of interdependence and transnationalism universally apply. Reality demonstrates the features of a 'mixed actor system' (Young, 1972), in which actors coexist with no settled hierarchy between them and with no overriding consensus on the rules by which the international game is to be played. Within this heterogeneous system, there are high levels of interdependence and interpenetration – much higher than those assumed in unalloyed traditionalist thinking – and a fluctuating agenda of diplomatic, military, economic and social concerns which are difficult to disentangle either at the level of academic analysis or that of practical policy.

Perspectives on foreign policy in these conditions must take account of complexity and paradox. Policy content is neither wholly diplomatic and military nor entirely economic and social; it is not as completely dominated by 'high politics' as some theorists would claim, but it is not as thoroughy permeated by 'low politics' as claimed by others. Accordingly, the processes by which foreign policy is conducted can best be described as multilayered; the traditional view of elite dominance and broad consensus is inaccurate, but so is a view based on the merging of domestic and international processes. In the late 1980s, the conduct of foreign policy varies from issue to issue, with elite dominance largely intact in areas of national security but substantial pluralism in a wide range of economic and social affairs. Especially in AICs, it can be misleading to talk of 'foreign policy', since the term implies a unified and identifiable domain of policy with distinctive content and methods of conduct. 'Foreign policy' appears now to be an umbrella term for attempts by governments to influence or manage events outside the state's boundaries – events which may have either international or domestic origins. The implications are clear: traditional assumptions are no longer sufficient but they are still potent, whilst notions of transformation are substantially but not entirely to the point. It remains to explore these implications in the specific case of British foreign policy.

British Foreign Policy: Tradition or Transformation?

In this final section of the chapter, the aim is to relate the general argument about the changing nature of foreign policy and its implications for foreign policy analysis to the specific experience of Britain. The discussion is intended to be suggestive rather than exhaustive and to raise questions rather than to answer them, since many of the issues will recur in later and more empirical chapters. It follows the general shape of the preceding section, by looking at the 'traditionalist' and 'transformationalist' views of British foreign policy with particular reference to the context, content and conduct of policy.

A traditionalist approach to British foreign policy since the Second World War – and even before – would place great emphasis on Britain's changing position as a state within the international system of states and upon the role played by elements of power and capability. It is clear that one of the dominating trends in British foreign policy since the early years of this century has been a change in status from that of imperial and global power to that of a 'second rank' power (Northedge, 1970) and the traditionalist perspective is well equipped both to describe and to analyse this phenomenon. As a result, many of the most substantial works on British policy during the 1960s and early 1970s were explicitly focused on the causes and consequences of decline. A predominant image was that of the 'three circles' of involvement and responsibility (Empire and Commonwealth, Atlantic, European) and a central argument was that by the 1970s there was little left for Britain but to throw in its lot with the Europeans. Thus, entry into the European Community (EC) in 1973 had a dual significance in terms of Britain's place on the world stage: first, it represented the final adjustment to the harsh realities of life in the postwar era; but second, it also reflected a desire to rebuild the foundations for a more active British role in international politics. The traditionalist would certainly not deny that major changes have taken place in the context of British foreign policy, since it is central to the analysis outlined above that profound shifts of power and conflict at the global level – de-colonization, cold war, détente, 'new cold war' – have found their expression in an equally profound adjustment in the extent of British influence. The combination of such global shifts with the relative decline of British capabilities provides a potent explanation of the difficulties faced by every British government since 1945 (see Younger, 1964; Leifer, 1972; Northedge, 1974; Calvocoressi, 1978; Kennedy, 1981).

Whereas change in the international hierarchy and Britain's place within it looms large in traditionalist views of the international context, the agenda of foreign policy is seen as remaining relatively constant. Indeed, the fact of constancy lends weight to the arguments about the international setting, since it provides a consistent yardstick against which Britain's decline can be measured – that of national interest and national security. The British predicament in this case is an amalgam of several factors, chief among them the changing criteria of national status and security in the nuclear age. Successive British governments have been forced to recognize that they lack the capacity unilaterally to ensure their own security or to control the security of others. As a result, there has been a constant contraction of British security commitments, paralleled by a search for enhanced security through international arrangements such as the North Atlantic Treaty Organization (NATO). Despite – or perhaps because of – these changes, security needs preoccupy British governments of the 1980s as they did those of the 1950s. There is a recognition, though, that a combination of British economic frailty and the accelerating pace of military-technological change have reduced Britain's ability to set or to influence the handling of the agenda itself (see Hanrieder and Auton, 1980).

Constancy in a changing world is also seen by many traditionalists as characteristic of the conduct of British foreign policy. Indeed, it has often been claimed that continuity and the ability to avoid radical reversals are central virtues of the British style in foreign policy (see Waltz, 1967). On the other hand, it could equally be argued that in a world of radical change the inability to take fundamental choices and to reassess priorities constitutes a fundamental weakness (see Frankel, 1975). Whatever position is taken on the issue of choice in a changing world, traditionalists would agree that the conduct of British foreign policy has been, remains and should remain the preserve of a restricted elite centred

in the executive (Vital, 1968). Decisions at the level of broad
strategy are taken in the confines of No. 10 Downing Street and are
unlikely to be greatly affected either by party politics or by broader
public opinion. When it comes to the implementation of foreign
policy, that is essentially the task of the Foreign and Commonwealth Office (FCO), one of the 'great departments of state', which
takes the lead on all matters of external relations. This remains the
case according to the traditional view, despite entry into the EC or
the demands of other novel organizations or issues; other departments of government may well be involved in external relations,
but they play their parts within the broad parameters laid down by
the executive and the FCO. When it comes to the techniques of
policy, although the practice of diplomacy has diversified it is still
at the centre of foreign policy. Above all, and as demonstrated in
dramatic fashion by the Falklands War of 1982, the use of coercion
and force remains the ultimate instrument of the British state in a
world of states.

As noted above, the adoption of a traditionalist approach to the
analysis of British foreign policy by no means rules out consideration of change. Decline, transition, adjustment, collapse, all are
terms used frequently by traditionalist writers. Many of the most
damning criticisms of the effectiveness of British foreign policy
since 1945 have emerged from the traditionalist school, since
evaluation of the ways in which British policy-makers have
recognized and responded to changing power realities is central to
its perspective. None the less, the traditionalist position clings
more or less resolutely to a central assumption: that while conditions and policies may change, the fundamental character of policy
in general is constant. Such a position is challenged, as has been
seen, by the transformationalist view, and the implications for
British foreign policy are succinctly set out by Roy Jones:

> The course of modern British foreign policy can be described in
> terms of the inexorable decline of British national strength and of
> British exertions to compensate for the resulting loss of power.
> Accepting its assumptions, this explanation is at best only partial.
> If British foreign policy is undergoing not a decline but a transform-
> ation, the assumptions of this explanation become largely irrelevant,
> and explanation in terms of the complementarity of national and
> transnational government takes its place.   (1974, pp. 138–9)

The first challenge posed by the transformationalist view of British foreign policy relates to the nature of the international context. Although traditionalists can point to radical change, in their view this has taken place without shaking the 'power and security' foundations of the states–system; all that has happened is that Britain's place in the system has been altered. For transformationalists, this is simply not an accurate description of the new context for British foreign policy. Three features of this context mark it out as different in kind from those of previous eras: multilateralism, transnationalism and interdependence.

The first of these features – multilateralism – is expressed most clearly in the proliferation of international organizations which embody novel commitments and activities. For Britain, the plain fact is that foreign policy can no longer be pursued simply on a bilateral, state–to–state basis. What is even more important, perhaps, is that these organizations reflect the increasing difficulty of pursuing domestic policies on a purely national plane, since many of them provide for common action to achieve welfare or security objectives that are beyond the means of single governments. Alongside multilateralism goes transnationalism: the growth of contacts between groups within different national societies which need not necessarily fall within the competence or control of governments. To take just two of the more obvious examples, Britain is both host and home for a large number of MNCs and also sends and receives very large numbers of tourists and business travellers every year. Indeed, Britain rates as one of the most heavily penetrated countries in the world in these areas. Both multilateralism and transnationalism are expressions and reinforcements of growing interdependence between Britain and other societies, especially those in the advanced industrial world. No longer is this interdependence confined to governmental elites: rather, it extends across a wide range of dealings previously considered purely national in their scope, exposing British society to new influences and new avenues of interaction. The upshot is that the context of British foreign policy has effectively been transformed in several dimensions. This transformation does not render the relative decline of British power irrelevant, but it places the decline within a far wider and arguably more significant framework of constraints and opportunities (see Kaiser and Morgan, 1971; Jones, 1974).

It was argued earlier that one of the key elements in a transformationalist view of foreign policy was a distinctive conception of the foreign policy agenda. Not only has the agenda expanded, it is claimed; it has also become more fluid and prone to fluctuation, in the light of pressures both from the domestic and the external arena. In the case of British foreign policy, this transformation of content has claimed attention alongside the shifts in context outlined above. William Wallace (1976) has argued persuasively that the change has not simply affected the balance between 'high' and 'low' policies (that is, the traditional concerns of power and security, and the technical and welfare issues characteristic of advanced industrial life): there is in fact a threefold distinction to be made, between 'high', 'low' and 'sectoral' policies. Of these, the most interesting in many ways are the 'sectoral' issues, such as energy, technology, or trade, since these attract novel combinations of pressures and participants and they also involve major choices of values or allocations of resources. Importantly, the process by which items get on to the foreign policy agenda may not be within the control of any one government, since transnational and other groupings can exert a good deal of political influence and may have technical or other resources denied to national authorities. Another feature of the agenda according to transformationalists is that by definition many of the issues it contains are not the sole concern of the FCO; indeed, when it comes to economic or other technical matters, the traditional diplomat may be at a severe disadvantage *vis-à-vis* his or her counterparts in other departments of government. The agenda may therefore be set as much by negotiation between agencies of government or between government and societal groups as by any elite consensus on the 'national interest'.

This brings the argument to the conduct of policy. As the discussion above implies, the transformationalist image of the conduct of British foreign policy is at odds with many of the central tenets of a traditional view. Whereas traditionalists would see the conduct of policy in terms of the matching of resources to objectives, and the problems faced by the British in terms of the failure of successive governments to carry out the operation appropriately, the transformationalists would take a very different line. The growth of interdependence and transnational contacts means that the task of British governments has completely changed. Far greater attention has to be paid to co-ordination between the many departments of state interested in international affairs, and the possibilities of co-ordination are themselves reduced by conflicts of interest between different ministries. Not only this, but a plurality of interest groups and other bodies, from within and outside the country, has to be taken into account in the formation of policies. Finally, such policies as are decided must be implemented in the international context already described – a setting characterized by multilateralism, transnationalism and interdependence. James Barber (1976) encapsulates the problem of conducting foreign policy in such conditions in four images of the policy process, depending on the scope and level of involvement each entails. The point is not that any one of these images has replaced the others; it is that they coexist, creating novel problems of co-ordination and management throughout government and far into society at large. On any given issue, policy will emerge from several sources within government and be directed towards several targets at home and abroad.

Although it would be tempting to conclude that there has been a total transformation of British foreign policy, a word of caution is in order. There has indeed been a high level of change in the context, content and conduct of policy, but this has not eliminated the traditional features of Britain's approach to the outside world. The world of military security, of secrecy and of force as the final resort has not disappeared, and the patterns of past concerns and commitments have not been eradicated. To return to the general conclusion reached earlier, the world of British foreign policy is a mixed one, and the old coexists sometimes uneasily with the new. Not least do they coexist in the perceptions of policy-makers, as many of the chapters in this book make clear.

Conclusion

This chapter has addressed the problem of analysing British foreign policy in two distinct but interrelated ways. First, it has argued that the study of foreign policy in general, and of British foreign policy in particular, relies upon certain choices of method and level of analysis. Second, it has focused on the changing nature of broad perspectives about the status of foreign policy itself, by making the distinction between 'traditionalist' and 'transformationalist' approaches to the subject-matter. Two very general conclusions emerge from this twofold investigation: the first is that the study of British foreign policy is inescapably theoretical, in a broad sense, and that it is best to be aware of the choices that are made by any analysis; the second is that there is an intimate link between choices about how British foreign policy should be analysed and assumptions about its changing nature. Each of these assertions will briefly be examined here.

It is a truism that the facts never speak for themselves and that any account of social phenomena or processes will be based on decisions about what to include, about what is significant and about causes and consequences of events and behaviour. Such decisions, though, are not always made explicit and the first part of the chapter attempted to outline some of the questions that might be asked of studies in British foreign policy. The fact that there is a spectrum of possible approaches, ranging from 'history' to 'science', does not necessarily mean that the one is any less 'theoretical' than the other. It may mean, however, that in one case the theoretical choices are left implicit and the basis for selection and interpretation left unstated, while in the other the argument is dominated by the attempt to impose an explicit framework of hypotheses or 'tests'. Analytical awareness does not necessarily imply the attempt to construct general theories or all-encompassing frameworks – indeed, the record of such attempts in the foreign policy field is distinctly patchy (Smith, 1983; Hill, 1974) – but rather a sensitivity to the bases on which particular interpretations are constructed and a recognition of the limitations inherent in any explanation. The argument here has been that the most promising avenues for the analysis of British foreign policy are those that allow for the complexity of the real world and can be applied to specific problems, processes and areas of comparison. In terms both of methodology and of levels of analysis, this is where much of the extant literature on British foreign policy can be located, although there is still room for a great deal of diversity.

Diversity of approach, and the development of analysis which often uses historical evidence but does so within more or less explicit social science frameworks, is thus characteristic of much writing about British foreign policy. This situation is closely connected to debates – both in the academic and in the 'real' world

– about the underlying nature of foreign policy itself. The dichotomy between 'traditionalist' and 'transformationalist' views of the subject is in many ways overstated and artificial, but it does expose the complexity and contestability of the field. It also exposes the ways in which different schools of thought use historical evidence and analytical devices, by confronting the 'traditionalist' emphasis on continuity and the 'special' status of foreign policy with the 'transformationalist' stress on discontinuity and interconnectedness. Whilst this argument cannot be pushed too far, it is one that emerges from alertness to the links between subject-matter and method and between the academic and the practical world. As such, it underlies the thrust of the analysis in this book as a whole.

2 The Historical Background

Past and Present in British Foreign Policy

CHRISTOPHER HILL

History is made to be summarized. There is no other way to make sense of the mass of human experience which constitutes the past than to reduce, distil and dramatize it. Yet summarizing can easily turn into oversimplification, just as the opposite tendency – loving attention to detail – can lead to shapelessness and obscurity. Policy-makers in Britain, it can be argued, have a tendency to fall into the first error. The pressure of events encourages a cavalier attitude to the use of examples and language drawn from history, while the long adversarial tradition of party politics fosters virulent debates about past glories or failures which inevitably sacrifice cool analysis to high-running emotions. The struggle to cope with the consequences of massive, often deleterious, changes in Britain's position in the world has meant a preoccupation, even in the late 1980s, with past experiences and their myriad practical legacies. The importance of external relations to Britain, and of Britain to other states over the last two centuries, means that the actions of previous governments are still matters of live contemporary significance, as the debate about Harold Macmillan's apparent decision to return Cossacks to the Soviet Union in 1945 (Tolstoy, 1986), and the amount of attention given to the thirtieth anniversary of the Suez expedition, illustrate. Unhappily, an historical consciousness is no guarantee against the misuse of historical material and, in particular, the crude attempts to draw specific lessons from the past, whether by way of reaction or emulation.

The argument which follows starts from the premiss that Britain is a society in which historical thinking is particularly important and prominent. It goes on to develop the proposition that modern British foreign policy cannot be explained without careful attention to the dual impact of the past, both through events themselves and through the conceptions of history (general and particular) held by decision-makers. This raises certain important theoretical issues of the kind which occur in foreign policy analysis, for instance the gap between the operational and psychological environments, the nature of belief systems and the flexibility of the policy-making system. In particular, the problem of change will be addressed. All the major points of debate over British foreign policy centre on change, which is inherently connected to ideas about the past, at once promising a break with history and being defined by it. For at least the last thirty years, those concerned with Britain's international relations have been arguing about the extent to which major choices need to be made over changes in direction, involving possibly radical reassessments of some long-cherished axioms. (In this sense the foreign policy debate anticipated by some years the rising tide of impatience with the domestic order in politics and economics, which produced the polarization of the parties in the second half of the 1970s.) The nature of the changes debated – in the geographical scope of foreign policy, over the institutions of foreign policy and over defence – can only be properly understood through an analysis of the dominant images in Whitehall and Westminster of our past experiences, as well as through the actual origins of Britain's current place in the world.

Accordingly, the discussion begins by looking at the conventional ways of relating the past to present foreign policy problems, before moving on to suggest an alternative model, designed to cope with the fact that while history provides the overall matrix of the present, some legacies from history are shaken off more easily than others. It then moves on to evaluate attempts at change and ends by considering how far the British foreign policy-making system is adaptable and how far it is still weighed down by the past in its various guises.

Nostalgia

There are two orthodox, and therefore important, ways in which the conceptualization of history (as opposed to the causal chain of events) affects British foreign policy. The first is nostalgia, or the reluctance to abandon anachronistic ways of thinking. Lord Franks said in 1954 that 'it is part of the habit and furniture of our minds that Britain should be a great power' (Darby, 1973, p.22). It is arguable that this attitude has persisted throughout the postwar period, influencing the determination to have an independent nuclear deterrent, the antipathy to compromising sovereignty within the European Community and the various attempts to mediate between the superpowers.

If it is true, as Lord Salisbury said, that 'the commonest error in politics [is] sticking to the carcase of dead policies' (Kennedy, 1981, p.377), then there can be little doubt that the great Victorian Foreign Secretary and Prime Minister's injunction has not been followed by his successors. The Suez expedition of 1956 was influenced both by considerations of imperial security at a time when the empire was on the point of dissolution and by Eden's harking back to the 1930s in an attempt to demonstrate the unwisdom of appeasement. Over a longer time-span, the whole commitment to military bases 'East of Suez' lasted well beyond the independence of India in 1947, which removed their supposed rationale (Darby, 1973, *passim*). Even in 1968, when it was announced that Britain would withdraw its forces from Singapore and the Persian Gulf, it was as a result of the financial crisis of late 1967, not a considered acceptance of the impossibility of such a world role for Britain. Only three years before, Harold Wilson had asserted that Britain's frontiers were 'in the Himalayas'.[1]

'Nostalgia' must, of course, be seen here as a useful summarizing term rather than a full explanation in itself of such major lines of foreign policy. British policy-makers were neither so blind nor so unsophisticated as to launch wars and commit billions of pounds out of a mere sentimental desire to prolong the conditions of their youth. What is really being referred to here is the immense power of traditions of thought about policy, and the difficulty of escaping from the intellectual and emotional constraints of the time in which one lives. Although when a new era opens the assumptions of even five years ago can suddenly seem bizarre and inappropriate, there are usually long periods of transition while ideas whose time has come and is passing, work themselves through. The conservative, routine-bound nature of human society, and the human brain itself, means that decision-making does not take place in terms of endless sharp, radical jumps, but rather through long, evolutionary periods of adaptation (Steinbruner, 1974). Moreover, when revolutionary change does occur, it tends to be after generations of particularly marked resistance to innovation and, as often as not, policy quickly reverts to type in key respects.

The nature of international relations certainly tends to reinforce, in all states, the conservative quality of foreign policy. In Britain, however, 'historical thinking' in the sense of attitudes which are rooted in images of the country and its interests as they were in preceding generations, has been particularly marked.[2] Churchill's sense of a heroic tradition, evident in his immensely popular *History of the English-Speaking Peoples* (1956–8), was not wholly typical and Churchill himself displayed considerable realism in accepting Britain's reliance on the United States as early as the 1930s (Gilbert, 1976, pp.700, 897, 957, 1009), but there was certainly a widespread reluctance in the Conservative Party in the 1930s to envisage full independence for India that was only dispelled by the necessity of war. Equally, Labour's postwar governments were active in creating and sustaining Britain's strategic nuclear weapon capacity, more concerned to avoid the accusations of pacifism which had dogged them before 1939 and to maintain British prestige, than to give priority to considerations of cost and what is now called 'arms control'. As Ernest Bevin said in 1946:

> I don't want any other Foreign Secretary of this country talked at or by a Secretary of State in the United States as I have just had [*sic*] in my discussions with Mr Byrnes. We have got to have this thing over here whatever it costs . . . We've got to have the bloody Union Jack flying on top of it.
>
> (Bullock, 1985, p.352)

These are contentious matters. Bullock sees Bevin as having merely given his successors the option of pursuing the nuclear path rather than 'saddling Britain with a world role she could not sustain' (1985, p.847). It is not possible even for historians to make definitive judgements about which policies were doomed and which far-sighted. What can be said, though, is that there are few instances in modern British foreign policy of decision-makers consciously attempting to plan for the future and to work through

the practical implications of Britain's rapidly changing circumstances and reduced capabilities. When responsibilities have been
shed, it has usually been in an atmosphere of urgency if not actual
crisis, and the hasty decisions have tended to compound the
original problems. The longevity of established images and belief
systems is extensively discussed in the theoretical literature (for
example, Jervis, 1976; Axelrod, 1976; Cottam, 1977; Janis and
Mann, 1977) and the British aversion to *a priori* or forward thinking
merely compounds a problem which is inherent at both individual
and collective levels of decision–making.

The 'Givens'

Nostalgia in a loose sense, therefore, has continually affected the
formulation of modern British foreign policy, even if we must be
wary of facile images which portray Lord Home or Michael
Stewart as foreign secretaries who differed from Rosebery or Grey
only in their modern dress and political vocabulary.[3] A more
deep-rooted way in which the conceptualization of history affects
policy, however, is through the notion of enduring, timeless
interests given credence by Palmerston's famous remark of 1848.[4]
From both a Realist and a sentimental perspective on foreign policy
it is easy to assume that while a country may change its domestic
arrangements, it neglects the eternal verities of international politics
at its peril, given the obvious dangers of a world lacking over-
arching social and governmental institutions. In the British case,
what are sometimes called the 'givens' of foreign policy centre on
the geopolitics of Britain's island position. It has been conventionally argued, both by practitioners and observers of policy, that
the English Channel has simultaneously separated Britain from and
bound together Britain with the continent of Europe. Unwilling to
participate fully in European affairs, but unable to ignore them
completely, Britain has intervened spasmodically to maintain a
balance of power favourable to itself and sought leadership rather
than integration. The result has often been an uncertainty abroad as
to British intentions, as in 1938 over Czechoslovakia, or 1962 over
the negotiations for entry to the European Economic Community
(EEC).
    Other aspects of the apparently geohistorical continuities of

British foreign policy include its global reach (the Atlantic sea-lanes 'beckon' an island race), its commercial basis (the British Isles apparently being unable to support its peoples in food) and concomitant reliance on a navy as the main instrument of military influence, rather than the massed armies which would prove difficult to raise and transport abroad. Some of these notions are half-truths at best: for example, the British people managed to feed themselves in a surprisingly effective way when forced to go short of imports in the Second World War (Calder, 1971, pp.438–47, 466–8, 474–93). They have also applied with differing strengths at different times; for example, Britain showed recognition of declining global capabilities as early as 1902, when seeking an agreement with Japan, while twelve years or so later it was to fight one of the greatest and most prolonged of European land-battles, losing about 9 per cent of all men aged 20–45 during the Great War (Marwick, 1965, p.290).

But despite these caveats, it is going too far to suggest, as Paul Kennedy has done, that what have often seemed to be ineluctable truths of geography and history are in fact only the characteristics of a specific period (1981, pp.379, 384). In this view, Britain's 'global role' is really an interlude from about 1558 to 1939 in the longer tradition of integral involvement in European politics. This, however, takes insufficient account of the gradual emergence of an international economy and Britain's deep involvement in it. When technology and trade together made possible a reaching out beyond Europe to systematic contacts with the Americas and India, Britain's position and seafaring capabilities gave it an advantage long before the Industrial Revolution established political and economic primacy. This in its turn has widened horizons and created traditions which cannot simply be reversed, regardless of the 'descent from power'. Britain's own demography, financial system, trading needs and political contacts are now so diversified that a falling back into European parochialism is hardly an option.

Retrospection and an emphasis on the enduring interests behind British foreign policy are the two most commonly observed ways in which the past has an impact on contemporary decision-making. The one is largely (if not entirely) a matter of perceptions, the other is largely (but not entirely) a matter of objective constraints. So far as 'nostalgia' or anachronism is concerned, there are clearly large elements of both judgement and ideology at work. Burkeans may exaggerate the difficulties of change, revolutionaries may underrate the value of established practices. But to a certain extent it is impossible for decision-makers to free themselves from habits of mind and language which were forged in previous eras, particularly when the successes of past foreign policy still weigh heavy. Long-established perceptions and conventional wisdoms can become more or less objective parts of an individual's environment. This is an important qualification to the otherwise helpful theoretical distinction between the psychological milieu (in which decisions are taken) and the operational milieu (in which they have to be implemented).

Equally, although the givens of foreign policy are by definition factors over which particular generations have little control, all constraints *can* be challenged (for example, the charge of the Light Brigade, indeed the whole Crimean expedition) and some overcome successfully, as with the (French) construction of the Suez Canal in the 1860s to create a faster route to the East. So far as modern British policy is concerned, the 1930s saw the 'enduring interest' in the European balance of power once again reasserted, in a war for Poland against Germany, but only after prolonged and almost fatal hesitancies. Long-established positions in China and Africa, and even commitments to the security of the United Kingdom island fortress itself, were called into question as a result of the conditions of the time, in particular, domestic opposition to rearmament and a perceived lack of resources to cope with simultaneous threats in the Atlantic, Mediterranean and Far East.

There is, therefore, no justification for taking an excessively determinist view of the way British foreign policy has worked out in the twentieth century. The 'weight of the past' is mediated through the preferences and capacities of each new government in office. In the very long term, it may be true to say that Britain's loss of pre-eminence in the international system (always qualified) was inevitable, but the meaning, pace and impact of this relative decline were partly determined by the contingent way in which decision-makers viewed that very history in whose thrall they lay. The 'belief system' of the practitioner is a deep-rooted legacy of experience and political culture, but it is also an organic set of attitudes which is capable, within limits, of self-transformation.

Alternative Approaches

In order to explain more fully the interplay of perceptions and reality, we need to go beyond the account that we have given so far of the impact of history. There are two reasons for this. First, reference to neither nostalgia nor enduring interests can explain why certain images or factors endure powerfully for generations, even centuries, while others might atrophy or become transformed. Concern for the Commonwealth, for example, appears to be lasting well beyond the period of decolonization which shifted British foreign policy's central focus away from the empire. On the other hand, the nineteenth-century criterion of a two-power navy was abandoned with brusque realism when the rise of German, then American and Japanese fleets began to present a challenge (Kennedy, 1976, pp.205–37). Both the historical perspectives we have discussed would lead us to expect a greater continuity in foreign policy than is the case, with change either being retarded by conservatism or being calculated on the basis of how eternal interests can best be kept in focus as circumstances alter. Other forms of change would have to be ascribed to personality, chance, or human nature, but probably not to the influence of the past except in the tautological sense that everything has its roots in history and can therefore be seen as explained by it.

These weaknesses are like those that plague many forms of generalization based around single factors and are serious enough. In the same category, as a model used to explain British foreign policy, is power analysis, with its emphasis on capabilities. Britain's decline in (relative) military and economic power as new rivals arose and internal unrest rent the empire, has been seen by many as a sufficient explanation in itself of the course of British foreign policy from 1939, 1914, or even 1870. But this can only provide a very crude explanation over a long time-period. There are so many intervening variables and strands of activity which do not conform to the general pattern, that at best we need to look for extra dimensions to the model. For example, Britain's diplomatic influence is still considerable in the late 1980s and certainly beyond its ranking on economic indicators. British culture is also capable of exerting a formative influence on millions of people in many different kinds of society, independent of military capability (Mitchell, 1986, pp. 15–17; Parsons, 1984–85), while in the latter field, successive governments have decided to maintain formal nuclear weapon status despite the impossibility of matching the destructive capacity of the superpowers. Power, like history, only provides the substructure of an explanation of such variety.

The second reason why we need to look deeper into the relationship between British foreign policy in the closing years of the century and its glorious past, is because by now British policy has reached a stage where self-consciousness has set in about the deleterious impact of anachronistic thinking. Indeed, over the last two decades there has been something of a reaction against the notion of excessive continuity, with attempts (some actually successful) to establish alternative policies and procedures to those tested by time. This may be conveniently dated from 1969, when the publication of the Duncan Report (HMSO, 1969) served as a vehicle for those who felt that Britain was slipping behind in the international struggle for commercial survival, partly as a result of preoccupations with orthodox diplomatic prestige and military power. It has produced a fairly agonizing reappraisal of British foreign policy among practitioners and the attentive public since then and has culminated (although there are other factors at work here) in the break-up of cross-party consensus.

There are now clear distinctions between the three major party groupings on external policy, going beyond the more publicized arguments on nuclear weapons. Moreover the concomitant is the emergence of a conscious radicalism on foreign policy, if of different kinds, in each party's programme. The Conservatives have belied their name by taking a steadily more sceptical approach to the Commonwealth and even to the usefulness of the Foreign Office, ironically the source of a steady trickle (through early retirement) of such Tory politicians as Douglas Hurd and George Walden. Labour has moved away from the status quo policies of its periods in office during the 1960s and 1970s, to a commitment to remove American nuclear weapons from Britain which would undoubtedly have important repercussions if attempted. The Liberals also want a major change in nuclear weapons policy, although a degree of ambiguity still exists. They certainly stand for a radical commitment to increased European integration through more powers for the European Community. The Social Democrats are perhaps the exception to the rule of a desire to usher in a new era in foreign policy, but even they would cancel the

Trident missile system and insist on dual-key arrangements for Cruise.

Levels of Analysis

It is, therefore, not enough in the late 1980s to recite a list of apparent failures in British foreign policy since the war and to link them to an inability to let go of past attitudes and commitments. Although the elements of truth in this picture should not be forgotten, it is to a large extent an oversimplification and misses out the fact that decision-makers have already begun both to act on its supposed lessons and to transcend the debate it has produced. What is needed, by contrast, in any appreciation of the role of historical factors in contemporary policy, is some analysis which *discriminates* between (1) those legacies from the past which are so much part of the weft and warp of daily thought and business as to be almost indistinguishable from the present; (2) those which shape reality profoundly but are still capable of being transformed; and (3) those which constitute concrete but limited constraints.

Taking these three categories in order, it is clear that in a fundamental sense every action taken, or problem confronted, is connected to the past. However forward-looking we may wish to be, there can be no collective amnesia, no possibility of *tabulae rasae*. A state's past successes and failures, friendships and enmities, live on in the minds of present-day decision-makers both at home and abroad. However dramatic the attempts to cut the cord with the past, as with the Franco-German rapprochement since 1945, when the wider context is considered it becomes clear that constraints are still powerful. The experience of 1940 has left France with a determinedly independent defence policy, the Germans with a high nervousness about national self-assertion, and both countries with hypersensitivity about their muted relationship. Thus even breaks in continuity are defined by what went before. Future change is conditioned by the nature of what is being reacted against.

There is also the time-lag factor. The impact of the Great War on British social and political attitudes, for example, is still being felt. Given the continuing flood of material, serious and popular, about 1914–18, and the perceptions of futility which commonly attach to that struggle, it is not fanciful to suggest a connection between the searing experiences of the Somme and Passchendaele and the continuing strength of what A. J. P. Taylor and Martin Ceadel have identified as 'pacificism' (cf. pacifism) especially in nonconformist and left-of-centre circles in Britain (Ceadel, 1980, p.3).

Indeed, if history works through over generations, its impact will be especially persistent in the case of Britain and its foreign policy, given that the country is moving from primacy back to mere ordinariness. On the other hand, the 'descent from power' hypothesis, so often used to explain Britain's postwar difficulties, should really be seen as only a shorthand for the massive but various problems of historical adjustment faced by governments in London over the last half-century. Fewer capabilities and straitened circumstances are only half the story; what has been most difficult for decision-makers has been the persistent need to adapt to large-scale and primarily exogenous change in almost every area of policy. Moreover, the full impact of change, and adaptive responses, is only experienced over decades. There has been no once-and-for-all reduction in Britain's advantages, no obvious start or end to a period of contraction.

Handling persistent change is particularly difficult when behaviour has become well-grooved through constant success, and adaptation has only been necessary within a narrow range of variables, as was the case for Britain until about 1933. The pressure for extensive change when it finally comes is all the more disturbing and produces that reluctance to face new realities which psychologists explain through the theory of cognitive dissonance (Festinger, 1957). It becomes difficult even to think of altering the now long-established patterns of commitments, connections and concerns. Thus, when breaks do take place, as with the process of decolonization, the substance tends to fade much more slowly than the form, unlike the Cheshire Cat. Economic interests, political ties and cultural memories on both sides continue to bind Britain and its ex-colonies together for longer than purely rational calculations might predict. In such cases the past is more than an influential memory; it is seamlessly stitched in to the present.

Yet much of the imperial past really belongs on the margin of our second category – that of historical legacies which are powerful but not wholly irresistible. Because they are identifiable in concrete (often institutional) forms, they become susceptible to alteration by means of conscious policy efforts. The categories are hardly watertight: a prospect which is almost literally 'unthinkable' in one generation (say, a second world war in 1919) may become a clear choice or even an unavoidable change for the next. None the less those responsible for foreign policy in any state are uncomfortably aware that much of their working environment is made up of commitments or policies which are simultaneously structural and potential handles for innovation. Alliances can become semi-permanent, or cold wars institutionalized, but neither is immutable, and decision-makers are aware (although they usually prefer to suppress the thought) that each new government or period has the chance of reinterpreting the conventional wisdoms and arrangements which it has inherited. Karl Deutsch once said that 'decision-making is about combining new information with old memories' (1978, p.85), but he might have added 'and new possibilities'. Whatever decision-makers decide, in fact, the wider external and internal environments will continue to change around them and may ultimately compel reconsideration at a higher price than was available earlier on.

In the case of Britain, the major not-quite-givens of the 1970s were: possession of the nuclear deterrent, membership of NATO which included the provision of sites for American nuclear bases, and attachment to the Commonwealth. All of these have been such long-established parts of the British foreign policy scene that it takes a massive effort (or dislocation) to get them on to the policy agenda. But it is not impossible – as illustrated in the 1980s by the Labour Party's change of preference on the deterrent and the Conservatives' growing impatience with the Commonwealth. On the other hand, the European Community, which in the late 1970s was still such an ill-fitting piece in the whole jigsaw, is now accepted across the board as a permanent part of Britain's environment – perhaps because the battles fought over it are still in the recent past and the need to avoid further destructive conflict is paramount. In such ways does the 'verdict of history' get established and become a self-fulfilling prophecy.

But even if the debate is now uninhibited about US bases or Trident, and a newly retired senior British diplomat can write an article arguing that 'we can live quite well without the Commonwealth' (Butler, 1986), the fact is that the country is so deeply embedded in the multiple strata of institutions, expectations and personal contacts which these policies represent, that it will prove an immensely painful, slow and perhaps impossible task to implement such proposals even should a party committed to them win a clear majority in a general election. Two examples may serve to make the point more concrete.

First, let us take the question of the American bases. The interested general public is well aware that the United States would strenuously oppose any British request to remove nuclear weapons from its forces in the UK, even if it were eventually to comply. A major political struggle would ensue, with the costs for the British government to weigh in the balance being made as clear as they were to the New Zealand government in 1986, when Wellington refused to provide facilities for US warships carrying nuclear devices. What is perhaps less clear to those who do not take a professional interest in these matters is that the practical difficulties of carrying through the policy are likely to be immense and would seriously compound the political problems. For instance, if the purpose is to make Britain less of a target in a nuclear exchange, would it not be necessary to dismantle the early-warning station at Fylingdales, which is so central to US strategy as to cause a major crisis in NATO? Would American F1-11 bombers with their dual nuclear and conventional capacity be banned along with Cruise missiles? Would the intelligence flights over Soviet territory made from bases in Britain have to be transferred elsewhere in European NATO? If other member states refused to allow this shift in the balance of vulnerability, would a Labour government in London be prepared to see the whole alliance unravel? The USA has about sixty-three military bases of various kinds in Britain (Baylis, 1984, pp. 198–201), and a committed anti-nuclear government would find it difficult to accept that they related only to the alliance's conventional strategy. On the other hand, an attempt to grasp this nettle would raise the painful wider question of the whole US presence in Britain. These dilemmas can be brushed aside in the first flush of theoretical enthusiam for a new policy, but they would remorselessly come out once the first steps towards implementation were taken and would exert a strong braking effect.

The second example of constraints which can be confronted but then prove to have formidable sets of historical roots, relates to Britain's economic ties with Southern Africa. On the face of things we have here a case of steady adaptation to changing interests. A Conservative government in 1960 recognized the need to grant independence to African colonies and at the same time chose good relations with a reconstructed Commonwealth over closeness to South Africa, which left the Commonwealth in 1961. Over the subsequent twenty-five years the perception of the importance of relations with black Africa, especially Nigeria and Kenya, has increased in proportion to the share of Britain's exports taken by these countries (it overtook South Africa's share in the early 1970s).[5] The relinquishing of the naval base at Simonstown in 1975 was also in part a statement about the end of intimacy between London and Pretoria.

It would therefore seem a logical progression, or at least not an implausible proposition, that Britain should join in with economic sanctions against South Africa when a consensus of opinion among other states deemed the time to be right. History is, however, made up of many currents, not all of which move at the same speed. Discounting for the moment the theological objections to sanctions which have been common in Whitehall, and the various pressures from Washington, it is clear that any long-term strategy that official policy might have is always going to have to cope with an enormous 'tail' of complications consequent on the great span of activities undertaken abroad by private British citizens and enterprises. In the case of South Africa this means a British investment portfolio of £12 billion amounting to 38 per cent of total foreign investment, family links estimated at nearly one million white South African British-passport holders, and a central role in some of the country's largest banks, chemical and mining companies.[6] This is to say nothing of the extensive cultural and sporting links which have so often embarrassed British governments in recent decades. Thus Mrs Thatcher's administration, like her predecessors' and successors', has had and will have to cope with the fact that the historical primacy of Britain's place in South Africa's economic life is diminishing only slowly and that consequently the interests of British *society* in that troubled country will continue effectively to narrow policy-makers' options with regard to economic sanctions, the breaking of diplomatic links and alignment with the forces of black opposition to the regime.

In most important areas of policy, therefore, it can be seen not only that language and thought are indelibly affected by past experience (our first category), but also that the nature of choice is determined by commitments and patterns of activity which cannot simply be wished away. The central paradox here is that the movement of history compels constant reconsideration and dangles endlessly (in our change-dominated century) the attractions of a break with the past, of the dawning of new progressive eras. But the very millstones which seem so burdensome are not at all easy to cut loose from. This, then, is our second category: the past as matrix, structuring choice but not preventing it.

The third category is more easily disposed of. A state like Britain still has to deal with the detritus of its own past, in terms of many discrete problems which cannot be ignored but which essentially constitute little more than high-level nuisances. The most obvious cases here are the remnants of empire, most of which Britain would get rid of if only it could be done without political embarrassment. A deal has already been done to hand over Hong Kong to China by 1997, Brunei has been encouraged to take over responsibility for its external affairs (1984), troops would be withdrawn from Belize if Guatemala would agree to détente (and if the United States did not want to keep the British in Central America) and Gibraltar would almost certainly be leased to Spain if only the Gibraltarians could learn to trust Madrid. The Falkland Islands are similar: despite the understandably high feelings and moral questions which now attach to them, the islands would undoubtedly be relinquished gladly by Britain if the islanders were to decide that they could live under Argentinian sovereignty.

These are serious impedimenta to have been bequeathed, but at least policies can be constructed to cope with them which do not simultaneously have to attempt the reordering of large parts of the international system, which is the case with problems in category two. Of the same type, limited in scope, are such questions as the expectations which Portugal tends to have of good treatment from its old ally and now partner in the EC (despite the fact that this special relationship now presents far fewer advantages to Britain than it did in the eighteenth century), and the complications added to relations with India by the fact that many Sikhs who call for the violent overthrow of the Gandhi government, do so from their English domicile. Similarly, modern British governments have had to cope with criticisms from Australians angry at the anachronistic role of the Governor-General in the fall of the Whitlam administration in 1975 and claims made by others harmed by British nuclear tests in the Outback during the 1950s (Hocking and Warhurst, 1986). Another example of the endless unfinished business which keeps diplomats hurrying back to the archives, was the signing of an Anglo-Soviet agreement on the settlement of financial claims arising out of the freezing of assets after the revolution of 1917, no doubt an important small piece in the rebuilding of Anglo-Soviet relations (*International Herald Tribune*, 16 July 1986).

These then are the levels at which the past affects the making of contemporary British foreign policy. At each there is a process of causation at work, ranging from the irreversible impact of history on language and attitudes, through the provision of particular, knotty problems which have to be unravelled, to the structural dilemmas which demand attention but involve far more than just bilateral relations. This three-level approach is more helpful than the crude polarization between voluntarism ('policy-makers should not have been so backward-looking') and determinism ('Britain's offshore island position dictates various eternal interests, in sea-power, independence, free trade *et al.*'). With such a model it is possible to appreciate why the ubiquitous weight of the past bears down more heavily on some governments, or some issues, than on others.

The Capacity to Change

It is not as if changes have not been attempted in postwar British foreign policy at both particularist and structural levels. There have even been conscious efforts to change the decision-making culture in order to loosen the very grip of historical thinking (among other things). Over forty years Britain has come to divest itself of an empire, withdraw from far-flung military bases, reduce the nominal value of the currency by 75 per cent, enter the European Community, scrutinize the purpose and efficiency of its Diplomatic Service on at least three occasions and introduce a Foreign Affairs Committee in the House of Commons. On the other hand, all these things have been done partly by accident and certainly much later than some early critics advocated. Certainties hardened in the forge of time are difficult to shift from the policy-making mind. Moreover, it is arguable that they have been implemented with something less than full commitment, for the same reason. To the extent that hindsight suggests that British interests have suffered in consequence, individual politicians and officials must take their share of the blame for excessive conservatism or caution.

But it would be foolish simply to fall back on explanations based on 'guilty men' or the evasions of an elite trying to hang on to power and old policies. For foreign policy, *as an activity*, makes rapid or substantial change inherently difficult, while states like Britain which face major downward change from a position of great comparative advantage, are bound to drag their feet. In particular there is the problem of knowing where to go to, that is to say, what scope and function for foreign policy to find acceptable. If the political culture of the country is also (as it is in Britain) predisposed towards pragmatism and gradualism, then the accumulated wisdoms of a past and dominant age become enormously powerful barriers to change. Pragmatism should mean a willingness to face facts and to accept unavoidable change without fuss. In certain cases this has happened in British foreign policy, as with the recognition of Communist China in 1950, or the volte-face on negotiations with 'terrorists' in Cyprus and Kenya towards the end of the same decade. More often, however, it has meant avoiding major choices and sticking with known assets at all costs. The limp history of Britain's pursuit of American approval since 1940 is only the most obvious case in point.[7]

The virtues of immobilism in foreign policy are very great if a state already enjoys peace and stability at a satisfactory price, together with sufficiently flexible conditions to ensure homeostasis. But where (1) the costs of existing strategies are essentially too high, and (2) the pressure of change is acting to degrade the means of homeostasis, then rupture is likely, causing more damage than would have been incurred through anticipatory change. The Falklands is the prime example here. In financial terms, the ostrich-like policy which prevailed before 2 April 1982 was not onerous, but it was a medium (and uncalculated) risk. Moreover, the potential instruments of adaptation, relations with Argentina and relations with Latin America generally, had been allowed to atrophy. The result was trauma, and almost catastrophe. Although in such cases the flow of events has been suddenly broken, history still tends to have the last laugh. With the Falklands it was through the restoration of the *status quo ante* in an even more frozen condition.

In other circumstances it can be through the pendulum effect, as with exaggerated expectations of EC membership after the reluctance to join had finally been dispelled, or through cyclical returns to previous practice, as with the return to Far Eastern commitments via the Korean War and the South–East Asia Treaty Organization (SEATO), after the humiliating losses to Japan in 1942 might have been thought to have ended such aspirations permanently. In general, Britain has suffered a good deal in this respect through the decay of the principal means by which it has become accustomed to preserve status in the face of change. The economy has proved less and less able to support either rearmament or diplomatic pressure (British oil firms could not resist sanctions-busting in Rhodesia in the 1970s and proposals for economic sanctions tend to horrify Whitehall), the Diplomatic Service has suffered a near 20 per cent cut over the last twenty years, and the 'special relationship' has produced fewer and fewer tangible benefits to match its rhetoric.

Thus, partly through the nature of foreign policy itself, partly through the nature of Britain's particular predicament, and partly through errors and rigidities of policy, themselves connected to conceptions of history, Britain has found change a painful process in the postwar world. How well then, in comparative terms, has the country adapted? How will future historians, looking back on this era with the advantage of perspective, judge the British performance in the perpetual contest with history?

Evaluation

In contemporary international relations Britain is usually compared with the other middle-range powers for the purposes of assessing performance and capability. These are the 'analogue countries' of the report on the Diplomatic Service produced by the Central Policy Review Staff – France, West Germany, Italy, Japan, Australia and Canada (HMSO, 1977). Alongside such states Britain scored poorly on the usual indicators of economic well-being such as growth and productivity; it still tends to be found wanting on the underlying question of adaptability to change. The contrasts between the prewar and postwar societies of the defeated powers, Germany, Italy and Japan, are obvious enough, but France has also undergone a major transformation, from the demographic and industrial entropy of the Third Republic, to a state which now matches Britain in population while enjoying a higher standard of living. Australia and Canada, of course, have also achieved both high average qualities of life and relatively trouble-free external relations.

Yet such countries are surely not the appropriate reference group for Britain. Certainly for the old Axis powers, it is now generally agreed that defeat in the Second World War had in the long run some important benefits. Their industries were rebuilt with the help of American investment, their defence burdens relieved and their populations forced to confront the need for radical socio-political change. By contrast, victorious Britain won the freedom to maintain continuity with the past, which meant among other things the pattern of heavy industry which was already becoming uncompetitive before 1939, the rigid antagonisms of class and region and, most importantly in this context, responsibilities for the international system which were to prove costly in a number of senses. Australia and Canada, also victors but not superpowers, were relatively new and vibrant societies with abundant resources for their size of population.

Even the analogue state which is perhaps closest to Britain in characteristics, that is, France, is not quite such a shining exemplar as it might at first appear. The achievements of the Fifth Republic were only made possible by the cathartic crises over Algeria between 1954 and 1962, which nearly plunged the country into civil war, at a time when it had just been humilated by the enforced expulsion from Indo-China. Furthermore, the continuing insistence on an independent nuclear force and a military role in Africa may yet turn out to be expensive indulgences, as France struggles also to become a high-technology society on the Japanese and American model.

Thus, when compared to another major state coping with the end of empire, Britain seems less rigid than when the amnesiac modernity of Bonn or Tokyo is the yardstick. This is even more the case when a longer perspective is introduced. The imperial declines of Spain and then the Netherlands from the seventeenth century onwards were slow and incompetently handled, although admittedly beginning in an age when the pace of change itself was slow. It may be that towards the end of the twenty-first century, when the 'end of the postwar era' can be seen in context, Britain's management of decline will be judged to have been relatively sophisticated and far-sighted and to have displayed a high degree of adaptability in testing circumstances. Despite a number of embarrassments, Britain has been comparatively quick to spot and abandon losing causes in the period since 1945.

Whether this favourable picture of British foreign policy is correct is the question which now needs addressing. Britain may not have performed so badly as facile comparisons with other states suggest, but has policy been as flexible as it might have been? The trouble with the plausible image of the British as having faced a uniquely traumatic period of transition and having risen realistically to the challenge, is that it is one-eyed. It focuses almost wholly on the successes of decolonization – although depending on one's political perspective on the Cold War, it might also be fair to give credit to Attlee and Bevin for committing the United States to the defence of Europe and constructing NATO. There are many other aspects of policy to consider, such as the long-term consequences of hurried partition in India in 1947, the abandonment of Palestine the next year and the humiliation of Suez in 1956. Then there is the non-colonial side of foreign policy, such as the maintenance of a high-cost defence posture to the possible detriment of the economy, the neglect of commercial policy, and the lack of a clear and vigorous policy towards Western Europe for almost the whole postwar period.

Even those responsible would probably admit that there have been many serious wrong turnings in modern British foreign policy. Below the familiar crises of war and peace, there have still been such regular embarrassments as Philby and Maclean, Skybolt, Rhodesian UDI, de Gaulle's two 'nons', the expensive support of a overvalued pound and such recent demonstrations of reduced status as the lectures administered to Foreign Secretaries Carrington and Howe by the leaders of Malaysia and Zambia in 1982 and 1986 respectively.[8] Mistakes cannot be avoided in the turbulent world of international politics, but they may be reduced through a sense of history which is sophisticated enough to serve as a theory of change – that is, an ability to see the present as a bridge between past and future, not simply a screen on which history is to be run again but with errors edited out. Too often British policy has seemed to be flying by the seat of its pants, even with its supposed successes, as with the 'wind of change' speech. There has been little impression of decision-makers attempting systematically to identify those forces which are at the end of their historical span, those which are in the ascendant and those just emerging. Marxists may have a peculiarly narrow view of which factors are important, but at least they have a theory of historical change which encourages discrimination. Western pluralists tend to fall back on static pictures of politics and therefore to be surprised when some elements in the image fall by the wayside and others emerge as if from nowhere.

This is particularly evident with the famous 'three circles' metaphor, which was one of Churchill's most enduring bequests to his successors. Successive governments have been reluctant to depart from the notion that Britain has unique advantages because it is at the point of intersection between the three interlocking circles of the Atlantic area, Europe and the Commonwealth. Although in practice there has been a certain move away from the Commonwealth as a forum for consultations, and it would be diplomatically needless to throw away a card by publicly announcing an end to the doctrine, it is still the case that Britain finds it difficult to change its self-image of major bridge-builder in international relations, with a consequent unwillingness to give up the hope of having the best of all possible worlds by making a fuller commitment to one circle, or accepting realistically the limited benefits of another. The three circles concept implies that Britain can engage in some kind of eternal juggling act, with no need to choose priorities between the groupings. It also produces an insouciance about the inevitable processes of change which take place *within* the United States, Europe and the Commonwealth, and which can affect their appropriateness as reliable partners.

Similarly, the endless quest to identify a new, post-imperial role for Britain, which was started by Dean Acheson in 1962[9] but seemed to preoccupy the establishment for the following decade, was conducted in static and simplistic terms (Hill, 1979). Realism about new status as 'a major power of the second order' was wholly necessary, but it was not sufficient as a way of thinking about the changes facing British foreign policy. Identifying the relevant place in a league table of power, or confirming that Britain still has a niche at the 'top table' of international diplomacy, tells us little about the nature of the threats facing Britain, the impact of external relations on British society, those relationships which are crucial and those which are subordinate, or the level of resources which should be devoted to defence.

The search for roles also encourages an emphasis on 'turning points' or the obverse, 'missed opportunities', which casts a misleadingly apocalyptic light on the processes of change. Politicians are in the nature of things always heralding major crossroads, or dramatizing key events in which personalities (their own if things have gone well, others if not) have played a central role. For their part, historians tend to be more cautious, seeing cataclysmic revolutions as in fact having begun generations before and making in the end little difference to the old regimes they were supposed to be supplanting. The historians are the more nearly correct. Although it is useful to look back on British foreign policy and to recognize the important symbolism of events like the Washington Naval Conference of 1922, which demonstrated the limits to British sea-power, or the August 1961 application for entry to the EEC, these are little more than convenient pegs on which to hang discussions of broad trends.

It is thus an illusion to suppose that agreement can be reached among scholars looking back, let alone decision-makers in the heat of battle, on specific dates before which certain choices were unthinkable and after which others became impossible – for example, not all would agree even now that the chances of agreement between Britain and Nazi Germany in 1939–40 were near to zero. All the interesting things about British foreign policy hinge on far more complex patterns of causation than dramatic years or single events: conversely, it is pointless to spend too much time berating dead or ennobled prime ministers for missing the boat, whether at Versailles, Munich, Yalta, Messina, or Suez. In the medium term there is always a period of transition. Just as what is done is always susceptible to being undone by those with will and determination, so that which is undone can be made good by vision and subtlety later on. It is only when time reveals a pattern of actions or inactions that the need for explanations and excoriations becomes pressing.

If decision-makers tend to oversimplify and overdramatize the past, they are encouraged to do so by the rest of us, particularly through the party political process. Debates on contemporary issues in long-established cultures like the British and French are

always likely to throw up ghosts like those of Tonypandy or
Dreyfus, Gaitskell or de Daulle. As often as not this produces
phoney, synthesized versions of the past which are used either as a
clarion call to continue some tradition of heroic gesture (such as
resistance to aggression) or to emphasize the difficulty of change.
Both tend to obfuscate the real issues and do violence to history,
but the latter is particularly prevalent. In discussions of British
foreign policy, it is common to hear that decision-makers 'could
not really have acted otherwise' or that such and such a choice
would have been 'ahead of its time'. This can come from all parts of
the political spectrum and is used to explain why Britain did not
choose earlier than 1961 to join the European venture of the Six,
why the Falklands question was not tackled seriously before 1982
and why appeasement was not abandoned before 1939.

Such versions tend to exaggerate the weight of the past as a factor
in decision-making. Decision-makers themselves could not operate
with the conviction they do if they did not believe that their task
was to take the inheritance of history and rework it in their own
time. They perceive the fact of choice as being real, although they
may, by way of excusing themselves, often subscribe in public to
the idea of the sovereignty of history. This is akin to the well-known
tendency of politicians to fall back on simple analogies from their
own grossly distorted readings of history (see May, 1973; Jervis,
1976). The 'lessons of appeasement' is only the most overused and
documented of many such analogies. In this politicians are, of
course, aided and abetted by scholars sympathetic to their political
position, which says less about the 'treason of clerks' than about the
essentially contested nature of historical interpretation.

It has been the contention of this chapter that the making of
British foreign policy has been particularly deeply influenced by the
images of history held by those responsible for it and that this has
often had detrimental effects. While the worst excesses of nostalgia
and determinism are now avoided, an alertness to the complexities
of change, and particularly to its asymmetrical nature, has too often
been missing. There is a tendency in foreign policy to pay attention
to movement in the international environment, but to neglect the
changes at home which might be undermining the country's
external stance – by reducing the resource-base or the degree of
public support. While British diplomats have been regularly criticized on the grounds that they operate on the basis of a frozen view

of the country which they are representing abroad, in some ways diplomats have been less prone than their political masters to slide over tensions between domestic and external needs. Politicians of all parties have been responsible for the greatest continuity of all – keeping foreign policy goals in the first rank of priorities and not considering the need to focus more on domestic concerns. The consequence has been that fundamental questions like productivity, industrial re-equipment and social change have been submerged, without even (until too late) the shock to insularity which a predominantly international outlook should have provided.

For its part, foreign policy itself has suffered from the neglect of the domestic base, and there has been an associated failure to integrate the different operational levels of external relations. For example, there is clearly a gap between Britain's military status, through its possession of nuclear weapons, and the reputation of its economic performance, just as there is a disparity between British cultural influence, through broadcasting, education, arts and letters, and diminishing political or economic influence in areas where London used to count, like South America and South–East Asia. There is always continuity with the past, but at different paces and to different degrees according to the issue at stake, and the fact and consequences of this variety have been obscured by the historical pre-eminence of foreign policy.

This has meant opportunities missed as well as exaggerated. According to Johan Galtung, when an actor's reputation or self-image in one sphere gets out of line with that in others, something called rank disequilibrium occurs (1978, pp. 105–96). This means that differences in status and performance across a range of indicators set up tensions which can (unnecessarily) prevent the proper functioning of the system, as credibility gets called into question and resources get out of balance. To some extent this model can be applied to the evolution of modern British foreign policy. An awareness of such tensions is certainly preferable to the stereotyped 'lessons of the past' which tend to be the intellectual stock-in-trade of Keynes's 'practical men of affairs' who eschew theory (but are in fact 'the slaves of some defunct economist'). Instead of one-dimensional obsessions such as avoiding the errors of appeasement, disarming unilaterally, emulating Churchillian leadership, or making up for sluggardliness in Europe, decision-makers should reflect on how far the conditions which produced the successes or failures on which they look back, have changed unevenly, and what is the peculiar constellation of old and new factors which constitutes their own policy-making environment. Which elements that were fixed are now malleable? Which elements that were contestable are now givens? The Conservative Party leadership might examine the independent deterrent in the light of the first question, as Labour leaders have had to answer the second with reference to the European Community.

Excellent accounts exist of the history of recent British foreign policy – although in depth only up to 1973 (Northedge, 1974; Medlicott, 1968). This book as a whole attempts to cover the years since then in analytical terms, and it might be thought that this chapter, explicitly dealing with the historical background, would provide some chronological ballast. That this is not so, is because summaries of the long-term trends in British policy would be familiar and excessively general, while a synopsis of the period since 1973 would duplicate other chapters and amount to little more than a glorified index. Instead, an attempt has been made to analyse both the way British policy-makers have thought about their influential past, and the inherent relationship between past and present. The conclusion is that the image of a monumental past bearing down on a divorced but dominated present should not be abandoned in favour of an image of flux. British foreign policy cannot escape the currents of history, but it need not be swamped by them. The diversity and contradictions of the unfinished past provide choices as well as constraints – the trick lies in knowing the difference.

Notes

1 Harold Wilson first made the remark in 1964 and repeated it at the opening of the Nehru Memorial Exhibition on 10 June 1965. It is worth quoting what Wilson said in the full context, because the phrase is so often cited without even a source being given, let alone the meaning being drawn out. The Prime Minister said that he had sent John Freeman (a political appointment) as ambassador to New Delhi, 'because India and her immediate neighbours sit at the crossroads of the world . . . our frontiers are in the Himalayas and in the standard of living of the people of India'. (He had previously said that the future of Asia depended on the outcome of the struggle between 'the democratic way' exemplified by India and other Commonwealth countries and the communist way 'exemplified by a determined and extrovert

China'.) 'This is true for Britain, it is true for America, it is true for Europe.' The text of this speech is to be found in Box 66 of Chatham House's Press Library files for 1965, now held at the British Museum Newspaper Library in Colindale, North London. It was originally produced by the Information Service of India and issued through the Indian High Commission in London.

2   Anthony Verrier's book (1983) takes as its main theme the argument that modern British governments have been obsessed with maintaining the status of a world power long after the resources for that role had run out. Although Verrier overstates his case, he provides a lot of compelling evidence in support – albeit without proper documentation.

3   Bullock (1985, p. 89) chides those who saw Bevin as 'Palmerston in a cloth cap', for missing his uniqueness and the changes in circumstance which allowed an illegitimate carter to reach such high office.

4   In the House of Commons on 1 March 1848, Palmerston said (another freely paraphrased remark): 'It is a narrow policy to suppose that this country or that is to be marked out as the eternal ally or the perpetual enemy. Our interests are eternal and perpetual, and those interests it is our duty to follow.' The speech is reproduced in Joll (1967).

5   In 1975, Britain's exports to black African countries amounted to £1,053,481,000 (to Nigeria alone they were £511,694,000) against £684,251,000 to South Africa. By 1985, the figures were £2,103,630,000 for black Africa and £1,009,629,000 for South Africa. Source: *Overseas Trade Statistics of the United Kingdom 1976 and 1985*, Department of Trade, London, HMSO.

6   See *Financial Times* 30 May 1986 and 31 July 1986. On Britain's impact on South Africa's labour market, see *UK Companies: South African Pay and Conditions* report by EIRIS (Ethical Investment Research and Investment Service, 9, Poland St, London W1V 3DG), and on family ties, see Austin (1986, p. 401).

7   Sir James Cable (1983) makes a powerful case for seeing the policies of successive British postwar governments as evidence of a damaging reluctance to take a separate line from Washington when interests have diverged.

8   In February 1982, Lord Carrington reportedly sat through an uncomfortable hour with Mahathir Mohamed, who was angry at British policy on raised fees for overseas students and at the operation of the London Stock Exchange (see Leifer, 1983; also *The Times*, 9 February 1982). In 1986, Sir Geoffrey Howe suffered the worse humiliation of a public dressing-down from Kenneth Kaunda of Zambia during his fruitless fact-finding tour of Southern Africa on behalf of the European Community. See *The Times*, 25 July 1986.

9   Acheson actually said: 'Great Britain has lost an empire and has not yet found a role. The attempt to play a separate power role – that is a role apart from Europe . . . based on a "special relationship" with the United States . . . on being the head of a "Commonwealth" which has no political structure, unity, or strength . . . this role is about played out.' (*Keesing's*, 1963–4, p. 19181).

3 State, Society, Culture and British Foreign Policy

CHRISTOPHER FARRANDS

In contemporary Britain, major social and economic changes have intertwined with tradition and established power structures in ways which are peculiarly complex. This chapter seeks to relate debates about social and economic change to developments in our understanding of British foreign policy. It also explores the growing range of effects which international processes have on British society and the domestic uses of external policy. The primary purpose of this chapter, however, is to argue for a more systematic approach to the 'domestic bases' of British foreign policy which have been rather taken for granted.

Foreign Policy and Domestic Society: the Conventional View

British foreign policy has often been seen as the outcome of a bureaucratic and elite process. Vital gives a succinct justification for this view, claiming that policy is managed by elites which are infrequently or ineffectually constrained by a wider public (1968). Barber contrasts four models which provide 'alternative' explanations of the making of British foreign policy. Two of these models, the 'formal office holder' and the 'departmental negotiated order', are concerned with formally empowered elites. The other two, the 'pluralist' and 'public control' perspectives, look to broader elites in the political parties and the media (1976). Beloff analyses some important bureaucratic dilemmas in policy-making but without any reference to the social and cultural context in which they are managed (1961). Younger gives some weight to the domestic cultures and structures of countries with which Britain must deal, including the United States, France and West Germany, but gives no consideration to the changing domestic context in Britain (1964). Finally Wallace, in a very influential study, argues that 'no government can afford to ignore the domestic content of foreign policy', but then notes that there are severe limitations on public influence on policy (1976, pp. 88, 277–8). Most of Wallace's book is an extended analysis of elite and administrative processes.

This chapter argues that a focus on administrative and elite processes is inadequate. The workings of policy administration are an important part of any foreign policy system and Michael Clarke considers them in the next chapter of this book. But we must also explore social and cultural processes within the domestic environment, their relationship to the state and their interrelationships with the international system. To do this is admittedly to come close to undermining the notion of 'foreign policy', but it is also to recognize that the ideas and assumptions which underpin that notion – ideas of state autonomy, boundaries between domestic and international activities, assumptions about the purposes of foreign policy and the interests of states, for example – need continual and critical revision in the course of foreign policy analysis.

Foreign policy is a social process. The members of a decision-making elite receive their values, assumptions and expectations about the world from a wider society. They also owe some responsibility to that society, whether it is organized on explicitly democratic lines or not, for the way in which they handle power and authority. Leaderships which rely on principles of nationalism and/or party ideology none the less depend almost invariably on more than brute force for their position, and their authority derives in some way or other from their society. In Britain, there is both a strong democratic ideology and a powerful tradition that foreign policy is in some way outside popular control, a matter for the Crown or for executive privilege. These two traditions coexist in an uneasy, and sometimes very complicated, relationship. Nevertheless, to understand foreign policy we need to consider questions of authority, legitimacy and values. Nationalism and the interaction between the traditions of the Whig constitution (modified liberalism) and the Tudor constitution (the supremacy of the Crown) are central to these questions.

Another reason for studying the domestic bases of foreign policy is that the administrative/elite model focuses only on one form of power. It is plausible perhaps to argue that 'power over' policy is held by a fairly narrow administrative elite. But, as Lukes and others have shown, 'power over' outcomes is only one aspect of power (see Lukes, 1986). We need to ask how the policy agenda is defined and by whom; how consensus and legitimacy are maintained and communicated. These two questions reflect what Lukes calls the second and third 'faces' of power in society. In order to understand the significance of these dimensions of power in British foreign policy, we need to look at relations between culture, social process, the state and the foreign policy system.

It might be easier to accept a neglect of these domestic bases of policy if they were unchanging constants. There are enduring features of British society, of course, but most of the existing administrative/elite studies were written against a background of expectations of domestic stability which were common in 1950s writing on British politics. A decade of recession, rapid technological change, growing divisions between social groups and between regions of the UK, however, has led many writers to talk about the 'break-up of Britain' and to analyse the rise of new issues which challenge accepted ways of 'doing' politics. In this context, it seems wise at least to suggest the possibility of a new approach to the study of British foreign policy which does not assume domestic stability and consensus (see Nairn, 1981; Marwick, 1982; Held, 1983).

If British society has changed, so too has its study. Writers both on the left (Stuart Hall, Raymond Williams, Anthony Barnett, for example) and on the right (Samuel Brittan, Roger Scruton and others within pressure groups such as the Institute for Economic Affairs and the Adam Smith Institute) have shifted the ground of discussion away from 1950s-style consensus. While divisions in British society have widened, they have also become more serious subjects for study and comment. Domestic issues such as the Ulster question or immigration refuse to stay behind the boundaries of 'domestic' politics. Attitudes towards the independence movements in Kashmir and Khalistan are important factors in local government voting amongst Muslim and Sikh communities in Britain. The chemical accidents at Seveso and Bhopal had an impact on environmental and chemical industry politics in the UK.

Equally, there was widespread public concern, which may lead to a permanent shift in attitudes, after the most significant event in the history of the nuclear industry, the nuclear explosion in the USSR at Chernobyl in Spring 1986.

British society, then, has changed in significant ways and the study of that society has begun to change, influenced partly by the work of continental writers such as Foucault, Hayek, Gramsci and Habermas, whose ideas have been only slowly absorbed by the rather insular British intelligentsia. To understand contemporary British foreign policy, we need to go beyond the policy-making of the administrative elite even though decision-making, narrowly defined, remains the preserve of a fairly small elite. We need to explore the patterns of relations between state, society and culture. What follows is an attempt to indicate some major themes and arguments though many of the conclusions are tentative.

Britain in Decline?

Many writers in recent years have developed the idea that Britain is in decline. Though this is manifested most clearly in terms of the British economy, the roots of this decline, many argue, are to be found in British society and culture. Gamble (1985) and Eatwell (1981), for example, suggest a link between poor economic performance and ideological and political problems of adaptation in Britain. Wiener argues that the principal reason for Britain's economic decline has been cultural (1981). The 'decline of the industrial spirit' is explained in terms of a class-based 'gentrified' economy. While this account is flawed to the extent that other countries, like Japan, West Germany and France in particular, have also had a class system and gentrified industrialists which have not prevented industrial growth, this type of explanation has been very influential. There is a powerful image of Britain abroad as a rather antique, conservative society with an economy which has creaked into the twentieth century with little prospect of surviving far into the next. This image may infuriate British diplomats and business-men who suffer its consequences, but it does affect Britain's capacity to act abroad.

Whatever the causes of Britain's economic decline, it has had important effects on British foreign policy over and above an

unfortunate image abroad, though these effects were largely concealed in official statements until the 1970s. It was almost certainly
an unwillingness to give serious attention to the nature and the
direction of long-term economic decline which led British leaders
to believe they could act independently of the emerging European
Community in the 1950s (see Charlton, 1981). Led on by illusions
about Britain's strategic independence which were fostered by
'standing alone' in 1940 and by illusions about Britain's economic
potential which were concealed by apparent industrial and trading
strength, decision-makers felt able to attempt to maintain national
autonomy by committing resources to nuclear weapons, the
Commonwealth and the international role of sterling. Historians
will argue about when these self-images became illusions. But
when tentative references were made to the realities of Britain's
economic position in official publications such as the Duncan
Report (HMSO, 1969), which nervously described Britain as only
a 'major power of the second rank', the press and Parliament
responded with cries of treason.

It was only in the Berrill Report (HMSO, 1977) that the full extent of British dependence on a weakening economy was officially
spelt out for the first time. Even then, however, Berrill was
publicly rejected by the Labour Government in a White Paper of
stunning conservatism. But if it was still not possible for official
sources to refer publicly to national decline, many of the ideas in
the Berrill Report were taken seriously in private, both in the
Foreign Office and elsewhere in Whitehall (see Clarke, 1978–9).
Very similar ideas were put forward by the retiring Paris ambassador, Sir Nicholas Henderson, in his valedictory despatch which
was leaked to and published by the *Economist* (1979). The Henderson despatch was a vigorous, well-argued attack on economic
illusions in British foreign policy. It argued that economic performance is central to foreign policy, both in terms of resources and
in terms of how others see Britain. Diplomatic skill cannot wholly
compensate for material weakness, however much it may be able
to conceal it in the short term. The paper also offered a comparison that haunted discussion of British foreign policy in the
1980s, suggesting that the decline of the Spanish Empire and the
Dutch Republic illustrate how relative economic weakness can
in the long term consign once-great powers to absolute political
decline.

Social Cohesion and Disintegration

If one dominant image of British society abroad is of antique, class-based conservatism, a competing image is of social disintegration. This image means something very particular to citizens in Copenhagen, Madrid, Barcelona and Brussels, who have a clear picture of British footballers in their memories. When Italian football supporters died in clashes with Liverpool 'fans' in Brussels just before a European summit, British officials said they faced a wall of embarrassed hostility, even though no one attributed direct responsibility to them. Soccer violence is only one widely publicized aspect of questions relating to the changing nature of British society and British values since 1945. What has happened to the apparent social cohesion of the past? What is the evidence for declining social cohesion and how does this affect British foreign policy?

The evidence of a 'breakdown of Britain' is contested to say the least (Marwick, 1982, pt 3, offers the best survey of this theme). But the evidence for increased social change and increased complexity in relations between groups, ideologies and power structures, seems to be overwhelming. Roberts has argued that the myth of a stable Britain has lost its empirical basis on three grounds: the decline in support for the two established political parties, the growth of civil disobedience and the increasing alienation of society from political institutions as revealed, for example, in survey data (1977, pp. 162–3). Support for Celtic nationalism, 'Green politics' and the activities of peace movements such as the Greenham Common women can all be cited in support of these three propositions. Interestingly, where Roberts discusses increased civil disobedience, three of the five areas he uses as illustrations (South Africa, nuclear weapons and Ireland) relate to foreign rather than domestic policy issues.

Goldthorpe suggests that basic class structures have not changed. He argues that, despite economic growth and improvement in material conditions, 'no significant reduction in inequalities has been achieved' and that the 'working class has become increasingly self-recruiting and hence more homogeneous as regards the social origins of its members' (1980, pp. 252, 262). Townsend has demonstrated that poverty levels have increased in some respects and that the welfare system has failed those for whom it was designed (1979). Crewe and Sarlvik have claimed that British politics have been 'de-aligned' as a result of changes in the pattern of class-, regional- and employment-based allegiances (1983). They argue that increased social diversity has been the main cause of a changing party structure. Whichever class people may 'objectively' belong to, they identify less strongly with the 'old' parties of nineteenth-century class society. People's motives for voting are more diverse and this produces more volatile voting for a wider range of parties.

Jowell and Airey brought together some of these ideas in a survey of British social attitudes. They argued that 'there are actually several publics and many opinions . . . the relentless search for consensus [by analysts] impedes the exploration of diversity. By far the most interesting and revealing findings [of our study] refer to subgroup findings' (1984, p. 8). Young, in a contribution to this study, explored political attitudes. He found that while there was broad support for some national institutions, including the monarchy, the BBC and the major banks, the public was divided in its view of the National Health Service, the press and the prison service. But there was a consensus that industry, trade unions, local and central government are badly run, and politicians of all parties, it emerged, were held in particularly low public esteem. Young reported the growing feeling that the country is badly managed (Jowell and Airey, 1984, p. 29). The proportion of people who said they would resort to direct action to resist an unjust or harmful law had risen from 47 per cent in 1960 to 77 per cent in 1983, and the proportion of those asked who said they would join some form of collective action had risen from 23 per cent in 1960 to 77 per cent in 1983. This suggests that public support for the legitimacy of the law-making process has declined very substantially.

These debates engage in political argument as well as academic analysis. Any discussion of the current level of social cohesion in Britain must involve values and political judgement. However, while all the writers cited above take up particular positions, there is no consistent pattern in their conclusions. There are Marxists, liberals, commentators on the radical right and the pluralist centre in each of the groups who argue either that social cohesion has declined, or that it has been maintained, or that it is hard to tell. Many Marxists, for example, would agree with Kenneth Minogue, a representative of the radical right, who has argued that the attempt to maintain consensus through a form of social contract in the 1970s was itself a symptom of social breakdown which needs to be addressed more directly (1978).

There is a common view that British society is changing and that it has become more diverse. But this does not automatically lead to the conclusion that British society has been *breaking down*. Indeed, Halsey (1981) and Miliband (1973), despite their sharply different political positions, provide substantial evidence that key institutions and structures, like class, the family and the economic structuration of society, have not changed. They highlight the strong bonds which pattern British society, which provide continuity over long periods of time and which are expressed in attitudes and institutions and articulated in the social myths of popular television 'soap operas' like *Coronation Street* and *East-Enders*. Giddens broadly accepts this view but qualifies it by pointing to the increasing complexity of social structures which are under pressure from patterns of economic change, growing cultural diversity and the globalization of important processes of information and production (1973).

What does this very ambivalent debate about the nature of British society mean for British foreign policy? One conclusion is to suggest that British people hold multiple allegiances, which may in theory be in conflict, but not in practice. They support local institutions but recognize national loyalties. Established sources of social cohesion in the workplace have changed as the nature of employment has changed, but class patterns remain the basis of social organization. Allegiances to ethnic community (amongst Poles, Ukrainians and Irish groups as well as 'New Commonwealth' communities), generation, or gender groups (feminists or gay communities), have become more prominent alongside other allegiances. These new social patterns are significant for foreign policy in at least four ways.

First, on whose behalf is foreign policy to be made and how is the success or failure of that policy to be judged? If we say with Miliband (1973), for example, that it is made on behalf of the ruling class, it is more difficult to assess what is going on and what should be going on if that class is becoming more complex and parts of it are more heavily integrated into an international ruling elite. If, as writers closer to the liberal tradition would hope, policy is made on behalf of society as a whole, albeit mediated through state institutions, it is also more difficult to judge which interests should influence policy as society becomes more complex, social divisions more pronounced and British society more interpenetrated with other developed societies. The Westland affair at the beginning of 1986 illustrates this problem. The British government faced an apparently domestic decision on the future of the British helicopter industry. But that future rested in part on foreign orders, especially orders from India which the Indian government had blocked because it objected to new immigration restrictions imposed by London. It also rested on a choice of foreign partners; whether to merge Westland with the American–led consortium United Technologies or a European consortium. The labour force at Westland favoured the American option, the Labour Party and Defence Secretary Michael Heseltine favoured a European link. Heseltine resigned when most of his Cabinet colleagues came down in favour of the US link. The conflict here arose not between two (or three) classes but between a diversity of groups and between competing images of Britain's industrial and strategic interests. Social divisions amongst an increasing range of groups and complex interests make policy judgement and policy evaluation more difficult.

A second dimension of the impact of increased social complexity on foreign policy, touched on earlier in this chapter, is the image which it promotes of Britain abroad. It may be that other countries have their social divisions, and it may equally be that the image of the average Briton as a football hooligan is recognized to be false by most people most of the time. What may well count here is not the absolute condition of British society, but the perception that something stable and orderly has changed rather rapidly in the recent past. This is certainly the view taken by officials at European embassies in London interviewed by this author. Those officials have also noted the obsessive interest taken by their national media in the decline of social cohesion in Britain. As with economic decline, people abroad may have a false and simplified idea, but the image of social disintegration is a powerful one. Moreover, industrial unrest and urban riots provide empirical evidence for this view. The image that Britain is weak and unreliable affects its capacity to act, its capacity to conclude agreements and its capacity to avoid conflicts. While it could be legitimately argued that in the Falklands War both government and society showed a stronger face, it is also plausible to argue that if apparent social and economic decline had not gone so far, Argentina would never have concluded that an attack on the islands would have been worth attempting in the first place.

A third dimension of growing social complexity and the apparent passing of an established order which has an impact on foreign policy is concerned with legitimacy. In recent years, the legitimacy of policy has been questioned in ways which would have been almost unthinkable earlier this century, when governments could build a large 'secret state' through the expansion of intelligence organizations and through decisions to develop nuclear weapons which were never referred to Parliament, or even to full Cabinet. This expansion of executive power was broadly accepted by elite groups because of the consensus of support for state goals. That this consensus has been seriously eroded is most clearly shown by the contempt and mistrust between the parliamentary leaderships since 1979 and by the expulsion of a score of opposition MPs from the chamber of the House for calling ministers liars. Equally, the conduct of Mrs Thatcher's Private Office in the Westland affair, where staff believed that unconstitutional action to blacken a Cabinet colleague was approved at the highest level, suggests that some peculiar ideas of legitimacy have crept into government. In November 1986, the Chairman of the Conservative Party, Norman Tebbit, publicly criticized the BBC for what he thought was biased reporting of the US attack on Libya in April of that year. BBC officials were able to defend themselves against the substance of these criticisms but, in the course of the debate which ensued, it became clear that part of the argument was about the nature of the 'truth'. The debate over this issue illustrates a growing division in society and amongst media professionals about values and the way news items are presented. This is important because news reporting helps to legitimize (or de-legitimize) the actions of governments.

The Glasgow University Media Group has explored the implications of this, concluding that the media have great power in shaping the public's view of foreign policy issues but that this power is often exercised in an uncritical way which implicitly reflects establishment interests (1985). These arguments over legitimacy raise questions about the growth of relativism in public views of morality, the balance between the state and the citizen's right of access to a full range of critical ideas on foreign policy, and the question of what constitutes 'truth' in the presentation of public affairs. The willingness of popular newspapers like the *Sun* to distort or simply invent news despite repeated reprimands from the Press Council, suggests that standards of judgement in this context have become diverse, to say the least. This has an effect on every area of policy-making because it makes all political pronouncements more sceptically received. This in turn makes it more difficult to establish the authority of particular policies and more difficult to see how in principle policy can be legitimized. When civil servants like Clive Ponting and Sarah Tisdall leaked material which was politically sensitive but which had little direct bearing on national security, they represented the tip of a larger iceberg of civil servants who appear to be increasingly unwilling to accept the conventions of the policy process. This must make policy-making and policy implementation more difficult.

The fourth and final dimension of social change which affects British foreign policy relates to the openness of British society to outside influences. This is not new in itself, as the impact of romanticism in the nineteenth or communism in the twentieth century illustrates. But in a society which is marked by a greater variety of groups and cultures, by more political information and disinformation and by an increasingly questioned idea of legitimacy, the interaction of British and foreign groups has grown, with diverse effects on policy. Appeals to outside sources may provide competing ideas of legitimacy, as in the case of the Cambridge spies, Philby, Burgess, Maclean, Blunt and possibly others. Transnational links between political parties certainly facilitate the exchange of ideas and help to shape attitudes to policy, although they may also establish the boundaries of future disagreements. Newman illustrates both processes in his study of the relations between socialist parties in Britain and France and their evolving views of European integration. He concludes by noting the importance of the dialogue between the two sides but points out that this dialogue has not produced much substantial co-operation or agreement on policy (1983). Outside influences on domestic society and culture have also been important with respect to the continuing links between immigrant groups in Britain and their former homelands. For example, Jewish groups, mainly of East European origin, have campaigned vigorously for the award of visas to Jews wanting to emigrate from the Soviet Union. Tamil, Sikh and Muslim fundamentalist groups, on the other hand, have their own policy agendas in the UK. Environmental lobbies in the UK also derive a large part of their agenda, and many of their methods, from the more developed 'Green' movements in Holland and Germany. Thus, outside influences have an important effect in shaping the agenda and the arguments in British politics, as well as providing additional sources of ideas and legitimacy to which diverse groups in British society may refer.

This section has concentrated on social divisions and their consequences for foreign policy. But Britain is also a society held together in important ways. While some social bonds may have loosened significantly, others remain powerful. The next two sections of this chapter look at two of the main sources of cohesion and continuity in British politics, nationalism and the network of interest groups and representative lobbies which draw together economic and social interests in British foreign policy.

Nationalism

Nationalism is a powerful but highly ambivalent force in British politics, given that the UK is a multinational state. British national-ism can be evoked by external challenges. The most obvious example is the Second World War, where a unifying British nationalism was encouraged by a sense of being under common threat. This feeling was also the subject of much casual humour, however, and state propaganda which tried to manipulate it often failed. Even at the height of the Blitz, local loyalties counted for as much as national sentiments (see Harrisson, 1976). A sense that the nation is under attack in some way can unify the House of Commons. In early August 1956, for example, a strong reaction in all parts of the House persuaded Prime Minister Eden that he could command general support for the use of force against Egyptian President Nasser's nationalization of the Suez Canal. On 2 April 1982, in only the second Saturday sitting of the House in modern times, a wave of nationalist pressure pushed the government into a commitment to use force in response to the Argentinian invasion of the Falklands. While it is clear that the Thatcher government hoped to get support for a military operation, had it thought other-wise it would still have been forced to retaliate militarily against Argentina by the intense pressure from almost everyone who spoke in the debate. The only dissenter, Ray Whitney, a Conservative MP who had formerly worked in the Foreign Office, earned criticism from other MPs for a speech which was regarded as typifying weak Foreign Office attitudes on this issue.

Nationalism is, therefore, a powerful emotional package. It is as strong in the 1980s as it has been in the past, even though the imperialist ideology of the nineteenth and early twentieth century has largely disappeared. Nationalism has two dimensions which are peculiarly British: loyalty to the Crown and the doctrine of parliamentary sovereignty. Significantly, loyalty to the Crown and/or Parliament rather than to the state may divert support from government. Those civil servants who leaked a stream of defence information to Winston Churchill in the 1930s did so on the grounds of a higher loyalty to the Crown and to Parliament, rather than to a government whose policies they despised. Loyalty to the Crown rather than to the government is important to the British military, especially to Scottish, Irish, or Welsh soldiers, who may feel little national allegiance to any London government. The Crown may not have powers in the direct sense which go beyond Bagehot's description: to advise, to warn and to be informed. But it would be difficult to exaggerate its symbolic importance as a focus for allegiance.

Parliamentary sovereignty is also an important aspect of nationalism. William Wallace has explored the role of sovereignty in the making of British foreign policy, both in practice and in ideological terms. He concludes that 'sovereignty remains a powerful and emotive concept in British politics', but adds that 'whatever the breakwaters set up to stop further erosion of British autonomy, the tide of informal integration will swirl around them and new waves of international collaboration come pounding in' (1986b, p. 389). The idea that British autonomy can in some way be maintained matters in parliamentary discussion and in the media, especially the popular press. It is a routine part of every opposition case on issues like foreign trade, arms procurement and economic negotiations, to argue that the government of the day has acted in a way which undermines the independence of Parliament. Judged in terms of maintaining national autonomy, the Heath government succeeded during the 1973 oil crisis in keeping open an independent line of communication to the Arab states, although this was achieved at some cost to Britain's allies, to European Community institutions and to the prospects for long-term co-operation. It can be argued that Mrs Thatcher's unwillingness to join the European Monetary System (EMS) reflected the same values.

In Britain, parliamentary sovereignty and nationalism are inextricably interlinked ideologies which powerfully constrain policy. Closely related to this ideological context are national and, indeed, racial images. Eden would not have handled the Suez crisis as he did if he had not shared with many British people a strong dislike, even a racial contempt, for Egyptians. Xenophobia never seems to be far below the surface of British thinking about the external world and, as the sudden discovery of the nastiness of the Argentinians in 1982 illustrates, such contempt can be synthesized to order (see Harris, 1983). Northedge has suggested in this context that national arrogance is the most persistent assumption in British thinking on foreign policy (1974, p. 360) and despite continuing change in Britain's external position, this remains a relevant observation.

The character of Britain as a multinational state is important in foreign policy terms, although only Irish nationalism has spilled out into the international arena. Scottish and Welsh nationalism have been successfully absorbed into the British state through the Crown and, while they remain important domestic foci of dissent along with growing regional differences, they have had less effect on British foreign policy than the multi-ethnic divisions noted above. This may not continue to be the case, but there is little evidence to date of Scottish or Welsh national politics developing international dimensions, however strong they are in their own countries.

Nationalism and the particular features of British nationalism are fundamental to political culture and ideology in Britain. They provide the main bases of foreign policy legitimation and they transcend other secular divisions, at least in times of crisis. Nationalism may be subject to manipulation, especially in the popular press, but it would be difficult to argue on the evidence that nationalistic attitudes are created by the manipulators: they also reflect genuine popular feelings. Nationalism has a strong appeal and governments and oppositions draw on this appeal to gain support on, for example, defence policy. Opinion poll evidence suggests that most British people dislike nuclear weapons and fear nuclear war. The attachment of a similar proportion of the public (a consistent 60–70 per cent) to the British 'independent' nuclear deterrent, however, can be explained as much in terms of its perceived potency as a national symbol as to the perception that nuclear weapons make a rational contribution to national security. More generally, debate on foreign policy regularly involves bids for support in terms of nationalist symbols. It is an important guide to and constraint on policy, and the ability to manipulate national sentiment is important to policy-makers of all political persuasions.

Networks, Groups and Corporatism

There is a wide range of interest groups operating in British society, some only concerned with domestic affairs. But there are some 'full-time' international interest groups, such as Oxfam, Amnesty International and the arms control lobby. Other groups have an intermittent concern with foreign policy; the Automobile Association (AA) and the Royal Society for the Prevention of Cruelty to Animals (RSPCA), for example. The AA has sought to influence the debate on common insurance arrangements in the European Community, while the RSPCA has campaigned to control the export of live animals from the UK, a successful and well-publicized intervention in trade policy. These groups can be classified according to three criteria: size, access and relationship to government. First, groups which command widespread support are more likely to have an impact, to hold media attention and to capture legitimacy for their objectives. Second, groups which, for some reason, have access to government have a greater capacity to shape the agenda, timing and direction of policy. Third, some groups develop an interdependent relationship with the machinery of the state. Groups which can offer something the state needs, like information or the compliance of their membership, are likely to be advantaged.

These three sources of influence deserve closer examination. But before discussing them further, it is worth remembering how compelling the international environment can be and the extent to which previous commitments can shape policy. Also, governments which do not want to respect the preferences of a significant lobby may be able to use the demands of the external environment to overrule them. For example, it has become fairly common for

British governments to use EC legislation as an excuse to deny pressures for trade protection which they do not feel they could adopt. In other areas, where Department of Trade and Industry staff have accepted the case for protection, in high-technology products and foodstuffs, for example, protective measures have been introduced. It is also conceivable that a future British government, faced with populist demands for a restoration of capital punishment, would use its obligations under the European Convention on Human Rights as an argument for not bringing back the death penalty.

How significant is the size of a group in determining its ability to influence policy? Two of the largest movements in twentieth-century Britain, the Peace Pledge Union of the 1930s and the Campaign for Nuclear Disarmament (CND) in the 1950s and 1960s attracted the support of millions of people. Neither, however, can be judged to have been very successful in its attempts to change policy. While both won substantial support from the Liberal and Labour parties, neither had much effect on the defence establishment; they did not gain 'power over' policy. But both groups can justifiably claim to have affected the policy agenda and the terms in which the defence debate was conducted, and to have won a forum for their views in both the media and Parliament. In the 1980s, there has been a revival of CND and it has won widespread support from socialists, liberals, church groups and many others. Again, however, it would be hard to point to ways in which it has directly affected defence policy, even though CND has also been significant because it has a high profile abroad and runs its own 'foreign policy' through its widespread links with other peace groups abroad. Size may be important to interest groups, but the example of CND suggests that it is no guarantee of effectiveness.

Access is a more direct source of influence. Membership of a social elite, or regular meetings with officials and ministers, may help to shape access. But the limited ability of organized groups of naval officers to prevent naval cuts in 1966 (when the Royal Navy lost its large carriers) and in 1981 (following John Nott's defence review), and the Thatcher government's apparent disregard of advice from the First Division Association (the union representing the most senior civil servants), suggest that access does not guarantee influence. One needs to ask in this context, access to whom or to what? Naval officers may have access both to information and to policy-makers on strategy, but if budget decisions are overseen from the Treasury, their access to policy-making is unlikely to extend that far. By contrast, the special position of the National Farmers' Union (NFU) does rest in large part on its special access to ministers and officials. Many would argue that the NFU is the most powerful lobby in Britain, with a formal consultative role under the 1947 Agriculture Act which is reinforced by EC procedures and by its informal links with the Ministry of Agriculture. Given the significance of the Common Agricultural Policy, agriculture has become very much a foreign as well as a domestic policy issue. The NFU monitors, advises on and occasionally helps to implement policy. In Brussels, where the NFU has had an office since before Britain joined the EC, NFU officials are always available to brief politicians, officials and the press.

Trade interests such as the Society of Motor Manufacturers and Traders and the British Textile Confederation also enjoy good access to government. The Motor Manufacturers are responsible for negotiating directly with the Japanese industry on trade re-straints which keep Japanese car sales in the UK below 11 per cent of the British market. Similar but more complex deals operate in some sectors of consumer electronics. These arrangements enable the state to supervise the negotiations, as trade officials do, but to deny the existence of any intergovernmental agreements which might be in breach of the General Agreement on Tariffs and Trade (GATT) obligations. The British Textile Confederation enjoys a similar standing to the Motor Manufacturers, although it has not been as successful in its attempts to limit trade. This is largely because the textile industry has fewer bargaining powers and is distributed on the whole in less influential regions of the country.

Interests groups may work independently but more often they work in the context of networks of political communication. They may well have links with similar groups abroad, in Brussels perhaps or in other EC member states. They will almost certainly have links with Members of Parliament. There is a parliamentary group interested in almost every country in the world, which aims to mobilize support or concern for issues relating to that country. There are also interconnected clusters of individuals and groups which operate in particular issue areas. The development lobby, for example, includes members of all parties, of both Houses, and a number of academics and researchers interested in Third World issues, as well as established groups like Oxfam and Save the Children. This lobby has transformed the debate about British aid policy over the last twenty years, mainly by a combination of expert argument and skilled use of the media. But the transformation has not affected the content so much as the presentation of policy. Government aid and development policy is now drafted almost entirely with a view to meeting the anticipated criticism of the development lobby.

Successful lobbying is a matter in part of access to government and in part of media expertise. It also involves building and using political networks effectively. It is sometimes said that organizations such as the Royal Institute of International Affairs, the Royal United Services Institute and the International Institute of Strategic Studies have significant influence over British foreign and defence policy. Some individual members may well have influence, indeed their leading figures tend to be very close to the establishment, and these bodies can lend authority to ideas by publishing them. But their influence as interest groups is easily exaggerated; all have diverse memberships representing very different interests. Their undoubted influence among the informed public in fact derives from their role as focal points for networks of information and argument rather than as pressure groups *per se*.

The informed public in Britain is a relatively small elite based largely in London. It is grouped partly around the readership of a range of journals from the *Spectactor* and *Encounter* on the right wing to the *New Left Review* on the left. It includes a number of academics, who may act as parliamentary advisers to committees; advisers to or members of party political groups; consultants to government or pressure groups. Personal networks of this kind help to transfer ideas, or to import ideas, from, for example, the French intellectual debate on structuralism or the American radical right debate on individualism. This elite does not 'make' policy, but it does act as a transmission belt and a test bed for ideas, and as a source of criticism which may feed into the policy process (see, for example, Baylis, 1986).

Pressure groups co-operate at different levels, but a new pattern of co-operation can be identified as the recession has deepened, as production, finance and exchange have been increasingly internationalized and as the demands of the state have grown. What is called 'corporatist' activity in this context refers to the mediation of interests by large groups acting on behalf of individuals and smaller associations. It also connotes the incorporation of groups within the state machinery, as those groups come to enforce or manage policy on behalf of the state. Finally, corporatism suggests a new style and structure of political activity where the nature of the state and of legitimacy and power are seen to be transformed by the degree and scope of corporatist behaviour. This notion of corporatism has dominated a debate about the relationship between interest groups and the state since the early 1970s (Cawson, 1985).

The corporatist debate has interesting implications for the student of foreign policy. It has revived interest among both pluralist and radical or Marxist writers in the complexity of the state and its relations with society. It has drawn attention to the limited capacity of the state to control economic interests, though liberals and Marxists have drawn very different conclusions from this. It implies a degree of penetration of the state by outside forces which poses both a problem of control and a problem of understanding, but which Andrew Gamble has seen as a direct cause of political change (1985). Governments in his view have failed both the instrumental test (they have not managed to control what they claimed to control) and the intellectual test (they have not understood what these related changes in economic and political structure have meant). The consequence has been an ideological lurch to the right in search of authoritarian, simplistic, or romantic 'solutions' (see also Anthony Barnett's argument for the 'necessity' of the Falklands War, 1982). Corporatist arguments have also been developed in less polemical studies which have suggested that corporatist groups reach outside Britain and co-operate with each other, in the European Community for example, although there is not a uniform pattern of corporatist activity there (see Sargent, 1985). A number of writers have concluded that corporatist patterns of activity straddle and to some extent undermine state boundaries and thus weaken the authority and the legitimacy of state institutions (see, for example, Keohane, 1984b; Maier, 1984; Schott, 1984).

If these arguments are accepted, it follows that corporatism has transformed international relations as well as domestic politics. Foreign policy in Britain, as in other advanced capitalist countries, is having to find modes of articulation, forms of control and policy co-ordination, ways of combining interests, to meet these new complexities in the social and economic organization of politics. One response, as in the motor industry, is to hand primary responsibility for issue management to relevant corporate groups. Another response is to trade power over policy for information which only the interest group and its members can provide, as in textiles and agriculture. But a third response is to admit the inability of government to satisfy demands – for lower interest rates, a steadier pound, or a British market for high-technology goods which is not dominated by the United States (as in the debates about Westland Helicopters and Nimrod-AWACS). This last option was increasingly favoured by the Conservative government in the mid-1980s. Although Mrs Thatcher was a strong critic of overt political co-operation between government and interest groups, her government encouraged international corporatist exchanges. The corporatist debate remains a key focus in the search for an explanation of political change and, therefore, of foreign policy in Britain.

Conclusions

This chapter has indicated both the changing nature of the domestic context of British foreign policy and differing interpretations of those changes. It has been argued that British society has become more complex. Social divisions are multidimensional and increasingly differentiated. British citizens have come to identify with a wider range of ideas, cultures and economic interests than was the case in the past. The British economy has performed badly, but it has also changed, providing a context for new social divisions and sharper regional cleavages. British society, economy and culture have been engaged in increasing interaction with world society in ways which are either unmediated by the state or at best only partially influenced by state regulation. While the international arena has provided issues for the domestic agenda, it has at the same time provided resources for government to manage domestic problems in the shape of both excuses for failure and institutional arrangements for agreement.

These changes in the 'domestic base' of foreign policy do not completely undermine the 'power over' decisions which an administrative elite holds. But they certainly weaken the degree of effective control it can exercise. An analysis of these changes also points to other conceptions of power which help to explain the relationship between British society and foreign policy; power over agendas, communications power, the implicit power of majority cultures, and the established power of habit and tradition which maintain certain assumptions about the world. The analyst of British foreign policy can no longer afford to assume that a domestic consensus underpins policy. Nor can he or she take on trust the single factor explanations which have characterized most established writing about British society, economy and culture, whether it be Marxist, liberal, functionalist or structuralist. Whichever approach is preferred and however the theoretical relations between state and society are constructed, an understanding of the role of society and values in British foreign policy has to start with a picture of complexity, of a society under considerable pressure moving in a number of different directions at once, but sustained by some established power structures, habits and ideas.

4 The Policy-Making Process

MICHAEL CLARKE

It is both easy and difficult to describe the process of foreign
policy-making in Britain. It is easy if we choose to interpret foreign
policy in a fairly traditional way; as diplomatic relations and
political manoeuvres directed towards other states or as Britain's
attitudes towards international issues. In this respect it is possible to
define clear areas of decision-making. The Prime Minister and the
Cabinet set the general direction of foreign policy and co-ordinate
the different branches of government. Together with the Foreign
and Commonwealth Office (FCO), the Ministry of Defence
(MOD) and their staffs abroad, they constitute what Vital characterized in 1968 as the 'central core' of the process – though at the time
he excluded even the MOD from this group (pp. 49–50). Then
there is what Vital called a 'surrounding mantle' of ministries
which have an involvement in foreign policy but are not primarily
responsible for it, such as the Department of Trade and Industry
(DTI), or the Treasury. Thus the machinery is not difficult to
define and the way in which it operates and the forces acting upon
it can be perceived through the patterns of historical practice
(Frankel, 1975, p. 2).

On the other hand, the process becomes extremely difficult to
describe if we assume that foreign policy covers the sum total of
Britain's external relations. On this assumption foreign policy
concerns trade, interest rates, monetary management, foreign aid,
agricultural policy, safety regulations, investment, cultural matters, overseas students in Britain, environmental protection, and so
on, in addition to standard diplomatic relations, security concerns
and the politics of negotiations in which Britain is involved. In this
case, to describe the foreign policy process is to attempt to describe
the nature and substance of British government in general, and we

may wonder whether it is possible to define such a thing as 'foreign policy'. We should not try to argue foreign policy out of existence, however, for there is something quite distinctive and important about the relations that governments have with the world outside. The problem is that much of foreign policy – strictly defined – is essentially intangible and yet it is mixed into a series of all too real policies; domestic issues having reciprocal effects in another domestic environment, or economic pressures deriving from international sources, for instance.

Both assumptions recognize an essential facet of contemporary British foreign policy: it is a highly dynamic process which defies easy conclusions. To characterize the process accurately, we should recognize that British foreign policy-making is a combination of unchanging realities and evolutionary developments in response to certain demands and pressures. We should not characterize it as a policy-making 'machine' or a 'map' of power and responsibility. Such analogies are misleading. Rather we should see the foreign policy process in organic terms as something which varies in size, shape and consistency and which has a remarkable tendency to adapt to its surroundings and remain alive.

Unchanging Realities in the Foreign Policy Process

The most obvious unchanging reality which persists over the years is the fact of executive dominance in the foreign policy process. More than any other policy area, foreign policy is identified as that which must be conducted by the executive; it is concerned with the exercise of sovereignty in relations with the outside world. It is no accident that control over foreign affairs was the last major power to be wrested from the monarchy in the development of the British Constitution. Indeed, it remains the policy area in which the monarch's practical involvement – to give advice, to help build good relations, to provide continuity to the external world between a series of governments – is probably at its greatest. It is a trivial but revealing observation to note that a British ambassador is the Queen's own representative abroad. As such, an ambassador is entitled to a nineteen-gun salute, only two less than the Queen herself. The Prime Minister, by contrast, is not entitled to any guns at all.

Foreign policy was always, and remains, in the hands of the executive, whether that be controlled by a monarch or a prime minister. In practice this means that the FCO is one of the most senior ministries in Whitehall and that the administration of foreign policy is concentrated around the centre of government and directed through the cabinet system. The formal involvement of outside bodies and domestic influences has always been low. As we shall see, this tendency towards centralization is being both reinforced and challenged by modern developments. Nevertheless, it is impossible to understand the process except as something which is derived and operates from the centre of government.

A second unchanging reality of foreign policy-making is the way in which the cabinet system operates. In practical terms, the 'British Cabinet' is not simply a committee of ministers meeting for two hours once or twice a week. It encompasses a network of at least twenty-five secret sub-committees, a powerful secretariat, the Prime Minister's own office, and an untold number of civil servant 'shadow' committees, liaison committees and *ad hoc* procedures between officials of different departments. In Wallace's words, the system 'is less a machine than a network of well-understood procedures' (1976, p. 48). Though it is undoubtedly a highly centralized decision-making system, it is also a curiously informal one. It operates through convention and practice; there are no rules as such. The role of the Prime Minister is therefore central, for the Prime Minister can determine how the system will operate, what will be on the agenda, how quickly a decision must be taken, who will be on which committees, and so on. In practice though, the nature of cabinet government alters with each Prime Minister. It is impossible to characterize cabinet government unless we first know *whose* cabinet we are considering.

For the purposes of foreign policy, then, it is clear that the personality of the Prime Minister is vital. This is manifested in two ways. First, prime ministers may choose to be more or less involved in foreign policy. Winston Churchill constantly and heavily involved himself in foreign policy. Clement Attlee, by contrast, was involved more intermittently and, generally speaking, involuntarily in the foreign policy of the Labour governments of 1945–51. Harold Wilson maintained a consistent interest and involvement in foreign affairs in all three of his governments. Mrs Thatcher was heavily and unavoidably involved in major foreign policy issues after 1979, though this was more as a result of circumstances than her natural inclinations. Prime ministers can hardly choose the issues to which they have to react; the world around them throws up problems which cannot be ignored. But they can determine how much initiative they are prepared to delegate to ministers or others dealing with them.

Secondly, therefore, the relationship between the Prime Minister on the one hand and the Foreign Secretary and the Secretary of State for Defence on the other, is always important. Prime ministers may appoint foreign and defence secretaries who share their views and who can thus be allowed a large measure of initiative in policy-making. They may appoint ministers who have a particular commitment to a major plank of policy such as entry into the EEC or a non-nuclear defence policy, in order to ensure its implementation. Finally, they may appoint senior members of the party to these posts in order to have strong voices in key positions or to reflect their standing in the party. The possibility of friction between the Prime Minister and senior ministers can hardly be predicted, but it is a potential problem that a prime minister must be able to handle. The Prime Minister can, of course, remove as well as appoint ministers, but resignations and dismissals are not good for any government and there is always a cost involved when a prime minister exerts such authority. Between 1979 and 1987, Mrs Thatcher may be counted unfortunate, or even careless, to have lost two foreign secretaries and two defence ministers, a Lord Privy Seal and two ministers of state, not to mention an industry minister, in dismissals and resignations occasioned by foreign and defence issues. It tells us something about her brand of cabinet government that after the resignation of Lord Carrington in 1982, she turned more to her own friends such as Cecil Parkinson and Lord (Hugh) Thomas for advice on foreign affairs (Riddell, 1985, p. 207). Such examples suggest that the personalities of key figures can affect the policy process. The problem for the analyst – more art than science – is to be able to spot *how* personality is having an effect at a given moment and which issues may be influenced or even determined by it.

Another major and unchanging reality in the process is the relatively subordinate role of the legislature. Parliament can involve itself in foreign and defence policy in a number of ways. There is normally at least one two-day debate on foreign policy per session, plus whatever debates take place on an *ad hoc* basis or in response to ministerial statements. Question time is devoted to foreign policy on the third Wednesday of every month. Early day motions, serving as a vehicle for back-bench opinion, provide a barometer of MPs' reactions, generally to immediate events. Such processes also take place in the House of Lords. Above all, there are the committees. Most important are the twelve Select Committees of the House of Commons which cover every major department of government. Thus, there is a Select Committee on Foreign Affairs and one on Defence. In addition to these, there are House of Lords committees dealing with external affairs and with European Community matters. There are also the parties' own committees on foreign affairs and the respective party organizations which can play an important role in formulating policy positions, particularly when a party is in opposition.

These devices, however, do not enable Parliament to play a central role in foreign policy-making. Debates tend to be generalized, ill-informed and ritualistic. Question time is not noted for its penetrating political analysis, though the volume of questions has grown considerably, and early day motions tend to be a reflection of the prevailing state of Government-Parliament relations. House of Lords committees have some important points of detail to raise, and party committees are a good source of indirect influence – what the party will or will not accept from its leadership. These devices allow Parliament to play a role in foreign policy, but it is an indirect one. Parliament can act as a general restraint on a government's foreign policy. It can express its displeasure at some aspect of policy, such as the recriminations against the government in April 1982 when the Falkland Islands were invaded, and governments would be ill-advised to try to outface Parliament on such occasions. These, however, are far from the normal run of foreign policy matters and they do not represent anything like detailed scrutiny or a thoughtful critique of policy options for the future.

This lack of detailed involvement in the policy process is particularly felt in parliamentary Select Committees, introduced in their present form in 1979. These committees have not lived up to their early promise and they are certainly nowhere near as powerful as their counterparts in the United States. Since 1979, they have tackled a number of important and controversial topics, but they have also been steered away from a number of other issues by the government. When they do investigate an issue, such as the replacement for Polaris, or the Westland affair, their deliberations are constrained by the need to examine the implementation of policy, rather than the policy itself; by the lack of an extensive staff to back up their investigations; by a restrictive government attitude which makes it very difficult for them to question civil servants on policy matters; and by a government majority on the committees which tends to make them split on party lines, producing a majority report which is acceptable to the government on most controversial issues. That said, the Select Committees do perform a valuable service and in their commentaries on the specifics of certain issues a powerful and authoritative critique can be discerned. Moreover, it is clear that the Select Committees are an evolutionary development and may be expected to gain authority and constitutional stature in the future. The fact remains, however, that they still have no real power save the power of publicity. Select Committee reports do not have to be debated in the Commons or anywhere else. If they fail to capture the headlines, they fail to carry any real political weight. In some respects, the committee system holds great promise for an increased role for Parliament in foreign and defence affairs, but it has yet to dilute the concentration of policy-making within Whitehall and the executive.

A third unchanging reality in British foreign policy is harder to define but may be termed the 'ethos' or the 'style' of British foreign policy. These terms refer to a mixture of factors including the way in which the political elite is recruited (Moorhouse, 1977, p. 71), the perennial concerns of British foreign policy (Hill, 1979), or the received traditions of practice or the preferred way of dealing with the world (Frankel, 1975, pp. 112–50). All of these factors are remarkably enduring. Much of the acrimony between Mrs Thatcher's No. 10 and the Foreign Office on the opposite side of Downing Street stemmed from the fact that the Prime Minister disliked the FCO ethos more than its particular policy recommendations. Mrs Thatcher was visibly irritated by the pragmatism of British foreign policy and the emphasis on continuity. She disliked the FCO tendency, particularly on EEC matters, to split the difference, to support the initiatives of others rather than to take them and to regard foreign policy as a matter best left to a particular Whitehall elite. Even a government as vigorous as that of Mrs Thatcher was not able to inject the 'ism' of its leader – Thatcherism – very effectively into the foreign policy process. Rather, the Prime Minister was forced to circumvent major features of the process on the issues which mattered to her government and to accept an uneasy coexistence between Downing Street and Whitehall on most of the rest.

A final unchanging reality is the generally low salience of foreign and defence affairs in the public debate, which has reinforced the persistence of a national style or ethos in foreign policy-making. There are, as we shall see, important respects in which this is beginning to change, particularly on issues relating to defence. In an overall sense, however, it has always been the case that external relations as such do not greatly move the British public. The 'informed public', expressing its views through the press and broadcasting and through the work of pressure groups, plays only a peripheral and reactive role in the policy process. Mass public opinion is scarcely involved at all, since the political parties do not see any votes in foreign affairs, and the amount of popular reportage on external relations, though not insubstantial, is patchy and sporadic (Barber, 1976, pp. 107–12). If the general public is not greatly concerned about foreign policy, then the informed public speaks easily for it, in a voice which has tended to express the traditions and the continuity of the policy process (Wallace, 1976, pp. 100–3). This reinforces the traditional character of the foreign policy process: the style, the lack of parliamentary power, the dominance of the executive and the personalities within it.

All of these unchanging realities are in themselves dynamic. They all apply, and continue to apply, but in different ways at any given time. There are other forces, however, which apply to the policy process but which are different in kind; new forces which are still being assessed but which tend to change rather than to reinforce the existing process. The next section reviews these forces and this is followed by a consideration of the ways in which the policy process has adapted itself in response to them.

Contemporary Pressures on the Foreign Policy Process

It is possible to identify at least four types of pressure on the foreign policy process, all of which overlap though they do not all point in the same direction. First, there are those pressures which emerge

from the evolution of British government itself: the pressures of
sheer complexity and the consequent problems of control. As the
business of modern government becomes more complex so the
enduring cabinet system has many more demands made upon it.
The cabinet system has shown itself to be highly adaptable, but its
adaptability may now have resulted in a loss of coherence. Several
senior ex-officials have criticized the system's inability to do more
than cope with day-to-day issues. Lord Hunt, a Cabinet Secretary
under four prime ministers, has argued that so much is now
imposed on the structure that there is a 'hole at the centre' of
government (Hennessy, 1965, p. 8). Others, such as Sir Douglas
Wass and Sir Kenneth Berrill, have made similar observations.
Immense pressure is now imposed on the liaison functions of the
cabinet system because so many issues straddle the responsibilities
and concerns of different ministries. In practice, the task of liaison
falls chiefly to the Cabinet Office and the Prime Minister's personal
office. This has correspondingly increased the importance and the
politicization of both officials and personal advisers. In 1986, Sir
Robert Armstrong, the Cabinet Secretary, Bernard Ingham, Mrs
Thatcher's Press Secretary in her Private Office, and Sir Percy
Craddock, her foreign affairs adviser at No. 10, all assumed a high
political profile over controversial issues. Such politicization has
reduced the deliberative power of the full Cabinet and this process
has been reinforced by other trends. It has been usual, for instance,
for a Cabinet to consider over four hundred policy papers in most
years. Mrs Thatcher, however, reduced this to sixty or seventy
papers, since she preferred to deal bilaterally, as it were, between
No. 10 and particular ministries (Hennessy, 1985, p. 9).

There are two interpretations of these trends. It is possible to see
them as a manifestation of the centralization of power: the office of
Prime Minister is now immensely powerful, such that the incum-
bent is bypassing all the other traditional centres of decision-
making. Power is exercised once more by a virtual monarch
surrounded by officials and associates who are not democratically
accountable and who are responsible only to the Premier. Alternatively, it is possible to see these developments as illustrating the
powerlessness of central government. Real power resides nowhere;
the centre is on a treadmill of 'liaison' and 'direction' in a vain
attempt to make sense of such complexity. In reality, the centre
does no more than troubleshoot from day to day, ministers do no

more than survive the enormous workload and 'co-ordination' passes for policy.

Whichever interpretation seems the more convincing, it is clear that such developments pose great problems for foreign policy-making. The FCO and the MOD are senior ministries in Whitehall, the FCO is second only to the Treasury in political weight. Yet this seniority counts for little if all the most important information and decisions are in the hands of officials and advisers at the centre. It was clear by the mid-1970s that there were major questions to be faced regarding the size and function of the FCO. Should it become a 'superministry' to direct all the major aspects of external policy – trade, agriculture, EC relations, defence industries – and receive only political direction from the Cabinet? Alternatively, should it be far smaller, concerned with diplomatic relations – narrowly defined – and leave all other relevant activities to the Cabinet Office or some new and powerful foreign policy executive? How, in other words, should the foreign policy process adapt itself to the growth of such complexity in British government? This was the essential problem faced by the Central Policy Review Staff (CPRS) when it produced its mammoth *Review of Overseas Representation* (HMSO, 1977): to define the requirements of 'overseas representation' and to try to decide which parts of the bureaucracy could best fulfil them.

A good example of some of the facets of this problem is provided by the administration of the secret services. There are many necessary inputs to the intelligence services; the four most important sources are M15, M16, GCHQ and the Defence Intelligence Staff. There may also be involvement, however, from the Home Office, the MOD, the FCO and the Northern Ireland Office, as well as the Allied Intelligence Services (which usually consist of representatives from the USA, Canada, Australia, and, until recently, New Zealand). Even for this specialized, sensitive function, therefore, the range of participants is both complex and international. How is it organized? The *budget* for security activities is determined within the Cabinet Office, worked out by senior officials in a Permanent Secretaries Intelligence Steering Committee which meets four times a year and is answerable only to the Prime Minister (Hennessy, 1986; Wilson, 1976, pp. 167–8). No other politicians are directly involved and ministers are consulted on a 'need to know' basis. The *operations* of the secret services are also co-ordinated through the Cabinet

Office. The office services the Cabinet's Joint Intelligence Committee which in turn transmits certain material, through a weekly 'Red Book' threat assessment, to the Cabinet's Committee on Defence and Overseas Policy. The chairman of the Joint Intelligence Committee and the director-generals of MI5 and MI6 have personal and direct access to the Prime Minister.

This is a cabinet government process that is at once centralized, complex and unaccountable. Until recently, it functioned well enough because it remained confidential and unquestioned. In the mid-1980s, however, in the face of leaks, memoirs, embarrassing failures and the disruption of the common allied effort to pool information, the system began to unravel (Hennessy, 1986). Clearly, intelligence has major foreign policy implications, and it is not obvious how it should be handled, or by whom. Secret services have to be directed at the highest political level. Yet this does not necessarily make for efficiency and cannot shield the process from international pressures for its lack of discretion, or from domestic pressures for its lack of accountability.

A second major source of pressure on the foreign policy process arises from the international environment in which Britain operates. This is not the place to discuss the nature of that environment in detail but the relevant features can be summarized briefly, if somewhat crudely. To begin with, Britain's foreign relations are predominantly and increasingly concerned with the western world: Western Europe, the Organization for Economic Co-operation and Development (OECD) countries, and the Atlantic Alliance. Within this complex of actors and issues, there is a very high level of interdependence. This does not imply that all countries' policies become the same: indeed, the states of Western Europe handle their interdependent problems in distinctively national ways (Wallace, 1986a, pp. 205–24). It does mean, however, that almost all issues will, to a greater or lesser extent, be multilateral. It also means that issues will characteristically straddle the boundary between foreign and domestic policy. Thus, interdependence does not create harmony, but it does produce great complexity and a management problem that leads us to question how foreign or defence policy should be defined. The CPRS, for instance, found that of the personnel working on Britain's external relations – broadly defined – 55 per cent worked in Britain and 45 per cent abroad; whilst only 46 per cent of the total were employed through the FCO and only

14 per cent were members of the Diplomatic Service (1977, p. ix, para. 21:56). Clearly, Britain's foreign policy is being handled by many people who would not traditionally have been regarded as part of the foreign policy community.

Though interdependence does not necessarily promote international solutions to problems, it does encourage the rapid growth of multilateral arrangements – more or less formal, more or less successful – which tend to structure the timing and the presentation of states' policies. In 1977, the CPRS recorded 126 international organizations to which Britain paid a subscription (pp. 408–10). The European Community, NATO and the OECD provide the most significant structures in which Britain is involved. But even these organizations, extensive as they are, tend to facilitate webs of contacts and meetings at a less formal level. They encourage patterns of multilateral behaviour which, by convention, become institutionalized. It is virtually impossible, in fact, to think of any aspect of British external relations which is not in some way contingent on a multilateral response.

The international environment, then, presents Britain with a web of commitments, difficult to visualize with any precision, probably greater than at any other time and showing every sign of a consistent increase. The 'overload' of domestic government is all part of precisely the same process which 'overloads' the international politics of the western world. A dramatic illustration of the nature of such a web of commitments is provided by public expenditure figures. Table 4.1 presents a conservative estimate of the amount of public expenditure which is wrapped up in Britain's external relations. This area accounts for just under 24 per cent of all central government expenditure and involves at least ten different spending ministries and numerous subordinate agencies. This is a good index of Britain's international commitments and it indicates both the degree of constraint the government must handle and the interaction of foreign and domestic issues.

A third source of pressure on the foreign policy process arises from the domestic environment itself. One of the symptoms of increasing interdependence is the way in which apparent foreign policy issues have domestic implications, and vice versa. In a world of 'mixed' issues, the foreign policy process comes under pressure from domestic interest groups who see their well-being affected by international developments such as high interest rates, trade

Table 4.1   *International Elements of Public Expenditure*

	1974/5 £	1979/80 £	1984/5 £
Defence Budget	4,215,000,000	9,226,000,000	17,186,000,000
FCO & Overseas Development Administration Budget	758,000,000	1,249,000,000	1,804,000,000
Ministry of Overseas Development	49,220,000		
Ministry of Agriculture	49,259,000	229,742,000	468,951,000
Board of Trade/DTI inc. Exports Credit Guarantee Dept	632,550,300	340,048,440	973,923,000
Home Office	15,512,000	9,576,000**	94,199,000
Dept of Ed. & Science	790,396	45,291,000	61,016,000
Science Res. Council	21,984,000		
Dept of Health/DHSS	3,332,510	6,001,100	9,307,000
Central Office of Info.	3,059,000		
Econ. & Finc. Assist.*	91,417,000	188,161,000	341,452,000
Dept of Environment		99,000	650,000
Scotland			80,182,000
Wales			35,757,000
Net payments to EC institutions (exc. overseas aid)[1]	−35,000,000	839,000,000	936,000,000
Total current prices	5,805,124,206	12,132,918,540	21,991,437,000
At 1980 constant prices	15,211,752,000	15,111,107,000	15,928,051,000
As share of central govt expenditure	21·5%	21·8%	23·9%
As share of GDP	7·25%	7·01%	7.12%

* Customs & Excise

** Does not include all the costs of control of immigration and nationality as in 1974/5 and 1984/5.

[1]EC net payments = Net payments to EC budget + contributions to the capital of European Investment Bank + receipts from European Coal and Steel Community.

Sources: Supply Estimates: HC 7439; HC 8494; HC 9702.
Extracted from Wallace, 1987.

policies, international take-over bids, anti-terrorist security measures, or whatever. The public's interest in foreign affairs, as such, may always be fairly low, but the interests of particular groups or sections of society with respect to certain issues seems likely to grow. To put it simply, many issues with which the foreign policy community has to deal are domestically sensitive, and complex trade-offs are thus involved in their resolution.

Thus, in time-honoured fashion, political leaders go to summit meetings and are seen by the world handling the great issues of state with their counterparts from other countries. Summits, however, are not what they were. There are many more of them, particularly within the OECD world, and leaders attend them under what can sometimes be acute domestic pressures to achieve (or thwart) certain agreements. In 1975, the 'big seven' of the OECD began to hold annual summit meetings to co-ordinate their positions on a whole series of issues. Within three years, these summits had become primarily concerned with agreements to harmonize domestic economic policies in ways which would be mutually reinforcing. The United States, during the Carter administration, was particularly keen to use these summits to organize the affairs of 'domestic' civil servants in the seven countries with the aim of creating 'interlocking co-operative actions' (Hunt and Owen, 1984, p. 658). Similarly, British leaders and officials have attended many an EC summit with almost the sole aim of bringing home the (price of) bacon to satisfy domestic interests. The need to achieve trade-offs between different interests has proved particularly acute in relation to the European Community. Officials trade off compromises in different policy areas – enlargement of the Community against agricultural prices – while politicians trade off compromises within one area – beef prices against fish quotas – when they present decisions to the domestic audience.

It is not surprising that there has been an increasing politicization of the domestic context of foreign policy. Certain policy areas cannot be insulated from public debate, no matter how centralized the foreign policy process may be. Thus, the whole range of Britain's relations with the EC is subject to domestic perceptions of that institution and to the vigorous party political debate which has accompanied Britain's every step in respect of the EC since before Britain joined. The Anglo-American 'special relationship' comes under fire as the public's confidence in the role of the USA continues to decline and the parties engage in specific battles over whether Washington should be supported on issues like the invasion of Grenada, attitudes to revolutionary Iran, or the bombing of Libya as a deterrent to terrorist attacks. The Anglo-Irish agreement of 1985 was a piece of international diplomacy whose origins and success were almost wholly determined by the domestic debate in both countries: an example of a highly charged domestic and international issue that is always subject to party pressures (Verrier, 1983, pp. 323–6). Above all, defence policy has ceased to be a bipartisan issue in British politics. The independent nuclear deterrent, Britain's role in NATO, the pattern of spending on conventional weapons, the future of Britain's defence industries themselves – all of these issues have been the focus of fierce party and public debates. It is not too much to say that, since the late 1970s, defence has been politicized as never before and on nuclear issues, in particular, the old consensus has been decisively broken (Clarke, 1987).

The final type of pressure which is now being exerted on the foreign policy process arises, in part, out of this. It can be characterized as the attempt to bend the foreign policy process to the needs of what Mrs Thatcher once applauded as 'a conviction government'. During the 1980s, the Conservative Party in government, no less than the Labour Party in opposition, became more committed to certain ideological stances. The Liberal/SDP Alliance, while trying to present an alternative to the 'politics of ideology', nevertheless found itself advocating a radical defence policy. Ideology is always difficult to translate into action, and foreign policy is an area which time and again blunts ideological fervour in favour of a more cautious pragmatism. Nevertheless, all major parties now have some radical commitments on foreign or defence policy and claim to be determined to carry them through. Less obviously relevant, but equally important, the parties have adopted radical and committed domestic policies which, as we have seen, may have important consequences for foreign policy. Thus, the seven-power summits that became an annual feature after 1975, underwent a significant change of character after 1980 as right-wing governments in Britain, the USA and the Federal Republic of Germany adopted monetarist economic policies. In political terms, these tended to be unilateral policies and they reduced considerably the scope for joint, detailed economic planning. This meant that the work and the outcomes of subsequent summits underwent a complete change (Putnam and Bayne, 1984).

In reality, 'conviction governments' make a difference which may turn out to be one of style rather than of substance; a matter of emphasis where a government tries to elevate certain priorities. But even a difference of style will affect the foreign policy process. It will affect a prime minister's appointment of key ministers and the relations that will prevail between them. It may lead to more political, as opposed to career, appointments in critical diplomatic posts – though past experience of carefully placed political appointees has not been particularly favourable. It will almost certainly lead to a greater degree of friction within Whitehall and between ministries and the Cabinet Office. Personal advisers become more influential, outsiders like Lord Rayner of Marks & Spencer are brought in to shake up the bureaucrats, and key appointments in the ranks of the most senior civil servants increase the politicization of the bureaucracy. In 1981, the government rode out a Civil Service strike, abolished the Civil Service Department 'which had symbolised the Civil Service being treated as an interest in its own right' (Fry, 1986, p. 103), forced the retirement of its Permanent Secretary and his deputy, and began to reorganize and cut the number of senior posts (Fry, 1985). In short, the adversarial nature of national politics has begun not just to affect the bureaucracy – it has always done that, even in the 1930s – but rather to structure it. In particular, it tends to affect appointments and channels of communication among the decision-makers. This may not, of course, be all bad. Nevertheless, it is a relatively new pressure to which the foreign policy process must respond.

The Evolution of the Foreign Policy Process

How then might we characterize the British foreign policy-making process in the late 1980s? Let us begin with the static picture as set out in Figure 4.1. This tells us that the Cabinet sits at the centre of responsibility. Of the secret cabinet committees, the most important is the Defence and Overseas Policy Committe, which plays a major co-ordinating role. The Joint Intelligence Committee is also directly related to external affairs. Other committees, such as the European Affairs Committee, have some involvement, and there

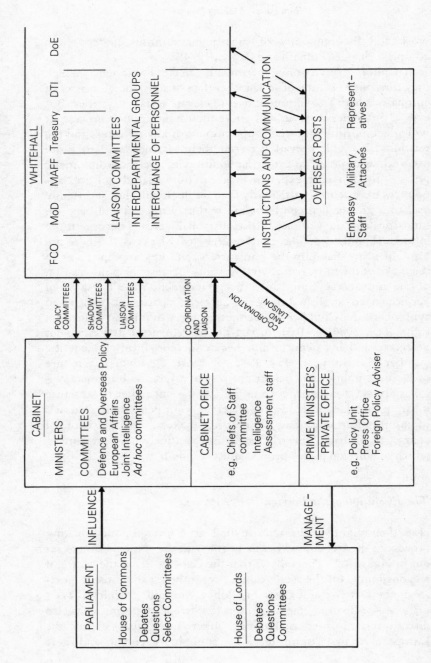

Figure 4.1 The static picture

will be *ad hoc* committees of a foreign policy nature such as the Rhodesia Committee (now disbanded) and the Falklands Committee (believed to be still in existence). Much of the work of such committees is facilitated by decisions taken in the Cabinet Office, in the Prime Minister's Private Office, and in the limbo between Cabinet and ministries where innumerable other committees meet. Some of these involve civil servants 'shadowing' the work of politicians; some are policy-making in their own right; others are there to liaise and back up the work of more formal cabinet committees and meetings.

Within Whitehall, ministries are concerned with their own responsibilities. The Treasury is a leading ministry and will have a voice in all major decisions. There is a traditional rivalry between the FCO and the Treasury since both are senior ministries and each tends to see an issue from its own perspective. The Ministry of Agriculture, Fisheries and Food (MAFF) has a large and active external relations branch and is noted for the detailed work it has to do in relation to the European Community. Issues, however, seldom fall exclusively into these ministerial categories, so there are numerous interdepartmental groups to provide consultation and liaison between ministries. These include outside bodies, such as the British Council, where relevant. Personnel is also switched between departments to provide advice and specialization where required. The static picture also shows us that in overseas posts, personnel from various ministries will work together, generally under an FCO structure. Some 35,000 civil servants are engaged abroad at a given time. On the other side of the picture, the influence of Parliament is in direct proportion to its political influence over the government at any one time.

Some response to the pressures outlined in the previous section can readily be discerned even in such a static picture. The vital importance of liaison and the role of key officials emerges very clearly. So too does the limited ability of ministers to keep up with the sheer intensity of business and the difficulty of being able to concentrate on more than a small range of issues at any one time. Ministers normally have to occupy positions in all three main areas of activity: in Parliament, as MPs, party leaders and constituency representatives; in Cabinet, either in full Cabinet or on some of the committees, or (in the case of junior ministers) on several liaison committees; and in their own ministries, running a bureaucracy and a sizeable budget. It is extraordinarily difficult for ministers to be familiar with and *be able to act* on more than a very limited number of issues at the same time. Lord Carrington, for example, resigned as Foreign Secretary over the Falklands invasion. Yet, as the Franks Report shows quite clearly, his analysis of the problem, even in 1979, had been uncannily accurate. His mistake was not that he misunderstood the problem, and neither did the FCO, but that he allowed it to be kept off the political agenda by more pressing issues (HMSO, 1983, paras 73, 75, 78, 187).

These points are reinforced if we look at the less static aspects of the process. It also becomes apparent that developments within the system are often contradictory. On the one hand, there is an inexorable shift towards a more horizontal bureaucratic structure across ministries and departments *and* across national boundaries. This becomes clear if we analyse the internal structure of the FCO. The structure of the FCO in 1974 was set out by Wallace (1976, p. 25). A similar snapshot in 1986 provides an interesting comparison, Figure 4.2 breaks down the 1974 and the 1986 structures into types of department. Some twenty-three departments are concerned with the administration of the FCO and its operations; there has been little change here over twelve years. Another twenty-one are geographical departments and show a number of understandable changes. The most interesting category involves the functional departments – those which deal with international issues rather than geographical areas. The number has fallen to twenty but represents a consolidation of what Wallace described as 'the main growth area within the Foreign Office during the 60s' (1976, p. 27). Many of the changes here are signs of the times. There is now a Nuclear Energy Department, the Consular Department fields a Football Liaison Officer, and 'Space' is now part of the bureaucracy. More significantly, the weight of these functional departments within the FCO has been steadily increasing, especially in such cases as the European Community departments, Economic Relations and Security Co-ordination. The Overseas Development Administration (formerly a separate ministry) also operates under the FCO umbrella and it too is structured around administrative, geographical and functional departments. This whole network is served by an extensive communication system which maintained, in 1986, 207 overseas posts in 162 different countries. It is presided over by a political team consisting of the Foreign Secretary, four

ADMINISTRATIVE DEPARTMENTS

1974	1986
Planning	Planning
Library and Records	Library and Records
News	News
Parliamentary Commissioner and Committees	Parliamentary Relations
Protocol and Conferences	Protocol
Research	Research
Inspectorate	Overseas Inspectorate
Personnel Operations ,	Personnel Operations
Personnel Policy	Personnel Policy
Personnel Services	Personnel Services
Security	Security
Training	Training
Communication Administration	Communication Administration
Communication Engineering	Communication Engineering
Communication Operations	Communication Operations
Communication Planning	Communication Planning
Communication Technical Services	Communication Technical Services
Finance	Finance
Accommodation and Services	Office Services and Transport
Overseas Police Adviser	Overseas Police Adviser
Permanent Under Secretaries' Department	Permanent Under Secretaries' Department
	Overseas Estates
	Management Review
Historical Adviser	
India Office Library and Records	

Figure 4.2a   The structure of the FCO: administrative

ministers of state to look after different areas of FCO operations
(one of whom is also Minister for Overseas Development) and a
parliamentary under-secretary.

A glance at this structure will make it clear how much of the
important work of the FCO is not merely 'cross-departmental' but
also 'cross-national-cross-departmental'. This is reinforced by the
intensity of British foreign policy in its contemporary European
context. A great deal of work has to be done to service commitments to the EC. In this respect, the FCO tends to take the lead
within Whitehall, in co-ordination with the Cabinet Office's European Secretariat. The FCO has always been more 'Euro-minded'
than most other areas of the Civil Service since Britain's entry into

REGIONAL DEPARTMENTS

1974	1986
Near East and North Africa	Near East and North Africa
Middle East	Middle East
East European and Soviet	East Europe
	Soviet
Ireland	Ireland
Western Europe	Western Europe
North America	North America
Latin America	South America
West Indies and Atlantic	West Indies and Atlantic
Far East	Far East
Hong Kong and Indian Ocean	Hong Kong
South Asia	South Asia
South-West Asia	South-East Asia
South-West Pacific	South Pacific
Central and South Africa	Central Africa
	South Africa
East Africa	East Africa
West Africa	West Africa
South-West Europe	Southern Europe
South-East Europe	
	Falkland Islands
Rhodesia	Mexico and Central America
Gibraltar and General	
Caribbean	
Pacific Dependent Territories	

Figure 4.2b   The structure of the FCO: regional.

the EC; its enthusiasm for European solutions has been a focus both for its leadership and for a fair amount of resentment against it in the Treasury. As the FCO itself observed, 'our membership of the European Community is central to the conduct of our foreign policy' (House of Commons, 1980, p. 106). More and more, officials from both the FCO and home departments are in regular and direct contact with their counterparts in other EC states. In trying merely to keep tabs on all of these contacts, the FCO inevitably plays a very vigorous liaison role. Moreover, with the development of European Political Co-operation (EPC), the range of subjects that are now considered in the European context has expanded and in this process, as Hill argues, the FCO 'has found an important new function' (1983a, p. 31).

FUNCTIONAL DEPARTMENTS

1974	1986
Overseas Labour Adviser	Overseas Labour Adviser
European Integration (external)	European Community (external)
European Integration (internal)	European Community (internal)
Trade Relations/Exports	Trade Relations/Exports
Energy	Energy/Science/Space
Marine/Transport/Science and Technology	Maritime/Aviation/Environment
United Nations	United Nations
Claims	Claims
Consular	Consular
Cultural Relations	Cultural Relations
Guidance and Information Policy	Information
Migration and Visa	Migration and Visa
Nationality and Treaty	Nationality and Treaty
Commonwealth Co-ordination	Commonwealth Co-ordination
Arms Control and Disarmament	Arms Control and Disarmament
Defence	Defence
	Information Technology
	Economic Relations
	Security Co-ordination
	Nuclear Energy
Cultural Exchange	
Information Administration	
Information Research	
European Integration (Information)	
Western Organizations	
Financial Relations	
Economists	
Passport Office	

Figure 4.2c   The structure of the FCO: functional

Most important of all, the overlapping of European foreign and defence fora has created a situation where European ministers meet on a weekly or a fortnightly basis in an EC, EPC, OECD or NATO context. A trilateral relationship of some importance has emerged between London, Paris and Bonn, which plays a major role in structuring the defence and economic policies of Western Europe. In 1980, for example, the four-power conversations over Berlin (which included the USA) were used as a cover for senior foreign ministry officials to work out secret accords to harmonize

European and American reactions to a range of delicate issues, without having to include all their other European partners in such discussions (Wallace, 1986a, pp. 221–2).

This growing cross-nationality of official contacts is particularly marked in the defence field. Since 1983, the European states have taken a number of institutional initiatives to strengthen the 'European pillar' within NATO and to promote European high-technology, defence and related industries, in response to renewed American competition. In 1986, the British government was involved in at least six different but overlapping institutions concerned with European defence co-operation: a revived West European Union, the Eurogroup, the Independent European Programme Group, European Political Co-operation, the European Space Agency and the Eureka programme to promote co-operation in civilian high technology. Day-to-day co-operation by officials involved in these programmes in France, the Federal Republic and Britain, is generally very good. What these organizations lack is more political drive higher up the authority ladder, in order to tackle some of the delicate trade-offs that are necessary to make them more effective (Taylor, 1987). The same can be said of military specialists within the NATO context: the degree of cross-national co-operation is impressive, even though it frequently operates within a constraining and somewhat incoherent political environment.

The effects of all this cross-department-cross-national liaison are not obvious. It may be that it indicates sheer confusion, as officials fight a losing battle to retain some shape to policy. More likely, however, given the expertise of senior officials and their proven ability to adjust themselves to new problems, what we are witnessing is the creation of several different, functioning, policy processes. It may be that we no longer have a 'foreign policy machine' in the sense that Vital used the term in 1968; but rather a series of them, which operate in different ways and establish their own *modus operandi* according to the scope, seniority and nationality of the officials responsible for them and the length of political leash allowed them by their overburdened ministers.

Despite all this, however, there has been a contradictory response in British government as the last ten years or so have witnessed a powerful move towards centralization. As we have seen, this is one of the pressures to which the foreign policy process has been subject, and at the higher levels it has responded to it.

There are two general motives for this centralization: to achieve greater political control and to contain expenditure. The foreign policy machine went through some impressive reorganizations in 1965 when the unified Diplomatic Service was formed, and in 1968 when the imperial structure of overseas administration was merged into a single Foreign and Commonwealth Office. This was paralleled in defence as the separate service ministries – Admiralty, War Office and Air Ministry – were merged into a reorganized Ministry of Defence. The Thatcher government further reorganized the FCO by winding up the Overseas Development Ministry for the second time in its history and putting it within the FCO as the ODA. There followed a series of manoeuvres in which Mrs Thatcher's style of cabinet government brought Downing Street into conflict with the foreign policy establishment. Though Lord Carrington as Foreign Secretary was trusted, his officials were not and when Francis Pym became Foreign Secretary, the Prime Minister seemed to regard him as thoroughly indoctrinated by the 'wet' ethos of the FCO.

Defence, too, was subject to close political scrutiny. When John Nott was Defence Secretary, he introduced reforms which strengthened the role of the Chief of the Defence Staff (CDS). Henceforth, the CDS was not merely a spokesman for the other service chiefs, but the government's chief military adviser. In 1984, the government created for the first time a combined Defence Staff, 'responsible to the Chief of the Defence Staff and the Permanent Under-Secretary' (HMSO, 1984, *Statement on the Defence Estimates*, para. 213), and backed it up with a Defence Policy and Operational Staff which aimed to provide an integrated civilian/military secretariat.

Inevitably, the desire to have more political control over the FCO and the MOD has been intimately bound up with the government's determination to cut the costs of its bureaucracy. In itself, the FCO can hardly be regarded as a big spender in Whitehall. Even including the budget for the British Council and the BBC's external services, the FCO's allocation in 1985–6 was £623 million, whilst the ODA's budget was £1,264 million. It can be argued that the FCO's overseas representation is well managed and good value for money. Nevertheless, fourteen overseas posts have been closed since 1983 in response to expenditure cuts (Wallace, 1987). Since some 80 per cent of FCO expenditure is on manpower and related services, it is difficult for the FCO to economize without reducing posts and/or restricting the scope of its activities. Cultural diplomacy, for example, has always been the poor relation of British foreign policy (Parsons, 1984–5). It is, however, an area in which other developed states make a much more concerted effort, on the assumption that it will provide incalculable long-term benefits to them. Yet money for such activities in Britain has been extremely scarce. Indeed, the withdrawal of Britain from the United Nations Educational, Scientific and Cultural Organization (UNESCO) in 1986 was counted as something of a windfall in the Cultural Relations department of the FCO, as some of the subscription could be redistributed to other programmes. The influence that Downing Street has tried to have on the FCO, first evident during the Callaghan government of 1976–9, has increasingly been that of a management consultant.

With respect to defence, the management consultant approach has been particularly forceful. Francis Pym, prior to being an errant Foreign Secretary, was deemed to be an errant Secretary of Defence, since under his stewardship the defence budget was felt, by Downing Street, to have run out of control. John Nott's brief was to contain and reduce defence expenditure. This he did in a painful review, *The Way Forward* (HMSO, 1981a), in which he chose to cut back the navy. The Falklands War demolished this policy and gave the navy a powerful second wind. But the problem of the defence budget remained. In 1985–6, it was again subject to cuts and it is almost certain to be the subject of another major review before 1990. In his term as Defence Secretary, Mr Heseltine introduced MINIS (Management Information System for Ministers and top management) to measure performance within the MOD. He also pushed through the establishment of an Office of Management and Budget within the ministry which echoed the procedures of the Pentagon.

All this may well derive from perfectly sensible and wise motivations on the part of government leaders. There is a desire to spend money more efficiently, to prevent the Whitehall bureaucracy from growing in numbers, to obtain political obedience, to give high-level ideological coherence to a series of controversial measures, and to find a way of making sense of an overloaded executive where issues fall less and less into the categories by which Whitehall is organized. Nevertheless, these objectives run counter to what is happening in the specifics of day-to-day administration. Faced with immediate, tangible problems, Whitehall officials tend to react as pragmatists. They follow standard operating procedures, they consult, arrange meetings, pick up the telephone and, like a railway timetable, find that as long as everyone keeps running, the system keeps performing. The fact that the Cabinet Office and No. 10 are so powerful leads inevitably to a plethora of committees and subcommittees which have some link to that part of the system. But more committees do not necessarily increase coherence and cannot encompass the sheer internationalization of bureaucracy in Western Europe. Thus all the major questions still remain. If so many ministries in Whitehall have a role to play in external relations, how should they be organized and their activities co-ordinated? If so many issues are both foreign and domestic, how should they be addressed? If the foreign policy process is likely to become even more domestically sensitive, how should it be accountable? Above all, if this analysis is correct, how should we define foreign policy?

One of the problems of thinking about foreign policy is that it is intimately concerned with the creation and the maintenance of symbols; of sovereignty, political identity and cultural cohesion. There are both historical and psychological reasons why this should be so pronounced in Britain's case (Wallace, 1986b, pp. 382–7). Western Europe of the 1980s, however, is characterized by the existence of a security community in which the specifics of so-called 'low politics' are both ubiquitous and very important. It is not just that the foreign policy process is *affected* by the forces of transnationalism and interdependence; rather that it is *part* of a transnational and interdependent structure which exists throughout the OECD world. In this situation, the price of fish is as important in Brussels as it is in Bridlington. So there is a paradox, more powerful in Britain than in some of its partners: we have to characterize foreign policy as having an important role to play in the maintenance of symbols of political identity, and yet also in the performance of functions which cannot be defined by reference to such identity.

PART II

Themes

5 Security and Order

The Military Dimension

TONY McGREW

Much of the academic literature on defence and national security policy still presents it as a distinctive issue area, insulated from the hurly-burly of domestic politics by a powerful societal consensus about how best to ensure the security of the realm. Defence is thus often characterized as largely a 'management' problem, implying that for the most part it involves a rational balancing of resources with capabilities in order to meet established commitments. Such a 'managerialist' conception of defence, though, is increasingly difficult to sustain given the turbulent environment which policy-makers inhabit in the 1980s. Defence has become a major political issue since the bipartisan consensus, upon which Britain's postwar security policies were founded, has been undermined by domestic and international developments. Cherished assumptions and long-standing policies are now open to serious challenges both from within and from outside the defence community – more so than at any time in the past (Baylis, 1983). Has British national security policy thus arrived at a new historical conjuncture demanding fundamental choices, or is the situation in the late 1980s merely a replay of earlier episodes in the management of Britain's decline? This chapter addresses these questions by exploring the forces that shape contemporary defence policy, in several key areas: first, the linkages between Britain's defence predicament and the dynamics of the international military order; second, the constraints and dilemmas that confront the policy-makers; finally, the relationship between military force and national security in the changing global political economy.

National Security, Defence Policy and International Order

According to Arnold Wolfers (1962) security is an 'ambiguous concept'. It is often equated with power and defence, yet it is in many ways conceptually distinct; indeed, the conflation of 'defence' with 'security' is often misleading, not least because security is a dynamic condition whilst defence is one instrument by which a given state may achieve that condition. In a global system of production and exchange, which can render the state vulnerable to a range of international economic forces, security clearly involves much more than simply the acquisition and deployment of military force. Defence policy is thus only one component of a national security policy and, as Jones suggests, 'the pursuit of defence and the pursuit of security are closely but ambiguously related' (1974, p. 87).

The suggestion that defence and security are only 'ambiguously related' smacks of heresy to those who take a 'realist' perspective on foreign policy. Most realists would argue that the lack of any over-arching authority in the international system places a premium on states' ability to defend themselves and protect their own core interests, if necessary by the use of military force. For them, military power is the currency of national security, and the more powerful the state, the more secure it is likely to be; thus security is 'reduced to little more than a synonym for power' (Buzan, 1983, p. 7). Since power is defined largely in terms of military capabilities, defence policy is easily elided with national security policy.

There are, however, a number of conceptual difficulties in equating defence with security in this way; three in particular can be identified here. First, there is a tension between security and defence arising from the 'security dilemma', which is a natural concomitant of international anarchy (Jervis, 1976, pp. 64–75). With no superior authority to guarantee their security, states arm to protect themselves, but in so doing they threaten those around them, who respond in kind. This can lead to a 'spiral of insecurity', in which efforts to increase or improve existing military capabilities merely result in decreased security for all. Defence policy and national security can therefore come directly into conflict (Buzan, 1983, ch. 6). Second, threats to national security are by no means purely military in character. External threats come in many forms – economic, technological, cultural, ideological. In dealing with such threats, the utility of military power is questionable, and as a result states have sought alternative instruments and mechanisms for achieving national security. Third, the dynamics of weapons technology have created what Buzan calls the 'defence dilemma' (1983, ch. 6). This is epitomized by the advent of nuclear weapons and advanced delivery systems, which make it virtually impossible for any state to defend its population against military attack. The doctrine of 'mutual assured destruction' (MAD), which still influences western military thinking, conceives security and stability as the product of a situation in which both sides tacitly accept the possibility of mutual annihilation. Attempts to establish a defence, such as President Reagan's Strategic Defence Initiative (SDI), are thus perceived as reducing security by increasing the chances of nuclear conflict.

Together, the three arguments summarized above lead to the conclusion that there is no necessary or simple correlation between increased military power and enhanced national security (Buzan, 1983, p. 253) and thus they lay open to question the whole concept of national security. Clearly, the idea of security entails more than just the absence of military threats or freedom from war. It concerns the relative abilities of states to counter threats to core values and interests, whether these are military, economic, ideological, or cultural. But security for any state also embodies a notion of order, or of the conditions necessary to maintain the smooth functioning and reproduction of existing society (Smith, 1980, ch. 1). National security thus has two central pillars: on the one hand, the maintenance and protection of the domestic socioeconomic order in the face of internal and external threats; on the other, the promotion of a preferred international order which minimizes the threat to core values and interests as well as to the domestic order. Thus in the aftermath of the Second World War Britain and the United States collaborated in the creation of a new international economic and political order which was seen as vital to the security of both states at home and abroad, as well as to their alliance partners (Reynolds, 1986). It follows that there are several distinct levels of security and order: the national, the regional and the global. In the case of Britain, perceptions of military security are profoundly shaped by regional security conditions such as the NATO/Warsaw Pact military balance, as well as the global balance of power. Security policy thus involves influencing international events and conditions – what Wolfers refers to in terms of 'milieu goals' – as well as the purely national concern with 'possession goals' (1962).

Military force is one of the instruments through which states can both counter certain types of threats and pursue broader milieu goals. British defence policy therefore includes the acquisition, management and deployment of military capabilities to counter threats to core values and interests as well as to promote a particular international order which is conducive to the country's security. For the most part, this means defending the western capitalist – rather than the specifically British – way of life, against the perceived 'seamless robe' of the Soviet threat (HMSO, 1986, Part 1, p. vi). As a result, Britain's military security is now defined not just in terms of threats to specifically national values, but also by threats to the shared values and interests of the Western Alliance.

Britain and the International Military Order

At the close of the Second World War, Britain was the largest military power in Western Europe, with more troops deployed on the continent even than the USA. Its position in the international military order gave it a seat at the negotiating tables of Yalta and Potsdam as well as considerable influence on the shape of the postwar international order. But the evolution of a bipolar international system, based upon the massive military supremacy of the two superpowers, combined with the structural weaknesses of the domestic economy, soon relegated Britain to middle-power status. Over the years the British defence posture has been adapted, albeit with considerable caution, to the realities of a new international military order – a process of adaptation which reflected the politics of necessity rather than the politics of choice (Wolfers, 1962).

Despite this forced adaptation, Britain still possesses enormous military capabilities and considerable defence commitments; in consequence, although Britain can be classed as a middle-ranking power in the international military order, this label is somewhat misleading. In comparison with other advanced industrial states, Britain spends more on defence, both in absolute terms and as a proportion of Gross National Product (GNP), and maintains larger professional military forces.[1] Britain has consistently spent more than the other NATO allies on defence, with the exception of the United States (Chalmers, 1985). It is the third largest spender on defence in the international arena and this, combined with its military capabilities, places it fourth or fifth (depending on the criteria used) in the military power hierarchy (International Institute for Strategic Studies, 1986; Russett, 1985). Along with France and the two superpowers, Britain maintains military capabilities that cover the whole spectrum of military force, from nuclear to conventional, strategic to battlefield, land, sea and air forces. The country has extensive defence roles and commitments to go alongside these capabilities; whether these can or should be maintained is a separate question, but the combination of capabilities and commitments means that the British defence posture is that of a major military power. This posture has four central features: defence commitments and political alignments; defence roles; military capabilities; and force deployments.

It is a truism that Britain's military power has not declined so much as it has been overtaken by the emergence of the two superpowers. The Second World War marked a historically unique and dramatic transformation in the global power structure (Ruggie, 1986, p. 137). By 1945, the United States and the Soviet Union had acquired military supremacy – a supremacy that was unchallengeable, and which became more so as each amassed a massive nuclear arsenal and invested huge resources in conventional forces. The bipolar structure of power has endured even though new centres of economic and political influence such as China, Japan and West Germany have emerged. In the 1980s the superpowers still retain an unassailable military supremacy, since no other state or group of states can match either the scale or the scope of their efforts. The massive growth of both American and Soviet conventional capabilities, particularly naval forces, has given them the ability to project force almost anywhere in the world; but their primacy is most visible in the area of nuclear forces.[2] Such nuclear supremacy makes any notion of a military challenge to superpower dominance unthinkable and militarily suicidal. It also means that few countries other than the superpowers can effectively pursue a national or independent defence policy. The political consequences are considerable, since the structure of power is 'frozen' and neither superpower could even contemplate hegemony over the other without risking armageddon. This ensures that the global ideological and political conflict between the United States and the Soviet Union remains one of the primary axes of world politics.

One of the results of the bipolar structure of world power has been the institutionalization of superpower conflict through the creation of rival alliance structures. In Europe, cold war politics led to the creation of both NATO (in 1949) and the Warsaw Pact (1955); on both sides of the 'Iron Curtain', collective security arrangements were seen as the only viable solution to the threat posed by the opposing superpower. NATO was little more than a formal treaty in 1949, but it soon became and has remained a highly integrated collective defence organization. It penetrates every aspect of defence policy and planning in its member states and takes collective decisions about strategy, weapons planning and procurement, force deployments and levels of military expenditure. As a collective defence organization, the alliance creates strong bonds of interdependence between its member states and generates pressures to conform to agreed policies, as with the 1979 decision to deploy Cruise and Pershing missiles in several West European countries. It also creates a 'strategic interdependence' between alliance members and the dynamics of the superpower military competition.

Alongside bipolarity and the growth of alliances, the advent of nuclear weapons has made the risks of confrontation between the superpowers so great that deterring war has become the primary objective of defence policy. To be credible, a deterrent posture requires the constant enhancement of military capabilities, both nuclear and conventional, just in case the other side might be able to establish a decisive military advantage. As Thompson notes, deterrence has become 'the ideological lubricant of the arms race' (1982, p. 66). In the context of technological, military and industrial pressures there is an almost automatic tendency on both sides to research, develop and procure new weapons systems to meet the challenge of existing or potential threats. This superpower competition creates a real dilemma for subordinate members of alliances, since they must either attempt to maintain the military effectiveness of their forces or witness their increasing obsolescence. In NATO, this poses a stark choice for member states: either they become increasingly reliant upon the USA for sophisticated military hardware or they develop it independently. Either way, the political, economic and industrial opportunity costs are enormous (Taylor, 1982). As the financial costs of weapons systems rise inexorably, the ability to maintain a viable independent defence industry is increasingly threatened – as both British and French governments have recognized. In addition, increasingly expensive weapons systems have to be paid for out of a limited defence budget, necessitating either additional defence spending or a contraction in the overall defence effort.

These three factors – bipolarity, alliance entanglements and the arms competition – define the contours of the mould from which Britain's contemporary defence posture has been cast. In terms of defence commitments, successive British governments have relinquished imperial ties, as decolonization took effect, and have reshaped defence policy in 'a painful recognition that of all her defence interests, only that in "European security" was, and will remain irreducible' (Kirby, 1977, p. 95). Thus as Britain withdrew from its global commitments one popular justification was that it 'made it possible for Britain to offer immediate increases in the availability of some of her forces to NATO' (HMSO, 1968, p. 6); Britain's frontiers were no longer on the Himalayas, but on the central front in Germany. NATO and the 'continental commitment' have become the foundation of Britain's defence posture and now account for over 90 per cent of the country's defence expenditure. As one *Statement on the Defence Estimates* explained, 'the North Atlantic Alliance remains vital to us and neither its strength nor its cohesion can be maintained without our crucial contribution. This is at the top of the government's priorities' (HMSO, 1981b, p. 1).

If commitments have been reshaped, so too have alignments. In terms of the 'three circles of influence', British interests have become increasingly aligned with Europe and the USA as the Commonwealth has declined in significance. The 'special relationship' with the United States was cultivated to give Britain some influence over the creation of the postwar international order, but the 'specialness' of the relationship concealed increasing British dependence, especially in nuclear policy (Reynolds, 1986). Not only this, but the 'special relationship' came into conflict with attempts to develop closer relations with Europe, particularly in the defence field – creating tensions which are still visible in the late 1980s.

Commitments are fulfilled through the organization of the defence effort into specific defence roles. According to the 1981 Defence Review, Britain's defence posture is based upon the fulfilment of four major defence roles: first, a contribution to NATO's nuclear deterrent through the dedication of Polaris to the alliance; second, the direct defence of the British mainland on land and in the air; third, a contribution to the forward defence of Europe through the British Army on the Rhine (BAOR); and finally, the maintenance of a maritime capability to defend the eastern Atlantic and the Channel (HMSO, 1981a, p. 5). To these established defence roles can be added another, namely the maintenance of 'a capability to intervene unilaterally or with allies either to protect our national interest or in response to a call for help from our friends' (HMSO, 1982, p. 32) – what might be termed the 'post-imperial' role (Smith, 1984). This reflects the post-Falklands defence debate, coupled with growing concern in NATO about the global nature of the Soviet threat. Despite this, Britain's defence posture remains structured almost completely around military roles defined by membership of NATO.

In a rational world, capabilities and deployments would follow directly from the specification of defence roles. This is only rarely the case, and in fact existing capabilities and deployments act to determine both the roles armed forces are expected to play and even defence commitments. Behind capabilities and deployments are the sectional interests of the armed forces, which are very powerful influences on defence policy. Thus it should come as no surprise to find that Britain continues to maintain 'balanced forces' – in other words, the ability to employ force across the entire military spectrum – and that each service obtains a roughly equal share of the defence budget (Smith, 1980). In effect, Britain's force structure reflects a desire to keep up with the superpowers, albeit at a much lower level of capability. This attempt to maintain a balanced force structure places enormous strain on the defence budget, since the increasing cost of sophisticated weaponry forces difficult choices on to the defence agenda.

Whilst it is possible to 'balance' capabilities, Britain's force deployments are largely concentrated. In particular, the continental commitment requires Britain to maintain its land and air forces in West Germany; the BAOR, with its 55,000 troops, consumes some 8 to 16 per cent (£3.5bn in 1986) of the defence budget, accounts for about 30 per cent of front-line forces and is a major drain on the balance of payments (House of Commons, 1982, p. ix; House of Commons, 1986, p. 136). The costs are so large – some 15 per cent more than maintaining the whole navy in any year – that the commitment has been regularly called into question. Not surprisingly, it is the 'navy lobby' which has been most vociferous on this issue, particularly after the reduction in the size of the surface fleet to fifty ships following the 1981 defence review (Freedman, 1983). The bulk of Britain's maritime forces are deployed on NATO-defined missions in the Eastern Atlantic and the Channel, but the navy desires a capability to project power further afield. Outside Europe, the only significant deployments of British military forces are in the Falklands, Belize, Cyprus and Gibraltar. Of these, the Falklands garrison remains the largest, costing some £250 million in 1986.

The critical issue that continues to confront the defence establishment is that of maintaining defence capabilities, roles and commitments within an increasingly stretched defence budget, at a time when defence equipment costs are increasing exponentially. But balancing resources with commitments has been an enduring feature of the defence policy process. The secular decline of the British economy has imposed its own constraints on the adaptation of the country's defence posture to the realities of the postwar international military order. Some would even argue that it is economic decline itself, rather than the changing nature of the international military order, that has been responsible for the painful and far-reaching transformation in Britain's defence posture.

Britain's Defence: Decline, Adjustment or Transformation?

The evolution of British national security policy since 1945 can be seen as a story of incremental adaptation to a new international politico-military order – the story of a former hegemonic power reluctantly coming to terms with a new position in the global hierarchy. To many writers of a realist persuasion, this 'coming to terms' is in effect a synonym for economic, political and military decline. At its simplest, their argument is that since the 1940s the secular decline of the British economy has made it increasingly difficult for Britain to maintain both its defence commitments and its military strength. The result has been a jettisoning of commitments and a reduction in military capabilities, leading to restrictions on Britain's ability to exert influence in the international arena (Northedge, 1974). This simple but elegant explanation has great intellectual appeal, since it appears to fit the facts well. But the various theoretical challenges to the realist approach, combined with more critical and revisionist analyses of British foreign policy, suggest that there may be other equally, if not more, convincing explanations. Greenwood (1977), for example, analyses the evolution of defence policy not in terms of decline but as a process of 'adjustment', and Jones (1974) points to a 'transformation'. There are thus at least three competing possible explanations of how Britain has arrived in its present defence predicament: decline, adjustment and transformation. Each will now be briefly explored.

A bold statement of British defence problems in terms of decline comes from Chichester and Wilkinson:

> Apart from a period of rearmament at the time of the Korean War, and the efforts of Mr Heath's and Mrs Thatcher's governments . . . Britain's defensive capacity has declined steadily since the end of the Second World War.
>
> (1982, p. x)

Although partisan in tone, this statement captures the essence of much of the literature. There has undoubtedly been a contraction of British commitments and force levels over the last thirty years or more. In 1955, the armed forces numbered 823,000, but by 1985 they numbered less than 326,000 (House of Commons, 1985, p. 11). Associated with this has been a reduction in military hardware, the termination of many major procurement programmes and the virtual abandonment of a number of defence roles, most evidently the ability to conduct independent military operations overseas. Underlying this process of contraction has been a faltering economic performance which, since the 1950s, has forced governments periodically to reassess defence plans in the light of available resources. The combination of low growth with rapidly rising defence costs has squeezed the defence budget from both ends; available resources are reduced whilst maintaining the status quo becomes more costly.

According to the theorists of decline, the 'dilemma of rising demands and insufficient resources' (Sprout and Sprout, 1968) has been responsible for the recurring need for difficult, if not agonizing, choices in British national security policy. The landmarks in this process have been the major defence reviews, starting in the 1950s and extending into the 1980s. Each of these reviews has played its part in the scaling down of the defence effort, and each in its own way has reflected the inexorable logic of economic decline. Thus in the late 1950s the 'Sandys' review, named after the Defence Minister of the time, called for a reduction in forces committed to NATO and emphasized nuclear weapons as a cost-effective deterrent. A series of incremental cuts during the early and mid-1960s were only the prelude to the dramatic debates of the late 1960s about the withdrawal from 'East of Suez', which was formalized in the decisions of early 1968. According to one commentator, these decisions 'were a genuine turning point in British defence policy. They marked an end to the attempt to maintain a permanent military presence in Asia, and a reluctant acceptance of Britain's reduced status in world affairs' (Chalmers, 1985, p. 88).

The agonizing reappraisals of the late 1960s, and the 'retreat to Europe' which resulted from them, did not mark the end of Britain's decline. In the wake of the 1973 oil crisis and the economic turmoil which accompanied it, it fell to the Labour government of 1976-9 to reduce still further the spending on operational programmes. By the end of the 1970s, though, there was a widespread perception that the Soviet threat was growing and that increased defence spending by NATO members was essential if the threat was to be countered. In 1979, the members of the alliance agreed to increase their defence spending by 3 per cent per annum in real terms until at least the mid-1980s and this commitment was backed up by rising support for the 'new right' in elections both in Europe and the USA. The Thatcher government elected in 1979 fully subscribed to the search for new military strength, but the onset of a severe economic recession during 1980-1 was enough to bring home the problem even to committed rearmers. In 1981, therefore, Defence Secretary John Knott introduced a Defence Review document optimistically entitled 'The Way Forward'. By concentrating cuts in expenditure on the Royal Navy, the review seemed to mark the end of any residual pretensions to a global role for Britain and it aroused strong opposition from the 'navy lobby'. The Falklands War led to a shelving of some of the harsher proposals, but the mismatch of commitments and resources remained.

Underlying this orthodox account of the evolution of British defence policy is a raw economic determinism. The logic of the argument is that economic decline has made it impossible for all governments, regardless of party, to avoid reduction of the defence effort. The evidence seems to corroborate this view: Chichester and Wilkinson assert that 'every defence review has been dictated by the considerations of financial stringency rather than military strategy' (1982, p. xvi). Furthermore, it seems apparent that the contraction of defence commitments and capabilities is a direct reflection of Britain's declining influence and status in the world. But there are flaws in this monocausal explanation, and a number of writers have been led to reject the orthodox account. The rejection of orthodoxy is based on two arguments: first, that the image of Britain as a declining military power is questionable; second, that changes in the international system have radically altered both the military role that the country is required to play and the significance of military power as an instrument of state policy. The evolution of British defence and national security policy is thus explained in terms of an adjustment to prevailing international conditions rather than as an automatic response to post-imperial decline. Indeed, some analysts would go further and point to a fundamental transformation of the conditions in which national security policy is made, demanding equally fundamental choices.

According to Greenwood, Britain's defence effort in the postwar period 'has neither contracted nor diminished but [it] has simply been reshaped' (1977, p. 191). In support of this argument, he points to trends in defence expenditure and to the nature of defence capabilities. With respect to expenditure, the argument for decline can either be strengthened or weakened depending on the baseline chosen. Comparing expenditure at the zenith of Britain's imperial power in the nineteenth century with the present-day situation, it is apparent that contemporary spending is markedly higher than it was at that time (Kennedy, 1981). Likewise, a comparison with the interwar period reveals that force levels and expenditure are much higher in the 1980s (Greenwood, 1985). Whilst British force levels have declined since the end of the Second World War, this is also true of virtually every other major military power, given the effects of demobilization and a return to 'normalcy'.

An examination of trends in defence expenditure shows that the resources devoted to national security have represented a relatively constant proportion of national income and that there have been periods of rapid growth since 1945 (Greenwood, 1977; Baylis,

1986; Chalmers, 1985). Apart from these fluctuations in spending, particularly the spectacular growth of the Korean War period, the evidence is that defence budgets have remained remarkably stable, at around 5 or 6 per cent of GNP (Greenwood, 1977, p. 191). Even the major defence reviews have not markedly reduced the burden of defence on the economy, since they have generally 'succeeded only in halting the growth of military spending' (Chalmers, 1985, p. 112). It seems that the relationship between economic power and military decline is a complex one and that the burden of defence spending may have contributed to Britain's reduced status rather than simply being a reflection of it (Smith, 1980; Chalmers, 1985, ch. 6).

Defence, it appears, has not been systematically starved of resources; nor, according to many commentators, has Britain's effective and usable military power markedly diminished (Greenwood, 1977, pp. 192–8). Rather, there has been a restructuring of capabilities to reflect technological and organizational change in the military sphere. This is evidenced both by the move to a professional (rather than a conscript-based) armed service and by the changing balance of expenditure between the demands of equipment and those of personnel. War has become more capital-intensive as qualitative improvements in weapons technology have occurred, and this is particularly true in the era of the electronics and informatics revolutions (Kaldor, 1982). Around 45 per cent of the annual defence budget is now spent on military equipment, with personnel accounting for only around 35 per cent (House of Commons, 1986, p. 127). Much of the qualitative improvement in military forces has taken place in the sphere of conventional weapons; this trend is likely to continue and to enhance Britain's capabilities in that area (Baylis, 1986; Pierre, 1986). While British capabilities in relation to the superpowers may have declined, the impact of qualitative improvements has been such that 'it is just not true that the UK now disposes [of] less military might than five, ten or twenty years ago' (Greenwood, 1977, p. 187; see also Baylis, 1986).

Although Britain's raw military power may thus not have declined, it is clear that there has been a contraction from a global to a regional military role. For Greenwood (1977) and Jones (1974) this contraction is evidence not of decline but of the reshaping of Britain's military effort to the changed realities of the international military order. As the United States asserted its hegemonic role in the postwar period, the rationale for a British global presence disappeared, quite apart from the pressure exerted by economic circumstances. As Bartlett notes, British forces East of Suez 'did not so much protect Britain as help to secure protection for the United States' (1977, p. 35). Indeed, these forces had been maintained largely to cultivate the 'special relationship' (Reynolds, 1986; Bartlett, 1977; Darby, 1977). As the process of decolonization accelerated, the case for Britain's global role was difficult to justify either politically or strategically. The economic crises of the mid–1960s thus provided the catalyst, rather than the fundamental cause, of military restructuring; and the resulting concentration of British defence efforts within NATO can be seen as a significant enhancement of Britain's security rather than as a symptom of decline. The process has increased Britain's effective military power and has enhanced its ability to protect its core interests (Greenwood, 1977; Jones, 1974, ch. 7; Baylis, 1986).

The evidence of adjustment and reshaping, as opposed to decline, is thus considerable. Some analysts would go further, though, and point to fundamental changes in the nature and role of military force in the international arena – changes that are bound to affect British national security policy (Morse, 1976; Keohane and Nye, 1977). The primacy of 'unusable' nuclear weapons, the development of a global system of production and exchange and the emergence of a 'new agenda' focused more on welfare than on warfare, have in their view conspired to sever the direct link between military power and political influence. Whilst military force has not by any means become obsolete, the system of nuclear deterrence has raised the stakes attached to the use of force and thus placed considerable restraints on its use. Not only this, but military force has very little bearing on the handling of most international issues, which are now largely concerned with questions of economic and social welfare and which require the cultivation of novel instruments of power. Economic power has come to the fore as a primary source of political influence, pushing military power into the background.

For Britain, one of the consequences of this transformation is that despite the reshaping of its military might its political influence in the world has continued to diminish because the 'currency of influence and power' has been transformed (Greenwood, 1977,

p. 187). It is a misconception that the decline of the country's military strength has eroded its political influence, since the former does not translate directly into the latter. Rather, it is the inability to mobilize other sources of power – economic or technological – that underlies the erosion of British influence. This does not mean that military force has no utility for Britain; to draw such a conclusion would be to ignore the many occasions in the postwar period when it has been used in pursuit of political objectives (Wyllie, 1984). The point is that whilst force retains considerable utility in some circumstances, for Britain as for other advanced industrial countries the range of such circumstances is increasingly restricted.

In the light of these arguments, it is difficult to sustain the orthodox interpretation of the evolution of Britain's defence policy, with its accompanying vocabulary of decline. At best this interpretation is an oversimplification of the processes at work; at worst, it may misrepresent them completely. Its crude economic determinism suggests that the policy-makers have been imprisoned by economic forces, with little scope for discretion or autonomy. This is challenged not only by the general arguments about the shape and nature of the British defence effort that have been reviewed here, but also by the evidence of policy-makers' behaviour. Indeed, one of the most frequent criticisms of postwar defence policy-making is that the defence establishment has consistently defied economic logic or power politics, and that a number of forces operate to insulate defence policy-making from the constraints emphasized in the conventional view. The relationship between British defence policy-making and the changing international arena thus requires exploration.

The Formulation of British Defence Policy

Implicit in the more orthodox interpretations of British national security policy is an assumption that the British state is a monolithic, unitary entity which has been forced periodically to adjust its defence posture in the light of available resources, external commitments and changing international conditions. Breakdowns in this process of rational adjustment, such as the delays in withdrawing from East of Suez, are ascribed to an irrational attachment on the part of the defence establishment to an outdated great-power status. Such accounts tend to gloss over the essentially political nature of defence policy, which influences both its formulation and its substance. The neglect of these factors arises in part at least from the latent realism of the orthodox account, which marginalizes the role of domestic or governmental politics in the pursuit of defence or foreign policy (Allison, 1971). Defence policy is conceived largely as management of the defence effort, with policy at least in theory conforming to the dictates of rational planning. Defence policy, though, can be seen as a fundamentally political activity, not reducible to simple rational or administrative calculation, and such a view gives a very different explanation of the course of British national security efforts.

Defence as an issue area is often seen as lying outside the arena of partisan politics, since it relates to core values concerning the security of the nation as a whole. In Britain, this view has been reinforced by the bipartisan consensus on defence policy which has been a central feature of the postwar political landscape. Although there has been disagreement over specific questions of policy, the fundamental framework of defence policy has been accepted largely without debate by successive governments, of whatever political persuasion. Until recently, this elite consensus appeared to reflect opinion in the country at large; but during the 1970s and 1980s the consensus at both elite and popular levels has been eroded by the emergence of competing ideologies of defence and security. The move towards unilateralism and non-nuclear defence within the Labour Party, the canvassing of alternative defence postures by the Liberals and Social Democrats and the tensions between 'Atlanticists' and 'Europeans' within the Conservative Party have combined to sweep away many of the accepted conventions surrounding the politics of defence. At the same time, public opinion on key defence issues has become fragmented and polarized, with the re-emergence of the Campaign for Nuclear Disarmament (CND) acting as a catalyst and a symbol for organized dissent. The domestic politics of defence policy are now turbulent and fluid and the halcyon days of the defence consensus seem to have disappeared.

Recent developments have thus highlighted the essentially political nature of defence decisions and have injected ideological controversy into the policy debate. In reality, though, national security policy has always been highly politicized and notions of bipartisan consensus have never adequately accounted for the ideological tensions or the political controversy surrounding the area. The bitter debates over withdrawal from East of Suez, and the long-standing conflicts within the Labour Party over the independent deterrent, are only two of the more notable examples that support this view. Defence and national security demand policy choices that are loaded with national symbolism and that are thus bound to produce political disputes (Wallace, 1976, p. 110). Thus, the cuts in naval forces announced in the 1981 Defence Review were furiously denounced within the ranks of the Conservative Party (but not only there) as a betrayal of Britain's prestige and the country's traditional maritime role, while criticisms of the Labour Party's non-nuclear defence plans also focused in part on the damage they would do to the image of the nation.

Another aspect of defence politics concerns the political ramifications of expenditure and procurement decisions, which can be highly significant for public spending and employment. In the first place, resources devoted to defence cannot be devoted to welfare programmes, and vice versa; in a slow-growing economy like that of Britain, such allocations are politically sensitive and often controversial. There is another side to the problem, though, since defence spending can produce jobs, profits and other benefits. In 1985, the Ministry of Defence (MOD) purchased £8.5 billion worth of goods and services from British industry, accounting directly and indirectly for 400,000 jobs (HMSO, 1986, pt 1). These global figures conceal the high dependence of certain industrial sectors or regions on defence contracts. Both in declining industries such as shipbuilding and in high-technology sectors such as the aerospace industry, defence contracts in 1985 accounted for over 40 per cent of output (HMSO, 1986, pt 1). Decisions about procurement are therefore inseparable from questions of industrial and economic policy, as evidenced in the Westland affair of 1986 (which led to the resignation of the Defence Secretary and the Industry Secretary) and the decision to drop the Nimrod early-warning aircraft project in 1987 (which saw intense lobbying from several of Britain's largest high-technology firms). As Miliband notes, 'decisions about defence are necessarily decisions about much else as well, from diplomacy to economic policy, and from social welfare to education' (1973, p. 123).

Defence policy is thus inevitably bound up with questions of politics and ideology, especially when it comes to decisions with large political and social consequences. This makes the rational 'managerialist' conception of policy difficult to apply, but it is not the only reason why that conception can be misleading. The process of policy formulation and choice frequently does not involve major decisions either of a rational or a political nature, and here a different set of factors can come into play. The idea of 'muddling through' or incrementalism sees policy as emerging not from rational choice or political authority but through a process by which ends are adjusted to means and what is desirable is adapted to what is feasible. Decision-making thus involves pragmatic rather than strategic reasoning, and it displays an inherent tendency towards conservative solutions to defence problems, requiring only marginal changes to the status quo. Darby concludes that 'there is little in the British record which offers support to those, either of the Left or Right, who see policy as a product of careful calculation' (1977, p. 53). Certainly, nothing demonstrates the incremental nature of the defence policy process better than the successive defence reviews, each making marginal changes to existing defence programmes without fundamentally disturbing the basic framework of defence policy. The emphasis has been on 'second order' decisions about procurement and deployments rather than on 'first order' issues such as the need for an independent nuclear force or the balance between an Atlantic or European orientation (Garnett, 1983). Apart from the period in the late 1960s, there has been little consideration of the appropriate roles and commitments for Britain in a changing world.

The reasons for this lack of fundamental reassessment in British defence policy are important to the broader argument about the country's position in the international military order. One of the most important factors is that governments inherit defence programmes and commitments that by and large offer little scope for radical restructuring. The Thatcher government came to power in 1979 facing a defence procurement budget already 90 per cent committed, and even in 1984 those past decisions accounted for almost 80 per cent of spending on defence equipment (Freedman, 1986). The six- to ten-year planning cycle of the MOD often locks governments into programmes and policy decisions which, given the choice, they might well never have embraced. Thus, Labour governments in the 1970s found it impossible to do other than continue the secret 'Chevaline' programme to update the Polaris warhead, largely because of the financial costs of cancellation (Freedman, 1980). Equally, the Nimrod project cancelled by the Thatcher government in 1987 had originally been sanctioned by a Labour government ten years earlier.

Quite apart from the constraints imposed by existing defence programmes, governments are constrained by the web of commitments and agreements in which the country is entangled and which create responsibilities and expectations at home and abroad. Any withdrawal from such commitments entails significant political costs and involves far greater political risks than the maintenance of the status quo – a fact which has made radical change less appealing both to politicians and to bureaucrats, and which accounts for at least some of the scepticism which greeted Labour's radical defence plans during the 1980s.

A third element in the bias against fundamental change in defence policies is the vested interests represented by a series of powerful military and industrial organizations. Perhaps the most obvious of these are the armed services, which have considerable power arising from their status as the 'experts' and the agencies of coercive action. Many policy decisions are naturally influenced by the predominantly conservative attitudes of the military hierarchy and by tensions between the needs of the major services. Thus, the Royal Navy played a key role in the perpetuation of the East of Suez presence during the 1950s and early 1960s, reflecting its concern to retain a global sphere of action. Successive defence reviews have seen efforts by each of the services to preserve its position and to shift any cuts on to its rivals. Such conflicts can increase the freedom of action of ministers and officials (as, for example, in 1981, when the navy was singled out for attention), but where the services unite in opposition to government wishes they can form a potent blocking coalition (as they did in opposing cuts during 1976) (Freedman, 1983; Chichester and Wilkinson, 1982). Governments in such circumstances can be deflected from taking hard decisions demanded by international or other pressures. As a result, there have been periodic attempts to counter the influence of the military by restructuring the MOD.

Defence contractors can also bring powerful interests to bear on the making of British defence policy. Though there is not in Britain such a tightly knit 'military-industrial complex' as there is in the USA, there is much evidence of close relationships between the MOD and major contractors. The contractors have 'insider' status within the MOD and are naturally inclined to define defence needs in ways that complement their own commercial prospects. The links between ministry and industry have been institutionalized through joint committees, industrial groups such as the Defence Manufacturers Association, and the 'revolving door' by means of which senior MOD officials 'retire' into industry while industrialists are seconded to the ministry (McLean, 1986, pp. 126–8). The linkages are reinforced by a shared defence ideology and by the relationships between technological change, profits and jobs. Governments find it hard to resist the political logic of the situation and their resolution is further eroded by the industry's ability to apply pressure in the most sensitive spots. As a result, even a determined Thatcher government found it impossible to ignore the pressure to reverse some of the naval cuts announced in the 1981 defence review (Freedman, 1983).

Industrial and service interests do not have the field to themselves, however; they have to compete with powerful bureaucratic and political actors in the policy process. Given the economic and industrial implications of defence decisions, it is inevitable that the Treasury – and more recently the Department of Trade and Industry (DTI) – will have an important role in policy formulation. The Foreign and Commonwealth Office, acting on the traditional assumption that defence policy should be the servant of foreign policy, is another department with a voice in the formal process of decision-making. Since each bureaucracy comes to any issue with its own assumptions and preferences, conflict can always arise, even though the natural attachment of administrative elites to consensual decision-making normally ensures that accommodation is reached. Where deep divisions exist or major political questions are raised, these have to be resolved at cabinet level within the Defence and Overseas Policy Committee or a specially convened *ad hoc* cabinet committee, such as that which dealt with the issue of Polaris replacement during the late 1970s (Smith 1986).

The net result of all these organizational and administrative pressures is to restrict participation in defence decision-making to a closed community of experts and ministers, and to rule out fundamental debate or shifts in policy. For students of policy-making, defence thus furnishes a good example of what has been called the 'mobilization of bias', a process by which the agenda includes those items reflecting the values and priorities of the most influential elites and excludes others (Schattschneider, 1960, p. 71). This helps to explain the way in which 'second order' choices have dominated, to the exclusion of debate about the appropriate role for a middle-ranking power in the contemporary military order. Such bias is not necessarily the result of overt manipulation or conspiracy; it can come about in more subtle and complex ways, through the institutions, procedures, rules and values enshrined in the organization of defence.

Significantly, the bias inherent in the organization of defence at the national level is reinforced by the secrecy which surrounds the whole area of national security. While there are often legitimate reasons for confidentiality and secrecy in defence matters, 'national security' can be used as a convenient cover for closing off political debate and ensuring that policy is left to the 'experts'. Many key decisions, including the inception of the atomic weapons programme, the agreements to provide bases for US nuclear forces in Britain and the decision to invade the Suez Canal Zone, have been taken without reference even to the Cabinet. The decision by the Thatcher government in 1980 to purchase Trident as a successor to Polaris was taken by a small group of senior ministers without any real Cabinet, parliamentary or public debate (Smith, 1986). Secrecy has had a number of important effects on the policy process. First, it has largely shielded the decision-makers from public scrutiny and has reduced their accountability to Parliament to little more than a formality. Second, by restricting the dissemination of information it allows the elite to set the policy agenda and to prescribe the limits within which effective political debate can occur. This immediately undermines any challenge to the prevailing elite consensus and allows government to depict dissenters as being politically suspect. Third, secrecy marginalizes Parliament as a policy-making body, since it lacks any real weapons against the barriers of official confidentiality (Smith, 1986).

The marginalization of Parliament and other bodies in the making of defence policy is a reflection not only of official secrecy but also of the growing internationalization of defence issues. This is most evident in the affairs of NATO, which not only commits its members' forces to the performance of alliance tasks but also integrates them into structures and networks of collective decision-making. The interpenetration of planning and policy-making has moved many decisions about strategic doctrine, deployments, procurement and operations outside the confines of Whitehall to Brussels and elsewhere. Collective decisions about alliance strategy and policy are now vital determinants of the country's defence posture and policies. The 1979 NATO decision that members should increase their defence spending by 3 per cent a year in real terms could be used at home to legitimize military demands for increases in the defence budget. Likewise, deployment of American Cruise missiles in Britain was part of a broader NATO package to modernize theatre nuclear forces and was implemented as such against a background of domestic opposition and public disquiet. The transnationalization of defence policy-making has thus created transgovernmental networks of civilian and military defence elites, which act as channels for mutual co-operation, but which are also beyond any purely national mechanisms of democratic control. These networks also buttress the national position of the defence establishment, by supporting its position within the state apparatus as well as shoring up the existing status quo on defence issues – thus constituting a further barrier to radical change or reappraisal.

A New Historical Conjuncture?

Despite the historical dominance of 'muddling through' in defence decision-making, and despite the constellation of powerful forces ranged against any radical shifts in defence posture, a number of factors suggest that a new historical conjuncture has arrived in the politics of British defence and national security. The specific combination of choices that presents itself to the policy-makers, allied to a turbulent domestic and international environment, 'could provide an unprecedented, and unrepeatable, moment of change' (Smith, 1984, p. 195). Four factors in particular lend support to this view. First, a 'window of choice' has appeared in relation to the independent nuclear deterrent: the choice is between maintaining the commitment to retaining a deterrent capacity after the demise of Polaris and abandoning a nuclear role altogether, and on this the major political parties fundamentally disagree. Second, the squeeze on the defence budget produced by the combination of economic decline and escalating costs has reached critical proportions in the late 1980s. The process of contraction and reshaping has been exhausted and real savings can only be found by redefining cherished defence roles and commitments. Clearly, this is connected with the nuclear issue, since expenditure projected for Polaris replacement is a central element in the squeeze on resources.

The combination of resource problems with a widespread awareness that a moment of choice has appeared can be seen as reinforcing a third factor: the increasing politicization of defence policy. As was noted earlier, the erosion of the domestic consensus on defence and the ideological fragmentation of party politics has gone alongside a change in public attitudes to produce a more critical and discriminating climate. This presents major obstacles for the legitimation of existing approaches to defence, but also prevents the easy adoption of alternatives (Capitanchik, 1982). The changing climate relates closely to a final factor in the new equation of defence and national security: the growing divergence of opinions within the major political parties as to the future orientation of Britain's effort. Should it be geared to strengthening independence (a 'post-imperial' option), or to developing closer collaboration with the European members of NATO (a 'Europeanist' option), or to reinforcing the bonds of the 'special relationship' (an 'Atlanticist' option)? These orientations are by no means mutually exclusive, but an attempt to pursue all three creates uncertainty and tension within the alliance, imposes enormous costs and undermines the coherence of Britain's national security posture. In the circumstances, it appears that hard choices cannot be delayed for long.

The result of these tendencies can be seen in the ferment of debate about alternative defence postures that has been apparent during the 1980s. Defence and national security are now politically salient issues and the demand for radical reorientation comes into conflict with the established process of 'muddling through' that has sustained defence policy-making for so long. It is not entirely fanciful to talk in terms of a profound crisis for British national security policy, both at the level of resources and forces and at the level of values and doctrine. Security and order in the military realm cannot be taken for granted as Britain approaches the 1990s.

Notes

1 The following table compares Britain's defence expenditure and manpower with those of other major advanced industrial societies. However, different definitions of what is included in the defence budget and
defence expenditure, together with different exchange rates used for
local currency to dollar conversions, make such comparisons difficult.
Thus a number of sources have been used here to make the comparisons more robust. The table none the less reinforces the argument
about Britain's relative position with respect to the allocation of
national resources to defence.

Table 5.1   *Comparison of Defence Expenditure and Manpower*
(US$ billions)

Country	GDP	Defence budget[a] IISS	1986 NATO	Defence expenditure IISS[b]	1984 SIPRI[c]	Defence % GDP 1984[d]	Armed Forces
Britain	480.6	28.01	28.70	23.29	30.49	5.5	323,800
France	511.41	22.34	27.71	20.21	27.89	4.1	557,493[e]
West Germany	621.74	22.487	27.20	20.12	26.99	3.3	485,800[f]
Japan	1220.70	20.12	—	12.01	11.37	1.0	243,000
Canada	469.7	7.18	—	7.19	5.77	2.1	83,000

a Two figures are given here, both from *The Military Balance 1986/87*. The 'raw'
figure from the International Institute for Strategic Studies (IISS) is a straight local
currency to dollar conversion based on prevailing exchange rates. The NATO
figure is the NATO definition of the defence budget which includes items (such as
certain R & D projects, for example) which may not be included in the official
defence budget but which appear under other budgetary heads.
  b This is defence expenditure as defined by the IISS: see *The Military Balance
1986–7*, p. 8.
  c The Stockholm International Peace Research Institute (SIPRI) definition of
defence expenditure can be found in *World Armaments and Disarmament Yearbook*,
1985.
  d This figure is taken directly from Table 4, pp. 212–14 of *The Military Balance
1986–7*.
  e Includes a figure of 253,000 conscripts.
  f Includes a figure of 228,850 conscripts.
  Sources: International Institute for Strategic Studies, 1986.
          Stockholm International Peace Research Institute, 1985.

2　The relative position of Britain in the 'nuclear club' can be seen from the table below.

Table 5.2　*Comparison of Nuclear Delivery Capabilities 1985*

Systems	USA	USSR	UK	France	China
ICBM/s	1010	1398	—	—	6
SLBM/s	640	944	64	96	24
IRBM/ MRBMs*	108	382	—	18	110
Bombers	260	160	48	34	120

Key:　ICBM: intercontinental ballistic missile
　　　SLBM: submarine-launched ballistic missile
　　　IRBM: intermediate range ballistic missile
　　　MRBM: medium range ballistic missile

* These two types of system have been conflated here merely for ease of presentation of the statistics.

Note: This table sets out figures for delivery systems, not warheads. It is, therefore, a fairly crude guide to the actual nuclear balance. However, it is merely intended to convey a picture of the relative position of the UK in the nuclear hierarchy.

Sources: International Institute for Strategic Studies, 1986, pp. 218–23.
　　　　W. M. Arkin and R. Fieldhouse, 1985, pp. 42, 44, 59.

6 Security and Order

The Economic Dimension

ROGER TOOZE

Part Two of this book considers the broad context of British foreign policy – issues, processes and outcomes – within the twin, and often problematic, themes of 'security' and 'order'. Both these themes are generally associated with military and defence issues and, as in the previous chapter, are normally discussed almost solely in this context. This chapter, however, looks at the achievement and problems of 'security' and 'order' within the economic dimension – a somewhat false distinction, as we shall see, but a critical, if not always explicit, aspect of British foreign policy. It has three principal tasks: to elucidate the concepts of 'economic security' and 'economic order', to construct an overview of British foreign policy from the perspective of these themes and to come to some judgements as to the success, or otherwise, of British policies and processes.

It is important to note at the outset that as far as the public analysis of British foreign policy is concerned there is a paucity of literature on the problem of 'economic security'. In a general policy sense the most relevant studies have been the careful analyses of process and issues by William Wallace, particularly on the management of foreign economic policy and the impact of interdependence (1974, 1986b). Where work has been done on the *issue* of 'economic security' it has focused on a specific form of external threat, that to British energy security, particularly since 1973 and the subsequent oil shocks. Similarly, the foreign policy debate within the British 'attentive public' has, with the exception of the question of membership of the European Community, by and large been confined to specific economic aspects of 'security', rather than 'economic security' as such, with energy security prominent in the 1970s and 1980s. The intellectual stimulus for policy reassessment that has occurred has principally come from outside the foreign policy 'community' and has primarily focused on the problems of Britain's relative economic decline from the perspectives of political analysis (see, especially, Gamble, 1985, or, from a different analysis, Alt, 1979) and economic history (see, particularly, Kirby, 1981). Hence one conclusion that could be drawn from the narrowness of the public foreign policy debate and the lack of a literature on the wider theme of 'economic security' is that 'economic security' is really not a problem for British foreign policy.

To come to this conclusion is to miss the point: the British policy process has defined the nature and achievement of 'economic security' in such a way, particularly since 1947, that it has been politically overshadowed by military and defence aspects of security. The achievement and maintenance of 'economic security', with the exceptions previously mentioned, have thus tended to be a secondary issue carried out in the general context of economic policy within and between members of the Organization for Economic Co-operation and Development (OECD) and, latterly, the European Community (EC). Only at times of great policy change, such as the setting up of the postwar monetary order at Bretton Woods in 1944 or the eventual entry into the European Community in 1973, have the broad parameters of external 'economic security' been considered at the public level.

To some extent this is explained by the fact that, in effect, these critical policy changes support a particular set of procedures, rules and norms of international behaviour that collectively form a framework for international economic activity. As such, the framework acts as a structure, underpinned by a series of core values, the maintenance of which is thought partly to provide for Britain's continued 'economic security' and partly to provide necessary and sufficient conditions of 'order' in the international economy. Once international economic structures have been established their maintenance becomes very much an implicit, even a non-political process until the structure itself is threatened, or until domestic changes raise questions (that are seen as politically salient) concerning the consequences of continued support for that structure. Both these phenomena have occurred since the British government helped to establish the postwar international economic order in 1944, but only on rare occasions have the basic values underlying British policy been seriously questioned. This is clearly because what constitutes 'economic security' for Britain is defined politically by the government of the day, both reactively as a response to the problems generated by the secular decline of the British economy in the context of a changing world economy and actively as a consequence of the ideological construction of that government's policies, domestic as well as foreign.

In an analysis of American economic issues and national security, Clark Murdock concludes that 'there can be no *a priori* definition of what constitutes an economic security issue . . . what makes an economic issue an economic security issue is defined by whether a government behaves as if an economic issue is a security issue' (1977, p. 72), and this conclusion applies equally to British policy. This chapter argues that the British government's definition of what constitutes an economic security issue and, hence, of what constitutes 'economic security' has been both narrow and inappropriate. Such an argument is itself contentious and, of course, political in the widest sense, and in order to substantiate this argument we need to look more closely at the notions of 'economic security' and (international) 'economic order'.

Security and Order in the Contemporary World Political Economy

Security is an ambiguous concept because it can be defined in many ways, each of which can be different but equally valid. It is, following Barry Buzan's excellent analysis, an 'essentially contested' concept which cannot be defined in a once-and-for-all sense because of the 'ideological elements' inherent in its meaning, interpretation and application (1983, p. 6). The precise interpretation of security can vary in different situations and at different times, although a minimal notion of security starts with the absence of threat, real and/or perceived. Yet this negative definition is insufficient if threat is interpreted only as threat to continued physical survival. To the extent that our needs and wants are derived from society, that society produces an expectation in each individual of the existence and the maintenance of certain values. The maintenance of values, however, emphasizes the importance of stability and order to the notion of security. Change, the pace of change and particularly change generated from outside the social unit to which the unit must adjust, are potentially destabilizing as they threaten the established means of securing key values. Hence, as Wallace puts it, when we experience 'periods of rapid domestic and international change perceptions of insecurity are . . . likely to become sharpened, unless the process of change is carefully managed and the states under potential threat have confidence in the mechanisms of management' (1986b, p. 370).

Although security is a difficult concept to define, most governments of territorial states have by their policies and actions defined security in the military-strategic context. Indeed, the conventional meaning of the concept of 'security' is one defined in national military terms, with consequent military-based policies and responses (see Buzan, 1983). The continued dominance of a military conception of security derives from the structure of international politics as well as the structure of foreign and domestic policy processes, in that actual physical survival comes before other values and tends therefore to predefine most security problems. The result is that military aspects of security are clearly and conventionally identifiable and evoke institutional and procedural responses, while non-military aspects of security, such as ecological threats, are intellectually and politically more difficult to define and to respond to (Ullman, 1983, p. 135). Moreover, governments find it politically more rewarding to focus upon military security as it is normally easier to achieve a domestic political consensus on the evaluation and response to a military security threat (Ullman, 1983; Buzan, 1983). For these reasons, security has been defined and operationalized by most governments primarily, though not wholly, in military terms.

This, however, is not to suggest that, for Britain or any other state, the economic dimension of security is never an important consideration. The link between military security and economic strength is clear, and is often stressed in policy terms, particularly for Britain over the last one hundred years (Kennedy, 1981). E. H. Carr quotes Hitler's *Mein Kampf* to support the argument that in British foreign policy 'economics and politics marched hand in hand towards the same objective: "Is it not precisely the hallmark of British statesmanship," he [Hitler] asks, "to draw economic advantages from political strength, and to transform every economic gain back into political power"' (1941, p. 147). Equally clear is the use of economic power and economic instruments to achieve military security (see, particularly, Knorr, 1973; Adler-Karlsson, 1982), and hence also the threat posed to one's own national security by the use of economic power and economic instruments by other states. But in both these aspects the *prior* determining conception of security is one which is based on a narrow interpretation of security as the absence of threat, real or perceived, to continued physical survival. Once we move beyond this interpretation to include within our notion of security a range of other key values, such as the expectation of the continued provision of economic welfare in its broadest sense, the nature of security changes.

Joseph Nye has suggested that security consists of three basic 'clusters of values': first, 'some minimal expected level of economic welfare'; second, 'a certain political and social autonomy as a group'; and third, 'a degree of political status as a group' (1974, p. 585). However, even at this level of abstraction, the choice of 'clusters of values' has a certain ideological element (here, perhaps, an American ethnocentrism). The notion of national security put forward by Richard Cooper is perhaps more appropriate because it does not impose a choice of values, viz: 'the capacity of a society (nation) to enjoy and cultivate its culture and values' (1975, p. 3). Using this notion, Wolfgang Hager concludes that 'economic security can thus be considered to be threatened seriously when external economic parameters change in such a manner as to cause the break-down of the preferred socio-economic system' (1982, p. 22). This conception stresses 'break-down' of the system itself; but what about changes that have 'harmful' consequences but fall short of causing actual 'break-down'? The adoption of the definition of security suggested by Richard Ullman enables us to identify threats that are relevant to economic security but do not necessarily lead to a 'break-down', viz:

> a threat to national security is an action or sequence of events that
> (1) threatens drastically and over a relatively brief span of time to degrade the quality of life for the inhabitants of a state, or
> (2) threatens significantly to narrow the range of policy choices available to the government of a state or to private

> nongovernmental entities (persons, groups, corporations) within the state (1983, p. 133).

This conception also enables us to look at specific policy aspects of security/economic security.

We now have a useful conception of economic security derived from Ullman's definition, but following on from the discussion we need to emphasize an important distinction. If we accept the political definition of security in the conventional, military sense then economic security consists of the traditional security consequences of economic relations. But if we accept the broader conception of security then economic security is a much more comprehensive policy problem, stemming in the main from the adoption of economic goals and responsibilities by states and made far more complex by the emergence of interdependence between states. In this sense (and following Ullman) any action or sequence of events that threatens abruptly to degrade the quality of economic life or significantly to narrow the range of economic policy options for the government of a state or for groups within a state constitutes a threat to national economic security.

Before we examine the further implications of this notion of economic security, we need to consider the second general theme of British foreign policy, that of 'order' in general and the 'international economic order' in particular. In a general sense, 'order' presupposes a pattern of relationships between entities – the expectation of a pattern enables us to distinguish between 'order' and 'disorder' in the physical relationship between 'things'. In political terms, this means not just any pattern but one that allows the political entities to achieve certain goals (Bull, 1977; McKinlay and Little, 1986). Hence, for states, an international order is a pattern of relationships that enables or supports the achievement of key state goals and, in so doing, enables some management of change. We can, however, be more specific and use the concept of an international order to mean 'the framework of rules, regulations, conventions and norms' governing a range of functional relations between states, for example, an international economic order, an international monetary order and so on (Cohen, 1977, p. 3). This idea has been extended into the seemingly ubiquitous concept of 'regime', with a similar meaning but with a much greater theoretical intent (the definitive statement is Krasner,

1983b). An international economic order, then, relates directly to economic security (as well as conventional security) to the extent that the achievement of a state's central economic goals is dependent on the establishment and maintenance of a preferred order and to the extent that the order brings increased perceptions of international economic stability.

With the creation of the postwar international economic order based on the principles of liberal free trade and backed by a negotiated monetary order, the liberal order itself became a key constituent of the process that led to the 'long boom' in economic activity, a boom sustained by export growth (Anell, 1981). Export-led growth and the large movements of capital in the form of 'multinational corporations' enabled many governments to achieve their economic goals, but at the same time changed the nature of the international economy by creating high levels of interdependence which not only linked national economies to each other but linked national economics further into the liberal international economy (see, particularly, Cooper, 1968; Keohane and Nye, 1977; Anell, 1981).

Each of these links has important consequences for economic security. First, the link into the international economy and the prevailing liberal international economic order produces a certain dependence on the international economy itself and a specific form of relationship to the liberal economic order, viz:

> The international economy, manipulated by its members, operates as a constant but unpredictable system of double distribution – of incomes, jobs, status within nations, and wealth and power amongst nations. But the domestic victims of this redistribution do not acknowledge the legitimacy of a haphazard or shifty mechanism that is external to the nation and competes or conflicts with the internal redistribution schemes that have been legitimately, authoritatively, or imperatively set up within the confines of the nation.
>
> (Stanley Hoffman, quoted in Anell, 1981, p. 90)

In addition to this dependence the nature of the liberal international order ultimately means 'that states must restructure themselves extensively in order to participate in it; once such restructuring has occurred states increase their vulnerability to adverse behaviour by others, or to breakdowns in the system' (Buzan, 1983, p. 144). This means that those states that have 'restructured' need to work to maintain the system and the liberal international economic order and need to 'adjust' their domestic structures and policies in order to maintain a high degree of 'fit' between domestic and international economy. Often this produces serious problems of 'adjustment' as people resist change they perceive as detrimental to their economic security, resulting in various forms of 'protectionism' and insulation from the world market. In the case of a hegemon, such as the United States, the international order would be a natural extension of the hegemon's domestic structure. In non-hegemonic economies the problem is clearly much greater, and it is in this respect that the liberal order faces its major challenge (Anell, 1981; Cooper, 1985; Keohane, 1984).

Thus, in Anell's word, governments become 'brokers' – they distribute available resources (many of which are 'supplied' through the international economy) between conflicting domestic interests. But, 'governments now have to play this role of broker in a world economy which has become so interdependent that it undermines national autonomy, i.e. the real power to manage the domestic economy' (Anell, 1981, p. 91). In general, if governments' power to manage the domestic economy has been undermined by international developments then economic security is potentially threatened as there is then a significant reduction in the range of policy options for government and other groups as well as the increased possibility that external action may seriously degrade the quality of economic life. If this is regarded as a threat to economic security in the OECD countries it must be noted that for most of the Third World countries it is the 'normal' condition of economic security.

Second, for the purpose of our analysis, interdependence has had two important consequences: as well as increasing the sensitivity of national economies to events outside the national economic boundary it has increased the vulnerability of national economies to external disturbances (Cooper, 1968; Cooper, 1975; Keohane and Nye, 1977; Jones and Willetts, 1984) and, as a result of the developments already discussed, interdependence has been instrumental in breaking down the policy process distinctions between domestic and foreign policy (see, amongst others, Nye, 1976). Both sensitivity and vulnerability interdependence have implications for foreign policy process and output, as well as outcomes (Smith, 1984), but vulnerability interdependence is perceived as the major instance of a threat to national economic security – in both senses of economic security. The reason for this is straightforward. The threat to disrupt supplies of a raw material, commodity, manufactured good or, perhaps, a service that is considered *essential* to a nation's continued economic well-being or *essential* to its continued capability to defend itself is both highly visible and direct. The different reactions of the USA and Europe to the actions of 1973–4 of the Organization of Petroleum Exporting Countries (OPEC) demonstrate the different perceptions of threat to economic security, as well as the enforced redefinition by 'oil-poor' European countries of their perception of economic security in a new and potentially destabilizing situation. In the case of oil, the threat was to the supply of a commodity which had become critical to the continued growth in the industrial economies (at least in the short and medium term), both as a source of energy and as the basis for industrial manufacturing (petro-chemicals) and the impact of large changes in the supply of oil could have had far greater political and economic consequences than actually occurred. That the perception of economic security did indeed change (particularly for those countries then without oil) is shown by the subsequent rapid development of the French and German nuclear power programmes and the increased efforts of the British government to speed up oil recovery from the North Sea.

Interdependence as it has developed in the postwar system makes the policy and conceptual distinction between 'foreign' and 'domestic' and between 'political' and 'economic' largely redundant, mainly because of the interpenetration of national economies and the centrality of economic and welfare goals to the continued legitimacy of contemporary governments. Hence, an analysis of the economic dimension of security and order *cannot* simply be concerned with 'foreign' or even 'international' economic (and political) policy; it must *necessarily* include domestic policy. As William Wallace explained in 1974 with respect to British foreign economic policy, 'the largest obstacle to the pursuit of a "coherent" foreign policy, in which political preferences and security objectives are integrated with economic goals, is the inseparability of foreign economic policy from domestic economic management' 1974, p. 253). This fact is reflected in the number of people in domestic agencies and departments who deal with 'foreign' policy. Moreover, the conceptual problems of 'domestic' and 'foreign' are translated directly into the political (that is, governmental) problem of assessing 'national interest'. Now, the concept of 'national interest' has many flaws and weaknesses but it becomes clear from even a cursory analysis of British policy that such a conception is present in the actual policies, if not declared aims, of successive governments. However, because interdependence spreads the costs and benefits of policies in different ways and new patterns of vulnerability are created for different individuals and groups, a purely 'national' policy becomes increasingly difficult to formulate, sustain and legitimate (Nye, 1976).

Confronted by the complexity of interdependence and the uncertainty of the world economy, governments have responded in different ways in a sometimes confused, and often implicit, attempt to maintain economic security through the pursuit of economic growth. Richard Cooper and Ann Hollick have characterized four possible policy responses to this situation (see also Chapter 10 in this volume):

1 *defensive* – which 'involves attempts by governments to stop erosion of the efficacy of their actions by steps that reduce the openness of their national economies'
2 *accommodative* – adapting policy measures to the new prevailing circumstances
3 *aggressive* – 'in the face of decreasing effectiveness in their action, [governments] try to extend their reach to cover the escaping parties'
4 *co-operative* – intergovernmental co-operation to overcome the erosion of policy measures (1985).

Each of these responses has particular costs and benefits: most OECD states have utilized a 'mix' of all four, and each of them can be perceived as a means of ensuring (non-conventional) economic security. However, within the ideology of the contemporary liberal international economic order, accommodative and co-operative responses are preferable because it is thought likely that these responses will support the order itself and lead to increases in global wealth and security. Defensive and aggressive responses are linked more to 'mercantilist' or economic nationalist policies and, from the perspective of liberal world order, are seen to detract from economic security, although this conclusion is the subject of much intellectual and political disagreement (Jones, 1986; Ward, 1979; McKinlay and Little, 1986).

What is clear is that governments have increasingly been forced to respond to the policy problems of interdependence and loss of control – in policy processes as well as outcomes – and, although not always perceiving these as economic security problems as is suggested here, they have had varying degrees of success depending on their economic power and position within the structures of the world economy (Strange, 1986). One development which is structural in the sense that it is difficult to avoid if the national economy is effectively to remain within the international economy, is the necessity for international policy co-ordination (that is, international co-ordination not just of foreign economic policies but mainly of *domestic* economic policies), and this is partly co-operative and partly accommodative (Cooper, R. N., 1985; Artis and Ostry, 1986). In the absence of effective hegemonic power to impose co-ordination, 'voluntary' policy co-ordination is (or may be) preferable to the costs of minimizing the impact of interdependence. The failure to co-ordinate will frustrate the achievement of policy goals (depending on the 'openness' of the national economy) and may damage the system itself. Conse-quently, we have seen new mechanisms and fora for co-ordination, most notably the 'seven-power summits' that have sprung directly from the political realization of the 'increasing entanglement of foreign and domestic politics that flows from economic interdepen-dence' (Putnam and Bayne, 1984, p. 1). Specific co-ordinating mechanisms may not always be necessary, however, in that 'liberal' interdependence and policy co-ordination have negative aspects for individual states: to the extent than any one economy is integrated into the international structure, that economy will be constrained from following policies (both domestic and inter-national) that are not also followed by the dominant economic grouping, the OECD states. The French attempts to apply broadly Keynesian policies to economic problems during 1981–2 and their subsequent failure when other OECD states adopted monetarist goals and instruments is indicative of the nature of the constraints.

The implications of 'liberal' interdependence for the achievement of national economic security are thus profound. The nature of the contemporary (predominantly liberal) system produces major contradictions in its structures and processes of growth and maintenance (Buzan, 1983). Robert Keohane comes to the sobering conclusion that 'unless its effects are cushioned by deliberate policy, the success of liberalism . . . tends to destroy the conditions of its existence' (1984b, p. 35), although he sees a way forward (1984a). In the dynamics of the complex relationships between state and international system, British policy has followed a unique path. Although Britain has shared many of the structural problems of other economies, both domestic and international, the values promulgated and the policies followed apparently owe more to an imperial past than to any rational assessment of Britain's position and interests.

British Foreign Policy, and Security and Order in the Economic Dimension: an Historical Overview

In assessing British Policy, it is important to examine the immediate postwar context because the commitments espoused then (as well as the assumptions those commitments were based upon) and maintained at an enormous cost over a lengthy period still have a major bearing on policy in the late 1980s (see, amongst others, Brett, 1985; Blank, 1977; Strange, 1971). In the ever-present tension of priorities which characterized postwar British policy, it is clear that military security was emphasized to a far greater extent than any notion or policy of economic security. Specific considerations of economic security were largely subsumed in the context of British support for the US-led liberal international economic order, at once identifying British economic security with the stability and maintenance of that economic order (although the end of imperial preferences caused a few problems; see Kennedy, 1981). Moreover, within this emphasis on military security we see the subordination of domestic policy to the 'goals of great power status and international responsibility' (Wallace, 1974, p. 252).

Given the experience of the Second World War and Britain's position as a (former) hegemonic power, the primacy of military security goals is not surprising. These goals were part of the conception of Britain as a great power with the range of international responsibilities and obligations that attended great power status. Inextricably linked to Britain's great power status was the international reserve role of sterling, linked to an exaggerated propensity to invest overseas (Strange, 1971). A strong pound, within the broad framework of Britain's support for the international order, was thought essential for world power status. Such was the critical nature of considerations of military power and the importance of maintaining the international system that British policy assumptions pointed to the 'subordination of national economic interests', when necessary, 'to considerations of international responsibility, to the obligations of a great power, and to the maintenance of good relations with the British Commonwealth' (Wallace, 1974, p. 261).

We have then in the formulation and implementation of British policy, a clear hierarchy of values and objectives which set the framework for the pursuit of economic security and order. First, the military dimension of security and the maintenance of world power status dominated purely economic matters. Sterling was viewed in power terms and hence as central, but for much of the period economic considerations were considered 'background factors' rather than a 'determinant of British policy' (Darby, 1973, p. 153.). Second, the international level dominated domestic considerations in that international obligations, themselves partly a product of continuing great power status, took precedence over domestic needs. With the ending of controls in the early 1950s the British economy was even more susceptible to change in order to achieve foreign policy goals, with the balance of payments the main arbiter of policy (see Brett, 1985). This combination of priorities and policies resulted in severe problems for British policy. As Stephen Blank concludes, 'for much of the postwar period, domestic and international economic policy was dominated by and subordinated to the goals of foreign policy, goals which Britain was incapable of realizing. *Yet the attempt to achieve these goals led successive governments to sacrifice the domestic economy again and again*' (1977, p. 675, italics added).

Some adjustment of the domestic economy is part of the general process of operating in a liberal international economy and, as such, can be expected. But, in the British case, the retention of world power goals and policies, the continuous movement of capital from the British economy and the particular methods of implementing adjustment that was used in Britain (macro-economic deflation), all made the adjustments far more painful and the policies far harsher. Whether in retrospect these policies achieved economic security (or even acknowledged economic security) is debatable, but the failure to react to change until 1966 led directly to the abrogation by governments of any responsibility for managing long-term growth and change in the domestic economy. British support of the liberal international economic order and Britain's particular monetary relationship with the USA (for contrasting views, see Brett, 1985 and Strange, 1971) could only help to achieve economic security as long as Britain was prepared to accept the necessary changes that integration into a liberal structure entailed, that is, prepared to follow policies of accommodation. But, in this matter, direct considerations of economic security were secondary to considerations of Britain's ability to influence the structure and operation of the system. As Susan Strange has pointed out, Britain took a highly conservative stance on the structure of the liberal system (as compared, for instance, to France) because Britain 'was seeking to maintain and perpetuate the existing American-dominated system that allowed her to play a junior but still important special role in it' (1974, p. 42).

In as much as economic security was a specific policy goal in the period before 1967–8, and there is little evidence to suggest that it was, British policy generally subsumed direct threats to economic security within the broad notion of traditional military security, although as previously suggested economic considerations were, more often than not, seen as 'background factors'. The more positive aspects of (non-conventional) economic security were subsumed and incorporated into British support for the international order and, more specifically, into support for a particular role for Britain in that international order. However, the relationship between military and economic security was not just one way, as British policy-makers originally intended. By 1966, the size of the deficit on the balance of payments, largely as a result of the level of government expenditure, the continuation of sterling's reserve role and the debilitating effect of governments' own policies on the national economy, led to a series of defence cuts (from a defence budget of £2.5 billion down to £2 billion) and the beginnings of a redefinition of Britain's world role (Darby, 1973). The 1966 cuts, together with the second Basle Agreement of 1968, by which Britain gave up sole responsibility for the management of sterling as a reserve currency, collectively changed the dominant elements of British policy (Strange, 1971; Brett, 1985). These events constituted for Teddy Brett 'a major shift in the country's international role and in the mechanisms which sustained it, but one which was made only after the damage to the underlying structures that had put Britain ahead of its major overseas rivals had been done' (1985, p. 155).

According to Brett, the delay in reshaping British commitments irrevocably squandered the economic advantages that Britain previously possessed over its international competitors and, in so doing, harmed the achievement of economic security for those that depended on the British national (as opposed to the British *international*) economy. One of the paradoxical features of the British economy is the relationship between domestic economic performance and the continuous outflow of British capital for foreign investment. 'By 1971 the value of foreign production by British business was more than double the value of visible export trade, whereas it was less than 40 per cent for Germany and Japan' (Gamble, 1985, p. 110). British foreign investment, then, encouraged the conflict between the international priorities and the domestic economy – a conflict which has normally been resolved in favour of the 'internationalized' sectors of the economy at the expense of the purely domestic sectors.

In addition, the events of the late 1960s marked the end of one of Britain's major policy commitments, 'the maintenance of a central role alongside the USA in the management of the international economic and security system' (Brett, 1985, p. 156). This argument is a strong one and the implications for the achievement of economic security and order are potentially severe. The 'surrender' of this policy commitment, in both military and economic dimensions, clearly alters the ability of British governments to achieve 'structural' economic security and order through the joint central management of the international politico-economic system. The 'special' role then is no longer available for Britain, although the problems of sterling foreshadowed deeper problems for the USA in the maintenance of the hegemonic order. The process of change that started in 1966–8 means that in theory the achievement of economic security and order slowly became less of a constituent part (and largely a by-product) of Britain's structural power and more a necessary and specific policy consideration derived from the needs of the domestic economy. In practice, though, changes in British governments have altered the political definition of what constitutes 'economic security' and how, or indeed if, it might be achieved.

The process of change and adjustment, usually forced by external circumstances, did not end with the 1967 devaluation and the Basle Agreement. The period up to the International Monetary Fund (IMF) loan in 1976 further highlighted the contradictions in British international and domestic politics and reaffirmed the importance of the balance of payments in British policy, with the eventual virtual abandonment of liberal Keynesian policies in response to conditions imposed by the external loans from the IMF in December 1976. Domestic policy was once again determined by the needs of the external balances. Also, and importantly, the formal framework of British policy was changed by the accession of Britain to the EEC. The slow and sometimes painful resolution of the tension between 'Atlanticist' and 'Europeanist' views of the direction of British policy in favour of Europe was a (belated) recognition of some of the changes we have discussed. European Community membership has increasingly provided the political and institutional focus for British efforts to achieve economic growth, to influence the structure of the international economy and to maintain economic security.

However, perhaps just as important a change has been the move away from the system of fixed exchange rates set up at Bretton Woods to a system of floating exchange rates, where, in theory, the exchange rate (the price of money in terms of another currency) is subject to 'market' forces of demand and supply. The pound was 'floated' in 1972 and by the end of 1973 most of the major currencies were floating. The series of developments that came with floating, particularly the creation of the Eurodollar markets, enormously increased the volume and volatility of liquid funds in the international system (see, amongst others, Lomax and Gutmann, 1981). The impact of this development was illustrated when the OPEC countries who had lent heavily to support sterling in 1976 lost confidence and began to take their money out – sterling fell from just over $2 at the beginning of that year to around $1.50 in September. The large movements in exchange rates that now take place, coupled with the uncertainty that is generated (even with the protection of the currency futures market), directly impinge upon the ability of the British and other governments to achieve economic security and order (Strange, 1986).

This broad overview of British policy has set out the priorities and changes that form the necessary context for an analysis of British policy. We can now assess the structures and processes that link the British economy to the other levels of economic activity and then consider contemporary British policy in relation to economic security and order.

Economic Security, Order and Contemporary British Foreign Policy

It is difficult to avoid the conclusion from the foregoing analysis that the dominance of the military dimension of security over the broad notion of economic security and the policy precedence of international considerations over domestic needs have generally been detrimental to the achievement of British national economic security as we have defined it – certainly in comparison with most other advanced industrial countries. This being the case we should perhaps look for changes in contemporary policy – domestic and foreign – that would indicate a revision of priorities, or at least, a specific consideration of the problems at issue. In this final section of the chapter we do not have the space for an exhaustive review of the extent to which British policy ensures national economic security. The later chapters of the book focus on 'arenas' of policy in more detail and so provide opportunities to consider in more depth some of the questions raised here. Here, we shall try to identify problems, contradictions and consistencies in policy output and process.

From the 'foreign' policy perspective, continuous changes in the nature of the international economy and the international economic order ensure that 'foreign economic policy' (if it can be identified as such) normally reflects these changes – for example, successive rounds of GATT talks, as well as changes in governmental policy. The real change in British foreign economic policy, although again not normally discussed in economic security terms, came in 1976 with the Labour government. The election of the Conservative government in 1979 confirmed and developed the policy direction already in place: a move to integrate the British economy into the

world economy within the context of a 'liberal' international
economic order. In other words, the implicit notion was that
economic security was to be provided through economic growth
but was rarely discussed as such because the concept of security was
still defined in a traditional, military way.

At the domestic level, however, (bearing in mind the problems
of separating domestic and foreign policy) policy in the 1980s
seemed even more set in the mould of the past, particularly the
operational, political definition of what constituted security. As
Wallace has argued, 'the sharp reduction in British public expenditure on trade and industry since 1979 . . . and the commensurate
increase in defence expenditure clearly indicates that the current
[1986] British government is much more concerned about military
security than economic security' (1986b, p. 389).

Given the emphasis on Britain's military and strategic 'role', the
presumed renewal of the 'special relationship', partly on a personal
basis by the two political leaders, and the ideology and leadership
style of Mrs Thatcher, it seemed that in the 1980s the 'traditional'
definition of legitimate British security concerns had remained
almost unscathed after twenty years of economic retrenchment.
That this policy definition of security also served immediate party
political and electoral objectives is reasonably transparent and to be
expected. This point suggests the continuing relevance of Stephen
Blank's 1977 analysis, that the 'attitudes, commitments and politics
of Britain's top political leaders' are far more important than other
groups, including the bureaucracy, in explaining 'Britain's economic problems' (1977, p. 174).

Moreover, the concentration in British policy on the traditional
military definition of security can be shown to have had a more
subtle but highly significant impact on economic security than we
have discussed so far. In an analysis of industrial competitiveness
and defence, Kaldor, Sharp and Walker comprehensively demonstrate that the 'civilian industry in Britain is adversely affected by
heavy defence commitments' (1986, p. 45). Their final conclusions
are important for the argument here in that they suggest that 'the
greatest threat to Britain's security comes from within – from our
continuing failure to reverse the trend of relative economic decline
and the erosion of a broader sense of national well-being and
stability which stems from this' (1986, p. 49). One element in the
reduction of this threat, they argue, would, therefore, be a major

cut in defence research and development and defence procurement (see also Chalmers, 1985).

Wallace's view that the Thatcher government was much more concerned about military than about economic security was trenchantly supported by the 1985 analysis of the House of Lords Select Committee on Overseas Trade. The committee's conclusions, which differed from those of the Treasury and the government, were that past policies had led to the decline of Britain's manufacturing capacity and this, combined with poor competitiveness in key sectors of the economy, had since 1983 created a grave deficit in the balance of trade in manufactures 'from a surplus of £5.5 bn in 1980 to a deficit of nearly £4 bn in 1984' (HL (84–85) 238–I, p. 7). The committee concluded that unless this trend was corrected the prospects arising from a continued deterioration in the manufacturing base would 'constitute a grave threat to the standard of living of the British people. Failure to recognise these dangers now could have a devastating effect on the future economic and political stability of the nation' (HL (84–85) 238–I, p. 48).

While this prognosis was alarming at the time, the objective conditions within which the British government implements its policies have become more generally problematic. The British economy in the 1980s is 'probably more open now than at any time in its history' and this means that 'the scope for achieving major economic objectives . . . by means of an independent macro-economic policy [is] extremely limited' (Panic, 1982, pp. 37, 46). Ironically, the Thatcher government greatly increased the openness of the British economy to external influences by abolishing exchange controls (on the movement of capital) in 1979, thus deliberately precipitating the further internationalization of key sectors of the British economy and simultaneously making its own task of control much more difficult.

As far as 'domestic' policies are concerned, then, two are of particular significance: first, the political resurgence of a predominantly military conception of security, with 'appropriate' funding, which allows for the (military) security consequences of international economic relations but seemingly not much else; and second, a domestic economic policy which by and large is based on a conception of the world economy as a (desirable) market and attempts to integrate the British economy into that market by replicating the processes that (are perceived to) constitute that world market at the national level. Hence, primary policies of accommodation are favoured as a route to economic growth (and, by implication, economic security), viz: 'the essential thrust of Government policy is to reduce market barriers and, by providing a favourable climate, to enable industry to respond flexibly and effectively to the requirements of the domestic and world markets' (HL (84–85) 238–II, p. 5). In effect this policy constitutes a continuation of the 'restructuring' necessary to benefit fully from the liberal international economic order (Buzan, 1983, p. 144).

In foreign policy the core aims of British economic policy are reflected in the overall strategy which includes the promotion of domestic economic growth and in the policies that support and influence the liberal international economic order. Externally, the policy process is located mainly within the context of the European Community, either multilaterally or bilaterally (Wallace, 1984). Not only does the Community form the key political and institutional matrix for Britain's economic policies, but the EC is Britain's biggest trading partner taking around 45 per cent of UK total exports and providing 44 per cent of UK imports. In comparison, the United States now takes 15 per cent of all UK exports and supplies 12 per cent of imports, while 19 per cent of UK exports go to developing countries and 15 per cent of UK imports come from developing countries. Over time, the British trade pattern has characteristically shown an increase in trade with other advanced industrial countries (AICs) and a decrease in trade with developing countries, confirming the institutional and political focus of British economic security in the trade (and capital) relations between Britain and the other OECD states. To the extent that we can identify a conscious policy on economic security, the OECD focus seems to be the working assumption of policy. Other bilateral relationships may be important (South Africa is exceptional) but in general they could be broken without major threat to British economic security.

Much of the influence that Britain now has on the political definition of the international economic order is, with perhaps the exception of money and financial issues, as a member of the EC, the world's largest trading bloc, operating through other international governmental organizations. Within these fora there is explicit British support for the maintenance of the liberal international economic order coupled with an awareness of the 'needs',

both political and economic, of the domestic economy, in agriculture, textiles and steel, for example. In the main, the basis of
British policy is co-operative – an attempt to solve the problems
of growth through increased control and the harmonization of
(ideologically) appropriate policy.

The identification with the prevailing liberal economic order
becomes, in effect, a process of reinforcing the international
economic structure in such a way as to use it to achieve domestic
economic goals. But ultimately the support for the liberal order is
ideological, deriving from a combination of the past and all its
implications and the world view of the present government. The
denomination of the 'market' as the provider of the highest
economic and political 'good' is a singularly ideological act,
whatever conventional economists might claim, and in the belief in
the subsequent success of (politically dependent) market structures
lies the definition of 'liberal' economic security: real economic
security is provided by a functioning, global wealth maximizing
'liberal' international economic order within which national market
economies freely operate (Ward, 1979; Buzan, 1983; McKinlay and
Little, 1986).

The arguments surrounding economic security are also essentially ideological: the relative benefits of competing economic orders
can only be assessed ideologically (McKinlay and Little, 1986).
Moreover, the political definition of what constitutes security for a
government is equally ideological – except that it has been argued
here that there are forces in the world political economy that will
create major problems for any government whose political definition of security does not ultimately include economic security.

Conclusions: British Foreign Policy and Economic Security

This chapter has argued that although British foreign policy (and
not *just* British foreign economic policy) is critical to an understanding of economic security and order, domestic policy is of
equal importance as conditions of interdependence make domestic/
foreign distinctions meaningless in practice as well as theory. The
political definition of British security has been shown to be narrow
as against a non-traditional formal definition of economic security.
It has also been suggested that this definition is inappropriate and

counter-productive to the achievement of real economic security in its exclusive implementation, particularly in the context of a liberal world economy. The pursuit of British economic security in the 1980s has meant ensuring continuity of supplies of strategic raw materials and ensuring beneficial economic relations with other AICs within the OECD. Because of the restricted notion of security, no real public debate has taken place within the foreign policy community, other than in the specific and limited form already mentioned.

British foreign and domestic policy has faced major problems in the formulation and achievement of economic security objectives. First, the adoption of a conception of military security that includes the key (and historical) element of a national industrial–defence base is incompatible with the adoption of a liberal economic policy that in the name of efficiency internationalizes the British economy. Second, the adoption of a conception of security that is primarily military only provided national economic security when Britain was the hegemonic power and largely determined the structure of the international economic order. Third, the underlying policy stance that 'Britain's international situation should provide the essential regulator for the domestic economy' (Blank, 1977, p. 705) is still operative. The dominance of the 'international', despite all claims to the contrary and for whatever motives, relegates national economic security to a subsidiary concern. Fourth, for Britain the adoption of accommodative policies, given the nature of government and the problems of political economic change, does *not* bring economic security, although it might in the longer term.

Underlying these four problems is the fact that British foreign policy-makers have not addressed the problems raised by an analysis of economic security. The reason is clear – a failure at the political level (Blank, 1977; Wallace, 1976). William Wallace's 1976 conclusion is unfortunately still valid: 'The crucial failure is at the higher level. Time and again, since World War II, questioning of the assumptions underlying foreign policy has successfully been suppressed. Alternatives have been denied, choices avoided; decisions once taken presented as inevitable, scarcely ever re-examined' (1976, p. 274). Until the process of questioning becomes a wholesale re-evaluation of foreign policy, real British national economic security will remain perhaps illusory and certainly partial.

PART III

Arenas

7 Britain and East–West Relations

BRIAN WHITE

The global environment of contemporary international relations and East–West relations in particular constitutes an important arena of activity and concern for British foreign policy-makers. This is not surprising, of course, given Britain's imperial tradition and the continuing predisposition of policy-makers to seek an effective global role in world affairs. This chapter has two related objectives. On the one hand, it highlights some important elements of continuity in British policy towards East–West relations, a policy arena which is taken here to subsume relations with the United States, the Soviet Union and Eastern Europe in both a bilateral and a multilateral context. British policy in the 1980s provides the specific focus but the object is to locate that policy within an historical context, to identify relevant attitudes which have under-pinned policy and to consider the extent to which this policy arena has provided and continues to provide a vehicle for attempts to maintain a global role.

Continuing global aspirations provide the link to the second, more general objective here. Given that Britain's position in the international hierarchy of states has declined sharply over the last forty years, the East–West arena is used to illustrate a major theme of postwar British foreign policy: the persistent efforts of policy-makers to substitute 'power', defined essentially by measurable indicators such as GNP and military force, with 'influence', defined by less tangible criteria such as diplomatic skills and personal relationships. The chapter concludes with a brief evaluation of British policy and some consideration of its appropriateness for the 1980s and beyond.

The Thatcher Government and East–West Regulations

The beginning of 1984 offers a convenient starting point for analysis because it witnessed a distinct if undramatic change in the approach of the Thatcher government to East–West relations. Having played the role of the 'Iron Lady' with some relish throughout the period of her first administration, Mrs Thatcher, with an overwhelming electoral victory behind her, now sought to convert that image into what she called 'an iron resolve for the easing of tension' between East and West. Speaking in Moscow at the funeral of Yuri Andropov, the Prime Minister took the opportunity to distance herself from the hard line she had taken in speeches in the United States and Canada the previous autumn and to signal her conversion to the idea of a new dialogue with the communist bloc. 'If there is to be progress on arms control – which I devoutly want – it will come, not through negotiating skill alone but because a broader understanding has been reached. The aim is that broader understanding. I do not know whether it can be achieved – I do know that we have to try' (*Guardian*, 15 February 1984).

The parlous state of East–West relations at the end of 1983 and the fact that 1984 was presidential election year in the United States provided both the immediate context and the opportunity for the Thatcher government to influence the international political climate. As well as seeking to improve bilateral relations with states on the other side of the Iron Curtain, the government, together with other allies notably the French and the West Germans, now sought to put pressure on the United States to adopt a more flexible attitude towards the Soviet Union.

The implementation of this new policy actually started just before the Andropov funeral when the Prime Minister and the Foreign Secretary Sir Geoffrey Howe visited Hungary at the beginning of February in the first of a series of official visits to Eastern Europe. Over the next fourteen months Howe became the first British Foreign Secretary to complete a full round of visits to all seven Warsaw Pact states including the Soviet Union. The visit to London by Soviet Deputy Foreign Minister Kornienko in March 1984 initiated a reciprocal process of reviving diplomatic relations with the Soviet Union. An important marker with respect to this process and something of a diplomatic coup for the British government was the visit by Mikhail Gorbachev in December 1984 a few weeks before he became Soviet leader. The announcement of a decision to lift a four-year embargo on ministerial contact with the Soviet Embassy in London was timed to fit in with this visit by the most senior Soviet leader since Kosygin in 1967.

Clearly this apparent volte-face towards the Soviet Union and its allies requires some explanation. After all, as Riddell has noted, the foreign policy of the first Thatcher government was characterized by high defence spending, a close identification with the Reagan administration and an equally tough anti-Soviet stance (1985, p. 227). To begin with, an element of what might be called pragmatic opportunism cannot be ignored. As President Reagan illustrated, it is not unknown for leaders to project a 'softer', more statesmanlike image in their second period of office. The 'peacemaker' label has a perennial attraction for politicians mindful of how history will judge them. The Prime Minister did say during the 1983 election campaign that if re-elected she hoped to play a more active international role. There was also domestic political mileage to be made out of pressing for a dialogue with the East in order to neutralize the 'peace movement' and help to recapture public support for a nuclear deterrence posture which had undoubtedly been undermined in the early 1980s. There are indications though that there was more to this change of policy than mere opportunism. The impression that this new approach fitted into a more considered, longer-term view of East–West relations emerges from the Foreign Secretary's speeches during this period and also from an interesting speech which Defence Secretary Michael Heseltine, hitherto the scourge of the peace movement, delivered to the Bow Group in the House of Commons.

On his forays into Eastern Europe, the Foreign Secretary pursued three themes in his speeches. The first was the need to create and develop high-level, personal contacts between European leaders. This, it was hoped, would gradually increase trust and contribute to an improved political atmosphere which might in turn facilitate progress in East–West negotiations. Howe stressed, however, that those negotiations should not be restricted to arms control. The aim should be to develop and sustain an East–West dialogue covering the broadest possible agenda. The other themes pursued by the Foreign Secretary were logical extensions of this position. The agenda for discussion, it was argued, should include trade and human rights issues. Thus, Howe was concerned to try to boost trade with Eastern Europe and the Soviet Union. He also raised whenever possible, and sometimes to the embarrassment of his hosts, particular human rights cases and the general human rights situation in the country he was visiting.

Speaking at the end of June 1984, just before the Foreign Secretary visited Moscow, Michael Heseltine called for greater mutual understanding between East and West. Both sides, he maintained, should seek better political and economic relations which would enable arms reductions to be achieved. As a contribution to that understanding, he was prepared to concede that the build-up of Soviet military strength in recent years was not solely designed to threaten the security of the West in accordance with some grand ideological design. Developing the theme of 'Russia in historical perspective', the Defence Secretary argued that Russian governments had been preoccupied for centuries with their security and the West should understand that the Soviet Union like the West has legitimate security interests to defend. His thesis was not that Western vigilance is inappropriate but that the West, in his words, should 'couple this essential policy of deterrence with a manifest willingness to talk and listen' (*Guardian*, 28 June 1984).

Significantly, Sir Geoffrey Howe's immediate predecessors at the Foreign and Commonwealth Office, Lord Carrington and Francis Pym, had both made essentially the same point in 1983. In his first speech from the back-benches after having been dismissed by Mrs Thatcher, Pym called for more top-level contacts between London and Moscow. In the Alastair Buchan Memorial Lecture delivered prior to the 1983 election, Lord Carrington criticized not only what he called 'megaphone diplomacy' but also a 'crude, one-dimensional moralism' in dealings with the Soviet Union. He was referring to the West as a whole, but as a comment on the 'Iron Lady' posture, the point was not lost on a domestic audience. What was being neglected, Carrington argued, was the 'broader political dimension of East–West relations'. What was needed was 'the peaceful resolution of potential conflict through energetic and forceful dialogue' (*Survival*, 1983, p. 151).

Perhaps Mrs Thatcher's *'Ostpolitik'* represented a victory for the co-called 'wets' in her own party or maybe she had come under the influence of the FCO despite her jaundiced view of the Office after the Falklands crisis? None of these hypotheses can be rejected out of hand but the argument to be developed here is that they take little account of the essential continuity in British policy on East–West relations since the Second World War. What emerges from these speeches is the idea that Western policy and more specifically British policy since 1979 had stressed the military component to the exclusion of the politico-diplomatic dimension of East–West relations. The prescriptions called for a return to a more balanced policy, to a 'sweet and sour approach' to the East as Carrington called it. Indeed, from an historical perspective, it is the 'Iron Lady' approach which appears anomalous.

The Historical Context

Mrs Thatcher is not the first Conservative prime minister with impeccable anti-communist credentials who has tried to initiate a dialogue with the Soviet Union. Her call for an 'easement of tension' with the Soviet Union even borrowed the language of Churchill's appeals in the early 1950s. More generally, however, there are striking parallels between the stated policy objectives of the Thatcher government after 1984 and persistent attempts by British governments since the 1950s to 'normalize' East–West relations. The emphasis may have changed at different times reflecting different circumstances, but British governments of all political persuasions have consistently taken the view that normal relations with the East should balance military strength with a preparedness to negotiate whenever possible or, to put it another way, should blend a structure of deterrence with a process of détente. Following the establishment of an effective structure of deterrence in the form of the North Atlantic alliance, British governments have been uncomfortable whenever the West has pursued a policy of deterrence to the exclusion of détente, or vice versa.

In the 1950s, for example, with the Americans committed only to 'negotiate from strength' with the Soviet Union, if at all, the governments of Churchill and Macmillan sought to act as mediator or 'honest broker' between the superpowers. Despite accusations that the 'British disease' as it was called threatened the solidarity of NATO, Britain played a significant role as a catalyst of détente during these years, helping to initiate and sustain an East–West dialogue. Whenever the solidarity of NATO genuinely was at risk, however, as in the latter part of 1954 or during the twelve months after the Suez crisis, attempts to mediate were temporarily abandoned and British efforts were devoted to maintaining the integrity of the alliance. On the other hand, once a superpower dialogue had apparently become self-sustaining in the early 1970s, British governments became concerned that a superpower preoccupation with détente might weaken the commitment to European security which, in the British view, underpinned the search for an East–West accommodation.

British attempts to influence the direction of East–West relations since the Second World War can be explained in various ways. The speeches of prime ministers and foreign secretaries suggest that the fear of a nuclear war sparked either by accident or design has been an important factor over the years. At various times, the possibility of electoral or commercial advantage appears to have loomed large in the calculations of foreign policy decision-makers. The persistence and the pattern of British efforts over a lengthy period, however, can perhaps best be explained as part of a continuing attempt to substitute declining material assets by manipulating the symbols of power such as diplomatic skills, nuclear status, personal and 'special' relationships, so as to maintain a global role. This attempt to adapt to Britain's so-called 'descent from power' by replacing 'power' with 'influence' has been a major theme of British foreign policy since the Second World War but, it can be argued, the East–West arena has been of declining utility to policy-makers. To pursue this argument in more detail, a useful if broad distinction can be drawn between the period up to the early 1960s and the period thereafter. In the first period, Britain played a central role in East–West relations but, since the 1960s, the British contribution has been more peripheral.

Britain, the Cold War and Détente

It may seem paradoxical but Britain was a leading 'architect' of both cold war and détente in the period from the end of the Second World War up to the early 1960s (Northedge and Wells, 1982, p. 128). It is clear from the historical record that the British perception of the Soviet Union as a major threat to Western interests predated similar American perceptions. Certainly Churchill's famous 'Iron Curtain' speech in March 1946 set the pace for the Americans in metaphorical 'bloc-building'. Parallel Anglo-American views with respect to the significance of the Soviet threat may have emerged by the end of 1946, as Bullock suggests, but the Attlee government and Foreign Secretary Ernest Bevin in particular had to work very hard over the next three years to persuade the Americans to take appropriate actions in response to that threat (1985, p. 239). The institutions that were established during that period, however, were a product in no small part of British diplomacy. Moreover, it can be argued that a separate West Germany, the Organization for European Economic Co-operation (OEEC) and the North Atlantic Treaty Organization (NATO) became the important cold war structures which severed West from East in political, economic and military terms and effectively polarized the postwar international system.

But the British contribution to an East–West cold war is not solely explicable in terms of perceptions of a Soviet threat. It was also a function of two other imperatives that governed British foreign policy after the Second World War. The first of these was Britain's economic plight. Such were the economic problems that faced the Attlee government, particularly evident after the harsh winter of 1946–7, that the burden of supporting the British zone in Germany had become intolerable. The agreement of December 1946, which fused together the British and American zones, was the first move towards the establishment of a separate, independent federal republic in September 1949. Similarly, the desperate need to ensure a massive influx of American dollars to fund industrial recovery and a welfare state in Britain is crucial to an explanation of Bevin's role in organizing the European response to the Marshall Plan through the mechanism of the OEEC. This role was also significant in terms of the second imperative, binding the United States to Britain and Western Europe. As early as 1946, much to the concern of the Labour left, the Attlee government had decided that British security as well as economic recovery necessitated a close alliance with the Americans. Hence the government signed the Dunkirk Treaty with France in 1947 and negotiated the Brussels Treaty with the Benelux countries the following year. These treaties, though nominally directed against Germany, laid firm and necessary foundations for the North Atlantic Treaty of April 1949.

As already suggested, however, a major consequence of establishing a structure of deterrence was a polarization of international relations with attendant dangers of East–West confrontation and the possibility of nuclear war. Even George Kennan, the architect of the containment doctrine, became concerned that these institutions would be 'certain to reinforce Soviet feelings of suspicion and insecurity, and, hence, to narrow opportunities for negotiations' (Gaddis, 1982, p. 71). The dangers posed by these structural consequences of Western policy were compounded by a hardening of American attitudes towards international communism. By 1950, as detailed in the famous National Security Council document published in that year (NSC-68), containment had become an end in itself, with the construction of what Acheson called a 'situation of strength' now regarded as the only viable strategy to meet the heightened threat of a monolithic, nuclear-armed, international communism. For the Americans, the Cold War had become synonymous with political warfare between ideologically opposed blocs. Normal relations including negotiations were effectively ruled out (see Gaddis, 1982, pp. 82–3, 104–6).

The more pragmatic British, however, could not wholly accept this overtly ideological approach to East–West relations. Containment was regarded as a short-term strategy and the Cold War as a necessary but temporary phase in relations. It soon became clear that the longer-term objective of British policy was the normalization of relations with the Soviet bloc. Though Bevin, like Churchill before him, was primarily concerned to bind the Americans to the fate of Western Europe, he was anxious to keep the door open to the East in the hope of a better political understanding (Bullock, 1985, p. 107). As Elisabeth Barker puts it, Bevin saw the 'alliance with the Americans not as a preparation for an inevitable war against Russia, but as an essential foundation for future efforts for détente' (1983, p. 185). If, for the Americans, cold war and détente had come to represent incompatible approaches to East–West relations, for the British they seemed to represent different aspects of the same strategy designed to normalize relations across the East–West ideological divide. Thus the British could neither accept the NSC-68 definition of the Soviet threat nor the prescribed response. Indeed, they became concerned that if the West tried to counter the threat by 'strength' alone, the result would be to rigidify East–West divisions and heighten the possibility of confrontation and war (see Bell, 1962). The appropriate response to the threat, from a British perspective, was to combine strength with diplomacy, deterrence with accommodation.

Anglo-American differences of approach to East–West relations became apparent in policy terms in 1950 with respect to China and the Korean War. While the 'loss' of China reinforced the American view of a monolithic communist bloc with which negotiations were impossible, the British explicitly rejected this notion by recognizing the new government in Peking and arguing that the West should negotiate with Mao (see Boardman, 1976). This illustrated very clearly a British determination to keep open East–West contacts, American displeasure notwithstanding. The outbreak of the Korean War in June 1950 and the reality of a major East–West conflict, on the other hand, underlined the dangers posed by the NSC-68 version of containment. The Attlee government loyally backed the American line on Korea, but the need to defuse the crisis persuaded Bevin to annoy the Americans once again by attempting to mediate. Little was achieved by British diplomatic initiatives at this stage, but they serve to indicate the extent of British concern about the direction of American policy and the state of East–West relations.

This concern was not restricted to the Labour government. The general election campaign in 1950 brought Winston Churchill to the stump on this issue. In an important speech in Edinburgh, Churchill appealed for an East–West summit. Picking up this theme in the first foreign policy debate of the new parliament, Churchill argued that it was all very well to build up 'situations of strength' and then 'negotiate from strength' but, as he put it, 'time and patience . . . are not necessarily on our side' (Bell, 1962, p. 22). The bipartisan nature of British concerns was confirmed after a Conservative government under Churchill was returned in October 1951. Churchill immediately returned to the issue of negotiations with the Russians. In a major speech at the Guildhall in London – to become a favoured venue for speeches about détente – he talked in characteristically Olympian terms about the need to keep the giants from colliding.

If an embryonic British détente policy can be detected as early as 1950, this policy had little impact on East–West relations until 1954–5. Thereafter, however, British governments played a central role in the détente process until the early 1960s. Churchill continued to push for East–West negotiations at a time when the Americans were doing everything possible to avoid them, the French were preoccupied with Indo-China and the European Defence Community (EDC), and Adenauer with securing sovereignty for the Federal Republic. The diplomatic skills of Foreign Secretary Anthony Eden were crucial in producing the agreements which eventually opened the way for the 1955 détente. Conciliatory British diplomacy later helped to contain the crises in the Middle East and Berlin while persistent British pressure led indirectly to the successful Camp David summit in 1959 and directly to the aborted summit in Paris the following year. The Macmillan government managed to keep open East–West contacts in the tense months following Paris, mediated effectively in the Laos crisis of 1961–2 and played a major role in steering the test ban negotiations to a successful conclusion in the form of the Partial Test Ban Treaty in 1963.[1]

Significantly, the antecedents of the 'new' British approach to East–West relations which surfaced in 1984 can be found in this period. In this sense, Carrington, Pym, Howe and even Heseltine can be said to be following in a Churchill-Macmillan tradition. In his famous speech to the House of Commons in May 1953, for example, Churchill too explicitly recognized the legitimacy of Soviet security interests and prescribed patient, piecemeal diplomacy at the highest level to reconcile East–West differences. Moreover, in his Bermuda talks with Eisenhower at the end of that year, the Prime Minister advocated what he called a policy of 'double-dealing' with the Soviet Union. According to Colville's account of the meeting, this typical example of Churchillian wit translated into 'a policy of strength towards the Soviet Union combined with holding out the hand of friendship' (1976, p. 240). Four years later, Macmillan also underlined the need for a balanced approach to East–West relations. On his return from a NATO council meeting in Paris in December 1957, he summed up the British position to the House of Commons. 'Our policy . . . is really two-fold, and I think in essence simple. It is a firm and powerful NATO, from the military point of view, but always ready to discuss and negotiate on a practical basis to obtain practical results.' In his memoirs, Macmillan adds, 'in a single phrase it could be described as "arm and parley" ' (1971, p. 340).

More recent references to the desirability of negotiating with the

East across the widest possible agenda also find an echo in the 1950s. Churchill's idea of a new approach to East–West relations in 1953–4 consisted not only of restoring and expanding politico-diplomatic contacts at heads of government level, but also of developing as many commercial, social and cultural contacts as possible (see Colville, 1981, p. 107). Speeches by Foreign Secretary Selwyn Lloyd in 1959 and 1960 suggest that the Macmillan government shared Churchill's 'open contacts' view that normalized diplomacy would not of itself 'normalize' East–West relations; it was necessary to buttress political contacts by developing contacts across the spectrum of non-governmental relations. The object of British efforts to promote East–West détente during this period, according to Lloyd, was nothing less than 'evolving a system of regulating international affairs' which would 'avoid a constant atmosphere of crisis'.[2]

But if crisis avoidance was central to the British approach, the potential of the East–West arena as a vehicle for distracting attention from the mounting evidence of Britain's material decline in the postwar period could not have escaped the attention of policy-makers. A tight bipolar structure, after all, not only heightened the danger of nuclear war but also imposed rigidity and inflexibility on foreign policy-making. If Britain was to continue playing a significant global role in international relations, it was necessary to create some room for manoeuvre within an hegemonial Western system dominated by the United States. Elisabeth Barker provides a useful summary in this context of the essential foreign policy problem which faced British governments after 1945. 'Britain's power to influence world events or even to pursue an independent foreign policy was . . . strictly limited. Skilful manoeuvring was required if the British were to retain some freedom of choice and the capacity to take initiatives' (1983, p. 69).

Even before the end of the Second World War, as Ritchie Ovendale has commented, 'Britain's position at the conference tables of world diplomacy . . . obscured the reality of Britain's diminished power' (1984, p. 3). By 1947, it was clear that the 'Big Three' concept was dead. Thereafter, the political task was to maintain the appearance at least of being as equal as possible with the remaining 'superpowers'. In hierarchical terms, this meant claiming a special position for Britain, just 'below' the United States and the Soviet Union perhaps but definitely 'above' the

other European allies. For policy-makers more and more interested, particularly after Suez, in manipulating the illusion rather
than the substance of power, a high-profile East–West role prom-
ised continuing status and no little prestige. This arena provided
valuable opportunities to deploy the types of influence that Britain
still possessed. Exploiting these opportunities enabled British
leaders to display qualities of leadership or even statesmanship on
a 'global stage' and British governments to exert some independent
leverage over the United States and, to a lesser extent, the Soviet
Union.

The test ban negotiations between 1958 and 1963 provide the
best example during this period of a British government maximizing its relatively limited resources to affect the outcome of a major
East–West issue. The Macmillan government, it must be said, had
been ambivalent at best about the idea of negotiating a ban on
nuclear tests until Britain's nuclear status was secured by the
restoration of a close Anglo-American nuclear relationship in the
summer of 1958. Once the Geneva talks were in progress, however, a series of British initiatives played an important role in keeping them going to a successful conclusion in the form of the Partial
Test Ban treaty (see Wright, 1964). The most important of these
initiatives in terms of affecting the outcome was Macmillan's
March 1963 proposal that personal emissaries of the three leaders
should negotiate directly in Moscow rather than in Geneva. The
Cuban missile crisis had finally impressed upon both Kennedy and
Khrushchev the need to make common cause on a test ban treaty.
But the strength of domestic opposition to a treaty which surfaced
in Washington and Moscow in the early weeks of 1963 produced an
impasse in Geneva and made it impossible for either Kennedy or
Khrushchev to make any further moves to break the deadlock.
Thus, Macmillan's initiative, which triggered what turned out to
be the final talks in Moscow four months later, was crucially
important and perfectly timed (Seaborg, 1981).

Specific British initiatives were arguably less crucial to the outcome, however, than the sustained pressure on both superpowers
and the Americans in particular over an extended period. As one
British negotiator, probably Sir Michael Wright put it, 'the initiative was in forcing the issue in private with the other two. We
looked at Britain as being in a position of being able to bring the
two sides together' (Nunnerly, 1972, p. 109). What the Macmillan

government managed to do remarkably successfully was to influence domestic political processes in the United States and, to a
lesser degree, the Soviet Union. The existence of powerful lobbies
in Washington and Moscow who were actively opposed to any sort
of test ban treaty meant that the respective leaders had very little
room for manoeuvre. The well-timed meeting or more often a
letter from Macmillan were only the most obvious manifestations
of a sustained attempt to reinforce the often embattled positions of
those who were fighting for a treaty. Leadership links and personal
friendships, ministers, diplomats and scientists on the ground in
Geneva were all skilfully orchestrated to maximize British influence. The fact that open disagreements with the United States
were usually avoided and that the semblance at least of a unified
Western negotiating position was maintained also served to increase the effectiveness of British diplomacy.

The Decline of British Influence on East–West Relations

From an historical perspective, however, the signing of the Partial
Test Ban Treaty in August 1963 emerges as the last peak of British
influence on the direction of East–West relations. Thereafter, the
ability of British governments to play a major East–West role
began to decline. If a single 'turning point' can be identified, it was
not the test ban treaty nor even the Paris summit débâcle in 1960, so
often pinpointed in this context, but the Eisenhower-Khrushchev
summit at Camp David in September 1959. This meeting was
crucial because, as Gaddis argues, it effectively 'legitimized' direct
negotiations between the superpowers at heads of government
level (1982, pp. 195–7). In the longer term, personal contacts
between Soviet and American leaders were bound to limit the
ability of third parties to influence East–West relations: personal
contacts of an exclusive nature were particularly ominous in this
respect, as Macmillan realized (see 1972, pp. 78–80). Paradoxically,
to the extent that unremitting British pressure on Washington was
responsible for the Camp David summit, the Macmillan government had been almost too successful. The more the leaders of the
two superpowers got into the habit of consulting directly, the less
they needed Britain's services as an intermediary.
  This does not mean of course that British governments have not

tried to influence the direction of East–West relations since 1963.
Indeed, there is some substance to the provocative Northedge
comment that the 'test ban agreement . . . had the effect of
fostering in Britain hallucinations of world power no longer
justified by realities' (1974, p. 292). Harold Wilson's attempts to
mediate in the Vietnam War provide a good illustration. Kosygin's
visit to London in February 1967 provided what Wilson hoped
would be, in Henry Brandon's words, 'an opportunity for him to
step onto the world stage as a mediator between the Americans and
the North Vietnamese' (1970, p. 82). A peace plan based on what
the government was assured would be acceptable to the Americans
was put to the Soviet leader. Meanwhile, however, the Johnson
administration had changed its view on what was required from the
North Vietnamese before the United States would suspend its
bombing campaign (for details, see Gore-Booth, 1974, pp. 335–
62). Not only did the British attempt to mediate fail but the
divisions in Washington succeeded in making the Wilson government look rather inept. As Foreign Secretary George Brown later
admitted though, the initiative failed in part because 'we were too
anxious to be intermediaries' (1972, p. 135).

By the late 1960s, residual mediation efforts notwithstanding, it
was clear that Britain's distinctive position within the Western
alliance had been usurped by France and the Federal Republic who
now, consciously or not, followed the British example by exploiting the potential of an independent, high-profile East–West role. A
series of Franco-Soviet ministerial exchanges culminated in de
Gaulle's visit to Moscow in 1966. This attempt to revive France's
historic links with the Soviet Union was a key part of de Gaulle's
'Grand Design'. As Alfred Grosser comments, 'ever since de
Gaulle's visit to Moscow in 1944, the aim of French policy [had]
been to promote whenever there was an opportunity . . . constructive relations with the Soviet Union . . . not as an end in itself, but
in order to strengthen the French hand in our dealings with the
United States' (Urban, 1976, p. 265). Not only was détente
regarded as a way of containing American (or 'Anglo-Saxon')
influence, it was a potential vehicle for exercising restraint on the
traditional enemy, Germany, and was therefore a central plank in
the Gaullist plan to restore French power and grandeur.

Much more significant in terms of its impact on East–West relations, however, was the *Ostpolitik* of the Federal Republic. This

policy represented a reversal of the premiss that the reunification of Germany must precede détente. While the uncompromising Adenauer line towards the East had been softened by the Erhard and Kiesinger governments, it was the Brandt government elected in 1969 which fully implemented this policy. Between 1970 and 1972, a number of treaties were signed which in effect secured the territorial stabilization of Europe with the implicit acceptance of the 1945 borders and provided a solution to the Berlin and the wider German problem. It is also significant that these independent European moves towards an East–West accommodation and *Ostpolitik* in particular had the effect of speeding up American plans to usher in what Nixon called an 'era of negotiation' in order to retain control of the détente process (see Kissinger, 1979, pp. 132, 382, 403).

What is interesting in the context of this chapter, though, is the extent to which by the early 1970s the British had become ambivalent towards a détente process which had now reached a critical phase. On the one hand, an East–West accommodation was still regarded as necessary, not least because of the continuing dangers of a nuclear confrontation between the superpowers. Kissinger's memoirs record the enthusiasm with which the Wilson government in 1969 and 1970 pressed Nixon both to support *Ostpolitik* and to engage in direct negotiations with Moscow (1979, pp. 89, 416). The second volume of those memoirs even details how the FCO helped to draft the Agreement on the Prevention of Nuclear War signed by the United States and the Soviet Union in 1973 (Kissinger, 1982, pp. 278–86). Those same memoirs, however, also indicate a growing British scepticism towards East–West negotiations which became focused on the Conference on Security and Co-operation in Europe (CSCE) (see Kissinger, 1979, pp. 938, 965; Dougherty, 1975, p. 88).

An ambivalent British attitude towards détente in part reflected the concern shared with the other European allies that the super-powers might reach agreements which were in their interests but not necessarily in the best interests of their allies. The Americans not surprisingly found this allied posture very frustrating. As Kissinger notes wryly, 'in times of rising tension, they [the Europeans] feared American rigidity; in times of relaxing tensions, they dreaded a US–Soviet condominium' (1979, p. 94). But more specific British reservations about superpower negotiations and the broader 'Helsinki process' centred on a concern that the potential of détente in terms of fundamentally changing the nature of East–West relations might be oversold (or possibly overbought) thus generating popular expectations that could only be met by the West 'going too far' or 'giving too much away' and possibly destabilizing the structure of European security (see Dougherty, 1975, p. 88; Williams, 1986).

This ambivalent British posture in the 1970s is consistent with the 'balanced' approach to East–West relations outlined above. Even before the détente negotiations of the 1970s began in earnest, the active British diplomacy to limit the damage done to NATO by the French withdrawal from the integrated military command structure in 1966 (see Gore-Booth, 1974, pp. 340–3) and the British role in the formation of the Eurogroup in 1968 were indications that a concern to maintain the cohesion of NATO (and being seen to be a 'good European') was beginning to have a higher priority in British foreign and defence policy than pressing for an East–West accommodation. Even after the signing of the Helsinki Accords in 1975, Roy Hattersley was warning the House of Comons that 'the policy of détente has to be pursued with the greatest possible caution. It can proceed only on the secure foundation of a strong and effective Western Alliance.'[3]

But it can also be argued that this ambivalence and a certain scepticism towards East–West relations simply reflected the fact that Britain, as Williams suggests, had been effectively 'marginalized' as far as the détente process and East–West relations as a whole were concerned (1986, p. 225). There was little to be gained in terms of Britain's international status from attempting to play a high-profile East–West role and this reinforced a preoccupation with Europe and entry to the European Community in the early 1970s. The British contribution to the CSCE negotiations, such as it was, focused on human rights and economic co-operation, consistent enough with the 'broad agenda' tradition perhaps, but scarcely the stuff of 'high politics'.

Britain and East–West Relations in the 1980s and Beyond

This review has highlighted the continuity of British policy in the East–West arena since 1945. If we turn in this final section to an evaulation of that policy and consider its appropriateness for the 1980s and beyond, two important points can be made on the credit side of the ledger. First, this policy can be located within a relatively successful British tradition of adaptation to change, a tradition which can be traced back at least to the turn of this century. Even in the late 1980s, it can be argued that British influence in international relations still exceeds British power measured simply by economic and military criteria.

Secondly, British governments have persisted over the years with a constructive approach to East–West relations. Moreover, the British conception of détente as a continuing process and the importance of maintaining a balance between the military and the political components of East–West relations can be said to have had a positive impact on this policy arena. It served to highlight the dangers of excessive reliance on a deterrence strategy in the 1950s and also the dangers of overselling détente in the 1970s. From an historical perspective, the Thatcher 'Iron Lady' posture can clearly be seen as an aberration. The more 'balanced' approach to East–West relations which re-emerged in 1984 is consistent with the general orientation of British policy since the 1950s.

On the debit side, however, it might be argued that British policy-makers have not looked hard enough at the 'lessons' of the last thirty years as revealed by the declining significance of British policy in the East–West arena. A fuller appreciation of changes in the international system and Britain's reduced circumstances might have produced more discontinuities in policy than have been evident to date. There continues to be something of a tension between maintaining a realistic approach to this policy arena and retaining certain assumptions about the bases of Britain's international influence which appear anachronistic in the late 1980s. The continuing attraction of the notion of a 'special relationship' with the United States, revived by the Falklands War, is a good example of the latter.

While the close working relationship between Britain and the United States in the context of the Second World War had some undoubted spin-off into the postwar era, to the advantage of both states, the relationship can no longer be labelled 'special' except perhaps in the particular areas of defence and intelligence collaboration (see Reynolds, 1986). Even in these areas, however, many would argue that Britain has simply become increasingly dependent upon the United States since the 1960s. However important the Anglo-American relationship might still be, the costs rather than the benefits of continuing to maintain such a close relationship with Washington in terms of Britain's status and the impact on relations with other states have scarcely been scrutinized.

With respect to status, neither a 'special relationship' with the United States nor for that matter the possession of nuclear weapons, both referred to earlier in this chapter as 'symbols of power', can any longer be said to guarantee political influence on a world stage. Britain has not had a 'seat at the top table' by virtue of either or both of these since the 1960s. Indeed, far from providing global status or special influence with Washington, the closeness of Anglo-American relations over the last twenty years or so may well have adversely affected the perceptions of other states with respect to Britain's independence. It was de Gaulle in the 1960s who raised suspicions about British independence in this context with comments to the effect that if allowed into the EEC Britain might serve as an American 'Trojan horse'. More recently, there have been several examples of an apparently excessive British willingness to underwrite American policy. A series of decisions in 1985–6, including following the United States out of UNESCO, agreeing to participate in SDI research programmes, sanctioning the takeover of Westland Helicopters by an American-led consortium and allowing the United States to stage the attack on Libya in April 1986 from bases in Britain, produced unflattering references in the media to Mrs Thatcher as 'Reagan's poodle'.

Whether these comments were justified or not, the continuing assumption of a special Anglo-American link certainly helps to explain why Anglo-Soviet relations have not been as important for either state as they might have been in recent years. Unless Soviet governments have been using London to test the temperature in Washington, they have tended to turn more and more to Bonn, Paris and other European capitals to exert influence in Western Europe. As far as exercising influence in the opposite direction is concerned, British governments now find themselves trying to catch up with their European colleagues who take their regular high-level meetings with Soviet counterparts very much for granted. Despite attempts to revive Anglo-Soviet relations since 1984, critics might argue with some justification that British governments continue to squander opportunities to regularize those relations. After their meeting in London, for example, Mrs Thatcher declared that Gorbachev was a communist leader with whom 'business could be done', but surprisingly little business has been done since 1984 in the form of expanding Anglo-Soviet trade. British governments still seem more concerned with expelling Soviet spies than with securing an increased share of Soviet trade with Western Europe. In part, this reflects the fact that trade with the East continues to be valued more as a political solvent than for its own sake. But it is difficult to resist the conclusion that it is an indication that the patterns of relationships which Britain maintains in the East–West arena have not yet received the reconsideration that may be necessary in the light of changing realities.

As Christopher Hill noted in an earlier chapter, the 'bridge-builder' image retains its attractions for British policy-makers, whether in the sphere of US–European or East–West relations. This cannot but obscure a clear appreciation of the limits of independent British action in both spheres. But if a Churchillian approach to British foreign policy is no longer appropriate in the late 1980s, this does not mean that Britain cannot make a significant contribution to East–West relations in a multilateral context. As Lord Carrington argued in 1983:

> Britain herself has an important role to play in developing a more sane and secure East–West relationship – not as a bridge, or an intermediary, not to spot the chance to split the difference. But contribute our knowledge, experience and mixture of firmness and flexibility to the efforts of our partners in Europe and America. We have a long and proud history of activity on this central question of international diplomacy.
>
> (*Survival*, 1983, p. 152).

Notes

1 For a more detailed discussion of the impact of British policy on East–West détente during this period, see White, 1987.
2 The relevant extracts from Selwyn Lloyd's speeches can be found in *Documents on International Affairs 1959* (1963), pp. 69–74; *Documents on International Affairs 1960* (1964), pp. 2–3.
3 See 'Extracts from a debate on East–West relations in the House of Commons on the 24th February 1976' in HMSO (1977), *Miscellaneous No. 17. Selected Documents Relating to Problems of Security and Cooperation in Europe, 1954–77*, p. 305.

8 Britain and Western Europe

DAVID ALLEN

Implicit in many of the chapters in this book is the argument that Britain has ceased to be a global power with global interests, and that one of the primary tasks facing British foreign policy-makers is that of adjusting to a new existence among the regional powers in the international system. Clearly, if there is any one region within which British foreign policy is concentrated during the late 1980s, that region is Western Europe. But the British position within Western Europe is not simply or necessarily a function of reduced status: it can be seen also as a reflection of fundamental changes in the substance and practice of foreign policy for countries like Britain. A network of relationships and institutions has emerged in Western Europe as an expression of the increasingly intimate connections between societies there, both in the traditional field of security and military relations and in the field of social and economic concerns.

The aim of this chapter is to explore the changing position of Britain in relation to Western Europe and to evaluate the extent and effectiveness of the shifts in British policy that have taken place, especially over the period since 1970. It will begin by looking at changes in the broad patterns of Britain's relations with Western Europe and it will then examine the major areas in which British foreign policy is entangled with the region and its institutions. Finally, it will attempt to evaluate the extent to which British policy-makers – and British politics – reflect the changing links to Western Europe.

Britain and Western Europe: Retreat or Readjustment?

In most academic writing and amongst the public at large, Britain's postwar relationship with Western Europe is seen as reflecting decline and retreat. At the end of the war Britain, unlike any of its European neighbours, had reasonable pretensions to exercise global power along with the United States and the Soviet Union. When the question of participation in the development of West European co-operation was raised, it was apparent that British policy-makers interpreted their role as one that was supportive of, but independent from, any integrative experiments. Whilst prepared both to shape and to participate in traditional intergovernmental organizations such as NATO and the OEEC/OECD, both of which were transatlantic in scope rather than exclusively European, British leaders were more suspicious of those institutions that they saw as leading towards any form of supranational European integration – this despite Churchill's advocacy of a Council of Europe and Bevin's half-formed ideas about a European 'third force' (Shlaim, 1978). Thus British governments first moved to ensure that the Council of Europe in no way reflected the federal aspirations of those who had called for its establishment at the Hague Congress; they then decided against participation in the European Coal and Steel Community, an institution whose success in the 1950s was to lead directly to the establishment of the European Economic Community which again Britain at first refused to join (Charlton, 1981).

Britain's 'global' perspective was in fact exercised through three distinct 'circles' of influence, two of which, the 'special relationship' with the USA and the evolving links with the post-imperial Commonwealth, took precedence over the third, European, dimension. As the first two circles progressively lost their credibility as foundations of British policy during the 1950s (highlighted in most people's minds by the Suez débâcle and Macmillan's recognition of the 'wind of change' in Africa), and as rapidly diminishing resources forced a reduction in commitments, so Britain found itself, more by a process of elimination than one of choice, turning towards Western Europe. The manner of Britain's formal approach to Europe was unfortunate: having initially tried to frustrate the development of the EEC, by attempting to organize a wider free trade bloc and by establishing the European Free Trade Area, Macmillan, for fairly obvious electoral reasons, changed course in 1961 and applied for EEC membership. Although the saga of de Gaulle's two rejections in the 1960s and Britain's eventual admission in 1973 is well known (Northedge, 1974, pp. 328–56;

Kitzinger, 1973), it is clear in retrospect that it was not until the end of the 1960s, with the enforced military withdrawal from East of Suez, that entry into the EEC was seen in Britain as anything other than a pragmatic economic move. In Europe, irritation arising from Britain's obsession with short-term economic gain and the niceties of legal sovereignty was further fuelled by ample evidence that British governments were by no means reconciled to a mainly European role. In 1964, Harold Wilson was still claiming that 'we are a world Power and a world influence or we are nothing' (Northedge, 1974, p. 297), and although in 1969 Denis Healey argued that his last defence review had completed 'Britain's transformation from a world power into a European power' (Kennedy, 1981, p. 376), the suspicion remains even in the late 1980s that Britain's European commitment is of a fundamentally different order from that of its West European partners.

It is a mistake to view this process of adjustment to a European role as necessitating an end to British interests and involvement in the rest of the world, just as it is also a mistake to view West European regionalism as a process isolated from the rest of the international system and limited only to changes in relations between West European states. In the contemporary international system, the global hegemony of the two superpowers is restricted to their thermo-nuclear capability: when it comes to exercising political and, in particular, economic power, they have the attributes of ordinary rather than super powers. Equally, other states in the system, acting alone or collectively, are capable of exerting significant influence outside their immediate regions. To be a regional power, as Britain along with France and West Germany is within Western Europe, or to exert power collectively, as all the EC member states do within the framework of the GATT or in bilateral trade negotiations with the USA or Japan, does not imply a qualitatively different role in the system from that of the superpowers. While it is certainly the case that the USA and the USSR may be able to exert more quantitative influence, the power structure that emanates from their relationship with each other is not all-pervasive, nor is the behaviour of all the other states in the system subject to their influence alone.

Nevertheless, it is not difficult to understand why those in Britain, mindful of the country's previous status and power, might regard its relationship with Western Europe as symbolic of loss rather than the basis for positive advancement. This feeling of somehow settling for a reduced international status in inferior company has been encouraged over the years by the changing American view of West European co-operation. Since the Nixon/ Kissinger years, the American tendency has been to contrast Western Europe's limited regional 'interests' with the USA's global 'responsibilities', usually coupling this with demands for more material burden-sharing in Europe and less West European 'interference' in the rest of the world. This view contrasts with the much more palatable, if less realistic, image propounded by Kennedy in the early 1960s, that Western Europe is one of the 'twin pillars' of the Atlantic alliance. Unlike most others in Western Europe, British leaders have always believed in a contrast between an internationalist (by which is meant global) and a narrow European perspective and they have thus often appeared to their European partners to be clinging on to the former image by rejecting attempts to improve European co-operation in favour of an increasingly obsequious and often unreciprocated relationship with the USA. Nowhere is this better illustrated than in the reasons advanced for Britain's initial rejection of membership of the European Monetary System during 1978–9. It was clear then that Mr Callaghan, the Prime Minister, regarded a European solution to international monetary problems as too narrow, and that he preferred to advocate an 'international' solution, by which he meant one including the USA and Japan (Statler, 1979).

Western Europe: Integration or Intergovernmentalism?

While it is certainly the case that the relationship between Britain and the West European states has been dominated by disagreements over the policies, procedures and future of the European Communities, there is a danger in allowing consideration of the rather nebulous notion of 'European integration' to dominate assessment of the significance of Western Europe for British foreign policy. Britain remains in a minority in terms of its distaste for the notion that the European Community might evolve into some sort of federation but serious attempts at converting such ideas into practical reality have in fact long since ceased to dominate all aspects of Community business. Within the EC Britain, like its partners, is primarily concerned with managing interdependence in a way that least offends domestic illusions of independence. Freed of the worst excesses of Community theology and integrationist symbolism Britain is even capable, in respect of desired objectives like the completion of the internal market or improvement of the foreign policy co-operation mechanism, of accepting attempts to develop the Community further, such as those embodied in the Single European Act of 1986.

The 'Western Europe' that now plays such a central role both as setting for and object of British foreign policy is much more than the European Community alone, even though that organization has now grown to include twelve of the eighteen West European states. International relations in the region now exhibit a high degree of institutionalization in the form of a number of organizations, all with slightly varying membership and responsible for a number of overlapping functions. Two major institutions, NATO and the OECD, whose membership extends beyond West European states, have their headquarters in Europe and, in the case of NATO in particular, have significant 'European' caucuses within them. What emerges from a mass of formal multilateral contacts, as well as less formal *ad hoc* groupings and an intricate pattern of bilateral relationships, is a 'Western Europe' recently characterized by Stanley Hoffmann as 'complex and messy' (Hoffmann, 1983).

It has now become impossible to describe or explain the process of change in European politics through the organizing device of integration theory. In particular, the 'zero–sum' notion of a progressive transfer of authority and tasks from a group of individual sovereign states to a new power centre – a kind of European state – bears no relation to what is actually happening in Western Europe.

Although none of its institutions shows any sign of evolving into a European state the West European region displays many of the features of advanced interdependence, particularly a broadening of the foreign policy agenda and a blurring of boundaries between domestic politics and foreign policy. Along with the other West European states, Britain has been forced to make a number of significant adjustments in response to what Wallace has accurately described as the 'transformation of European politics' (1984, pp. 4–20). The greatest change arises from the fact that with one or two possible exceptions (Greece and Turkey's ongoing dispute being the most obvious), the West European states have abandoned the use or the threat of the use of force in their relations with one another. In no other region in the contemporary international system is this the case, and although it is true that the internationalization of business, finance and the growth of world trade combined with the revolution in communications has changed both the procedures and substance of Britain's dealings with the entire OECD area, that change has been felt most intensely in Western Europe. Furthermore, to the extent that diminished politico-military influence and economic interdependence have altered the nature of Britain's dealings with states outside Western Europe, British governments have found that, in certain circumstances, action co-ordinated either formally or informally with other European states is more likely to succeed than a solo effort. Thus, in all its contemporary aspects – political, military-security, economic and social-welfare – British foreign policy both towards and in collaboration with the states and organizations of Western Europe (as well as towards the world outside Europe) has been fundamentally altered over the last fifteen to twenty years: Britain has been 'condemned to play the European game' (Wallace, 1984, p. 81).

Before turning to examine the way that Western Europe impacts on the various issue areas mentioned above, it is important to note that the overall shift to Europe in British foreign policy can in no way be seen as the result of a clear-cut decision. Britain has become progressively entangled in European diplomacy, with a series of *ad hoc* decisions all contributing in a relatively undesigned fashion to a situation in which 'Western Europe' constitutes a setting for the making of British foreign policy, a target of British foreign policy and, to the extent that Britain now collaborates with its West European partners, a part of the foreign policy decision-making process itself. Perhaps because the move towards Europe was the negative result of other avenues being closed, there has been within the British polity a great reluctance to accept that such a change has indeed come about. As we shall see in more detail later, significant changes in the general practices of government and the specific nature and management of foreign policy have not been accompanied by any similar shift in either the terms or the conditions of domestic political intercourse. One consequence of this is that there has been no attempt to build a domestic consensus to support British diplomacy in this still relatively new environment. In fact, precisely the opposite has occurred, with successive governments doing their best to maintain the illusion that real autonomy in both foreign and domestic policy has been preserved by stout defence of legal sovereignty in the West European arena.

Although Britain's involvement with Western Europe was considerably deepened by membership of the European Community after 1973, its participation in wide-ranging organizations like NATO and the Council of Europe as well as more specific functional bodies had already given a number of British officials and ministers wide experience in multilateral European diplomacy. In particular, as a founder member of NATO, Britain has been involved in the delicate art of collaborating with both fellow Europeans and the United States for nearly forty years; it is thus to the impact of Western Europe on the security aspects of British foreign policy that we will now turn.

NATO, Western Europe and Britain's Security

Since the Second World War, successive British governments have sought to achieve the prime objective of foreign policy, namely the security of the country, by collaborating with other states. In the immediate aftermath of the war the threat was perceived to be posed by a resurgent Germany. Fearful of once again having to stand alone in the event of an American withdrawal, British leaders first of all secured an occupation zone for France and then in 1947 signed with France the mutual defence Treaty of Dunkirk. This European alliance was then expanded in the 1948 Brussels Treaty to include the Benelux countries, but confidence in achieving security against the threat increasingly seen as coming from the Soviet Union rather than Germany, was only really achieved in 1949 when the United States agreed to formally join with the West Europeans in the North Atlantic Treaty. Since then, the security of Western Europe has been assured by this transatlantic collaboration, despite a series of disputes between the Europeans and the Americans in which for the most part Britain has sought to play the role of intermediary. The British assumption is that, among the West European states, Britain's relationship with the United States is unique and that above all it is in Britain's interest to maintain the US commitment.

Thus, when the proposed European Defence Community failed in the 1950s to provide the institutional basis for German rearmament, it was the British who resolved the issue. Their proposal to convert the Brussels Treaty Organization into a Western European Union, to which West Germany might be admitted, combined with their willingness to station 55,000 troops on the Rhine until 1990, averted the American threat of an 'agonizing reappraisal' of their European commitment if West Germany was not rearmed. In similar fashion, the British sought to resolve European fears about US nuclear predominance in the alliance with proposals for an Allied Nuclear Force in the 1960s and, towards the end of the decade, it was British Defence Secretary Denis Healey who was instrumental in setting up the Eurogroup – an informal meeting of European ministers who attempt to co-ordinate the European position before full NATO Council meetings (Taylor, 1984, p. 21). It was the Eurogroup that provided the framework for producing the 1970 European Defence Improvement Programme – Europe's response to threats from the US Senate that American troops would be withdrawn from Europe if the West Europeans did not increase their share of the defence burden.

By the end of the 1970s Britain was spending only 1.5 per cent of its total defence budget on non-NATO military commitments, compared with around 20 per cent in the mid-1960s. Although the unexpected costs of the post-1982 Falklands commitment altered this trend a little, there was no inclination in Britain to fundamentally change this total commitment of its forces to the alliance. There was considerable discussion about the size and composition of that contribution, given constraints on the military budget, but this did not prove to be a source of contention within the alliance itself. From time to time, though, concern has been expressed at what appears to be a British decision to maintain all its alliance commitments (the contribution to the Central Front, the Eastern Atlantic and Channel and the nuclear deterrent) by accepting a gradual weakening of the quality of the conventional forces and their support. An additional dimension to Britain's relationship with the alliance comes with the extensive political consultations which make NATO much more than a purely military alliance (Dannenbring, 1985; Wallace, 1976, pp. 238–43). These political consultations which, since France left the military structure of the alliance in 1966, have tended to be distanced from the considerations of strictly military matters within the Defence Planning Committee and the Nuclear Planning Committee, are primarily undertaken at official level between members of the large permanent delegations that member states maintain in Brussels. One clear indication of the impact of European developments on the implementation of British foreign policy is the presence in Brussels of three permanent British representations – to NATO, the EC and, last and most definitely least, to Belgium. The NATO and EC ambassadorships have become two of the most senior and important in the British Diplomatic Service, reflecting the growing multilateralization of diplomacy.

In the context of NATO, a number of trends that were to be enhanced by Britain's membership of the EC and in particular by European Political Co-operation, were visible from the mid-1960s. Not only did the expanded scope and quantity of multilateral business require a large permanent delegation; it also rapidly came to depend on direct contact in person or on the telephone between officials based in London, in an ever-growing number of departments, and their opposite numbers in other capitals. Thus, thousands of journeys were made each year on NATO business by officials from the MOD, the FCO, the DTI, the Procurement Executive, the Treasury and even the Department of the Environment. At the political level, NATO Foreign Ministers meet twice a year and heads of government less regularly within the Atlantic Council. It has usually been Britain's objective to use such fora to work for preserving the integrity of the alliance in the face of inevitable differences in perception of both the nature of the threat and the best way of meeting it. This strategy carries with it the obvious danger of falling between the European and American positions and thus antagonizing both sides – although to suggest this is perhaps to exaggerate the degree of European solidarity that exists. Nevertheless, during the Reagan presidency a number of issues from SDI and arms control to the question of the Soviet gas pipeline to West Germany and the American raid on Libya presented the Thatcher government with some delicate choices between adopting either a 'European' or an 'American' position. By and large Mrs Thatcher's gut reaction was to support the USA unquestioningly on all military issues (other than the US invasion of Grenada), and for the British position to be moderated thereafter through the process of European co-operation. The main point is that such matters are discussed within the framework of the alliance as well as within strictly limited European fora such as European Political Co-operation.

Fundamentally, Britain can be seen as a satisfied NATO power which would ideally like to preserve the current status quo. In this, Britain has much in common with most of its West European partners (even France in recent years has demonstrated a more overtly co-operative attitude towards the military side of the alliance). Those countries such as Spain and Greece which have domestic problems with the presence of US bases on their territories do not appear to see the resolution of these problems as requiring any reappraisal of their NATO commitment. For Britain, membership of NATO and collaboration with other West European states has involved no significant costs and it can be argued that the prime security objectives have been achieved. NATO membership has placed some financial constraints on British policy-makers because of commitments to agreed levels of military expenditure, and it has added a cautionary dimension to disputes that Britain has had with other member states, most notably with Iceland over cod and with Greece and Turkey over Cyprus.

Britain, Western Europe and Defence Co-operation

Apart from maintaining a domestic consensus over defence policy, Britain's major foreign policy concern in the military sphere has revolved around the question of European Defence Co-operation – an ever-present issue but one that has been particularly prominent on the agenda in the 1980s (see Taylor, 1984). In dealing with this question, British governments have firmly rejected any idea of a European 'third force'. In recent years only the Heath government, the most pro-European and anti-American in postwar history, has given serious consideration to the possibility of building a European political community around a separate European defence identity. However, even in that case, discussions about the possibility of a joint Anglo-French deterrent soon revealed the impracticability of such a proposal. In the scant year of EEC membership before his ejection from office in 1974, Mr Heath's actual European policy severely damaged his previously impeccable European credentials.

To insist on the continued integrity of the alliance is not, however, to be dismissive of European co-operation. British leaders' notion of the appropriate framework for this is rooted in the Kennedy image of the 'twin pillars' of the alliance. This was the basis for British interest in European procurement collaboration in the 1960s – namely, a desire to create a 'two-way street' in trans-atlantic procurement practices, previously dominated by US sales to Western Europe, and to attempt to achieve more defence for the same amount of money. The problem with collaborative projects such as the Jaguar and the Tornado fighter aircraft or the Lynx helicopter was that, as with conventional force structures, no state was prepared to give up national competences in a genuine pooling of effort. Thus the record to date, despite the existence of both the European Conference of National Armaments Directors and, to include the French, the Independent European Programme Group, is not an impressive one (see Gregory, 1982; Taylor, 1984, ch. 6). Attempts by the European Commission to get in on the act by building a European industrial policy around military procurement have similarly come to nothing. One major obstacle, national rivalries apart, is that for a number of projects Europe does not represent a natural focus of collaboration. British companies like Rolls-Royce, British Aerospace and Westland have close connec-tions in both the civil and the military sphere with both European and American counterparts – many of the European consortia are held together by their mutual connections with American firms. In other words, it is hard to carve a distinctively European procure-ment base out of a highly interdependent transatlantic system.

Nevertheless, Britain has been a firm supporter of procurement collaboration with other West European states, and such arrange-ments have been favoured by the Ministry of Defence – if only because joint projects are seen as being better protected against the dangers of cancellation on political or cost grounds than purely national projects. Even though there have not been significant savings of production costs, such projects do make it possible to spread research and development costs over more units, and in some cases make it possible to reduce the European dependence on American suppliers.

The renewed interest of the 1980s in the notion of a 'European-ized' structure for West European defence goes much further than a desire to create a European defence industrial base. For some states, though not for Britain, defence co-operation represents an opportunity to expand the scope of European integration along the lines of the failed European Defence Community. For others, Britain among them, the feeling has been growing that in the face both of new transatlantic disagreements and growing pressure on the Europeans to balance their economic strength and political interests with an enhanced security dimension, new forms of co-operation need to be found. While the chances of Western Europe actually shaping a defence identity of its own are extremely slim – 'on the agenda but not on the cards' to cite one American academic commentator (McGeehan, 1985) – all the major states have found themselves caught up in the game. British leaders, while advocating the extension of the European Political Co-operation agenda to include security matters, have been more hesitant in the face of Franco-German enthusiasm for reviving Western European Union. As with so many aspects of European co-operation Britain's interest in a revived WEU appears to have been inspired primarily by a concern that France and West Germany might just get their collective act together and jointly ensure their own leadership of a new development. In addition, WEU has certain attractions to a British government anxious to manage a number of challenges to the European members of the alliance; its membership happens to exclude the three states whose idiosyncratic security concerns made EPC discussions on such matters difficult – namely Ireland, Denmark and Greece.

While British governments are not basically interested in leading the West Europeans out from under the American umbrella the need for collective European thinking on defence matters was reflected during the early 1980s in the British-inspired call for discussion of security matters within the framework of EPC. This call was picked up by the Italian and German foreign ministers, who tried to link an increased security role with proposals for a major reform of the European Community. What is absent from all these proposals (which concentrate essentially on procedures) is any notion of what a West European defence identity would look like. The developments that interest the British are fundamentally defensive ones. There is concern about the USA's apparent disregard for West European interests when it comes to negotiating with the Soviets on arms control. There are fears that as the USA becomes more Pacific- than Atlantic-orientated the American domestic consensus on the value of NATO may be breaking down, and that it can only be revived by the West Europeans demonstrating a greater collective ability to pull their weight on defence matters. There are also worries about the implications of SDI for European security, although when it comes to scrambling for contracts the Europeans have readily accommodated a US desire to deal with them bilaterally rather than collectively. Concern about the dynamic technological effects in the USA of the massive funding associated with SDI gave rise to the French-inspired Eureka programme designed to give European technology a similar boost, although this scheme has neither an EC nor an explicitly military dimension (Arnaud, 1986).

If agreement on a European defence identity seems unlikely then so does the collective use of force by West European states outside the NATO area. At a time when the West Europeans even have problems in conceiving of opening a joint embassy, the chances of them agreeing to fight together seem negligible. What they may be able to do is build on the experience of the Falklands conflict, where support for Britain's unilateral use of force came in the form of symbolic economic sanctions against Argentina (see Edwards, 1984). While some commentators have stressed the problems that the West Europeans had in carrying out this act of support, others (particularly in the USA) compare the speed of response over the Falklands with the slowness of the Europeans to support the USA over both Iran and Libya. Furthermore, not all collective military action can be ruled out. Troops from Britain and three other European countries took part in the supervision of the Israeli withdrawal from the Sinai as part of the Camp David agreements, and their participation was collectively 'blessed' by a supportive statement from all the member states of the European Community (see Allen and Pijpers, 1985, ch. 12). Finally, European forces have played their part with no less success than the USA in attempts to keep the feuding parties apart in the Lebanon.

The main problem that Britain faces in the security sphere relates to growing doubts about the long-term compatibility of European interests expressed collectively with those of the United States. For European co-operation in foreign or security policy to have any meaning, the Europeans will have to articulate interests and perceptions that are exclusively European and this will inevitably lead to differences with an increasingly prickly USA. While there has always been concern in Britain that too great a show of European security togetherness might lead either to American umbrage or to an American belief that the Europeans no longer need their support, there seems at the same time to be very little basis for anything other than consultation among the West Europeans on defence matters. The harsh fact is that no European state is prepared to pay, or participate in paying, the enormous costs of building a truly independent European defence capability, unless such an action is forced upon them by a unilateral US decision. Britain's objective, apart from a genuine desire to improve the consultation process between European states for 'practical' rather than integrative reasons, is to try to preserve the alliance as it is presently constituted. At the same time, British governments have sought to limit the damage that could arise from the expectations that are created by ever more ambitious discussions of the concept of a West European defence identity, and the frustrations arising from the failure to match posturing with substantive action.

Britain's total commitment to reliance on NATO for achieving its security objectives brings it into contact with a number of West European states, some of which are not members of the EC. NATO provides a forum both for identifying and discussing the possibilities for greater West European defence co-operation as well as for squaring that closer co-operation with the need to maintain a decent relationship with the United States – a task which would appear to be becoming harder in the 1980s. Working within NATO creates a number of constraints for British policy-makers, but it also presents a number of opportunities for Britain, as a nuclear state and as a major provider of conventional forces, to exert influence. The intergovernmental structures of NATO, the Eurogroup and WEU mean that co-operation can take place without raising any of the alarms about parliamentary sovereignty and an inequitable distribution of resources that beset Britain's relationships within the European Community.

Britain and the European Community

When Britain joined the European Community in 1973, it was at a time when the process of economic advance, which had initially made the Community attractive to Britain, was coming to a halt.

Since 1973, Britain has found itself playing a negative, defensive role in the process of economic integration. British diplomats, having laboured long and hard over the admission conditions, found themselves almost immediately charged by the Wilson government with a superficial renegotiation of those terms. Even after the 1975 referendum that was expected to put an end to all argument about British membership, British policy-makers were constrained to spend another ten years arguing, drawing heavily on their partners' remaining goodwill, about the nature of the British contribution to the Community budget. Along the way, successive British ministers in the Council of Ministers made it clear that Britain was totally opposed to any extensions of supranationality. Often other member states were relieved of the task of having to veto European Commission proposals designed to wrest authority from national governments by the over-eager British, ever anxious to confirm their objections not just to specific proposals but to the very principles behind them. In the European Parliament for a period, numbers were distorted by the refusal of Labour members to attend. When the Parliament was eventually directly elected in 1979, one year later than agreed because of British objections, its representative nature was again distorted – this time by the vagaries of the British electoral system. When Roy Jenkins was President of the European Commission, his own country sought to have him excluded from meetings of the newly instituted European Council. The catalogue of woes could go on and on, and it contributed to what Jenkins himself described as a 'semi-detached relationship' (1983). Only when the question of the British budget contribution had been apparently resolved at Fontainebleau in 1984 was the Foreign Office able to get a British prime minister to deliver a positive paper on the direction that the community might now take. Even then, at the end of the third British presidency of the council in December 1986, Britain was once again accused of using its powers to keep potentially troublesome items off the European Council agenda.

There is, then, a continued perception that, apart from those economic policies which might directly benefit Britain and certain aspects of foreign policy co-operation, Britain remains only a half-hearted participant in the European Community. The implication is that Dean Acheson's much-quoted 1962 remark still holds true: that Britain has lost an empire but has not yet found a

(European) role (see Northedge, 1974, p. 220). While there is no evidence of any serious consideration of alternatives to closer co-operation with the states of Western Europe, the problem arises from the domestic politics of Britain's policy towards the European Community.

Membership of the EC has always been treated as a traditional foreign policy issue in Britain, and the political and administrative elite has never really attempted to create a domestic consensus to underpin Britain's European commitment. To the extent that membership was 'sold' to the British public during the 1970s, the measurable costs of entry were underemphasized and set against the unexplained and immeasurable political benefits. As a consequence, British attitudes to involvement in Europe have been extremely fickle, with 1966 being the highpoint for pro-Europeanism; at that time Gallup found that 70 per cent of the public favoured entry and only 10 per cent were opposed (Butler, 1979). In 1970, just 22 per cent favoured entry and 64 per cent objected whilst in the 1975 referendum 67 per cent voted for Britain to remain in the Community with 33 per cent against. By 1978, however, 48 per cent of the public were telling MORI that they would vote against membership if there was another referendum. By the spring of 1985, only 34 per cent of the British population, against an average for the Community as a whole of 61 per cent, felt that their country had benefited from membership of the EC.

What is most striking about Britain's relationship with the European Community is the level of public ignorance about the reality of British governments' involvement in West European politics and the changes in both the procedures and substance of foreign policy that this involvement has brought about since 1973. When Britain joined the Community, it committed itself to participate in two distinct processes of intergovernmental collaboration: first, the EC itself, and second, European Political Co-operation.

The EC itself generates a semi-supranational decision-making process centred upon the relationship between the European Commission and the Council of Ministers. The work of the council has expanded both procedurally and substantively over the years. Although the work of the Community is dominated by the Common Agricultural Policy and the existence of a (yet to be perfected) internal common market and common external tariff, there are also numerous other areas, ranging from regional policy to development aid to the Third World, where the member states seek to manage their mutual interdependence; in some cases this is achieved by the use of common policies at the European level, in others by concerting national policies. There are therefore few areas of national governmental activity which do not have a Community dimension of some sort or another. This means that the British state is in direct contact both with Community institutions and with other member states on a wide variety of issues, previously regarded as purely domestic in content but now with an international dimension. One consequence of all this has been a proliferation of international sections of domestic departments in Whitehall, and a parallel growth of functional departments in the Foreign and Commonwealth Office.

It is useful at this point to make a distinction between the notion of external relations and that of foreign policy. The many points of contact on the various issues referred to above have all contributed to a blurring of the boundaries of the British state and of the distinction between foreign policy and domestic policy. As such, they represent an expansion of Britain's external relations. Foreign policy in this context has to be understood as an attempt to bring some order to this expanded set of foreign contacts – an attempt in other words to design, manage and control Britain's external relations in order to try to achieve the objectives of foreign policy. It has already been argued that Britain's objectives *vis-à-vis* Western Europe in the medium- to long-term still do not seem to be clearly formulated; as a result, an essentially short-term notion of Britain's broad security and welfare interests has predominated and led successive British governments to impose negative restraints on the development of Britain's EC relations. The wide range of policy issues which is now dealt with in the Community framework has thus posed a considerable management and co-ordination problem for Britain's policy-makers, and it is one that they have primarily solved by compromise. The Foreign Office's natural desire to see all points of contact with foreigners, however mundane, as having political implications and therefore as part of its responsibility has been reconciled with the substantive European interests of most domestic departments by the creation of a European Unit in the Cabinet Office. This body is responsible for overall co-ordination of Britain's policy towards the EC, with both 'home' civil servants and Foreign Office officials jointly responsible for implementation under Foreign Office leadership. At the ministerial level, most members of any government will have had some experience of EC negotiations; while the Prime Minister and the Foreign Secretary play the leading roles, agriculture and finance ministers spend the most time in actual negotiation.

One major result of all this intergovernmental and transgovernmental activity – intensified rather than created by membership of the EC – has been a persistent questioning of the traditional role of the diplomat and the Foreign Office. The concentration on Western Europe and the expansion of the scope of foreign policy to include virtually all aspects of the British government's activities was the concern of both the 1968 Duncan Report and the Central Policy Review Staff's *Review of Overseas Representation* in 1977, both of which questioned the need for a separately organized, worldwide diplomatic service in the light of diplomatic trends in the West European area (see Shonfield, 1970; Wallace, 1978b; Hill and Wallace, 1979). One possible result of these developments might be the creation of a new European ministry charged with drawing together the threads of Britain's policy towards Western Europe in general and the EC in particular, under the responsibility of a European minister. The possible development of a European foreign policy and a European diplomatic service, or the more limited pooling of diplomatic resources, is more uncertain. What is clear is that the emergence of Western Europe as a significant 'area of concentration' in British foreign policy has put these questions on the agenda.

Regardless of future developments, the expansion of the Council of Ministers' role in the EC process has led to its vertical as well as horizontal growth. Thus at ministerial level, the foreign ministers remain in overall control of co-ordinating negotiations across all the various issue areas as well as being responsible for their own specialist area of external relations (which involves both the external policies of the EC itself and political co-operation), and finally for all institutional matters. Since the formalization of summit meetings in the form of the European Council, heads of government have also come to play a major role in the Community. One impact of this proliferation of senior ministerial meetings has been to undermine the coherence of national policies towards the Community as transgovernmental politics begin to exert their influence. For a number of years now, heads of government and their finance ministers have been calling for a reduction of agricultural spending, only to find that their own agriculture ministers have agreed to increase expenditure. Similarly, heads of government as statesmen (or women) at summit meetings often view European affairs differently when they return to their own countries and resume the role of partisan politician. The blurring of boundaries along with the growth of international communications and media activity can create problems for British politicians who can no longer rely on the mutual isolation of domestic and international audiences. This is a feature of international politics in general, but it is one that is felt most intensely in Western Europe.

The Council of Ministers has also expanded below the ministerial level, to produce a host of intergovernmental committees. Britain has a large permanent representation to the EC in Brussels and the ambassador, who to date has always come from the Foreign Office, and his deputy, who has always come from a 'home' ministry, head up Britain's team in the all-important Committee of Permanent Representatives (COREPER). Beneath them hundreds of officials, based both in Brussels and in London, meet more and more regularly whilst others talk daily on the telephone to one another in a growing network of European activity. This does not add up to integration as the 'Founding Fathers' thought of it, but it is a transformation of the way that West European states used to relate to one another. All this activity is managed through the rotating presidency of the Council. Britain held that presidency three times during the period 1973–87 (1977, 1981 and 1986) and each time the opportunity to take the initiative was effectively rejected in favour of 'competent' management of the business in hand (Wallace, 1986).

Substantially all this activity is directed both towards the management of Britain's interdependence with other West European countries and towards an attempted co-ordination of their joint approach to the outside world, in the hope that Britain's interests can be furthered through the collective bargaining power of what now constitutes the world's largest trading bloc. Britain's integration into that trading bloc has undoubtedly been enhanced by membership of the EC: by 1983 some 43 per cent of Britain's total trade was with its Community partners compared with just 30 per cent in 1973. Furthermore the European Free Trade Association

(EFTA), which is itself linked by a free trade agreement with the EC, accounted for a further 15 per cent. West Germany rivalled the USA as Britain's largest export market, and all the other EC partners with the exception of Greece and Portugal were among the top fifteen British export markets. Between 1972 and 1980, British exports to the EC increased by 480 per cent, while those to the USA grew by only 234 per cent, those to Japan by 237 per cent and those to the rest of the world by 295 per cent.

Just as the internal development of the European Community has become central to the achievement of Britain's major foreign policy objectives of economic welfare and security, so has the relationship between the EC and the rest of the world. In the disorder that spread through the international economic system during the 1970s and early 1980s, Britain sought to protect its own interests through collective defensive European action directed towards trading partners in both the developed and under-developed worlds. If such a system continues, then Western Europe will become more rather than less important to the protection of British interests, and if any progress is made towards re-establishing order in the international trade, monetary and financial systems, this will only come about through tripartite agreements between Japan, the USA and Western Europe. In broad economic terms, then, it would appear that co-operation with the other states of Western Europe has become essential to the achievement not just of Britain's 'possession' goals but also to its goals of 'self-extension' (see Wolfers, 1962).

Britain and European Political Co-operation: towards a European Foreign Policy?

The second West European policy framework of which Britain became part in 1973 was European Political Co-operation. EPC is an intergovernmental arrangement between the foreign offices of the EC member states, designed since its inception in 1970 to move through consultation, co-operation and where possible joint action towards the often stated (but rarely defined or clarified) goal of a common European foreign policy. In Britain, both officials and politicians have always been enthusiastic about political co-operation, although they have been inclined neither to explain this enthusiasm nor to share it with the wider British public. This reticence is surprising, since in the Single European Act of 1986 Britain participated in, indeed advocated, the legal formalization of the EPC mechanism. Britain is now committed not only to 'endeavour jointly to formulate and implement a European foreign policy' but also to 'take full account of the positions of the other partners' in 'adopting its positions and in its national measures'. Furthermore, Britain has agreed that 'the determination of common (European) positions shall constitute a point of reference' for its national policy and that it will 'endeavour to avoid any action or position which impairs the effectiveness' of the EC member states acting as a 'cohesive force in international relations or within international organizations'. This degree of commitment to foreign policy co-operation is in marked contrast to Britain's reputation for European 'foot-dragging'.

The Treaty on European Co-operation does not represent an ambitious but unlikely European blueprint for the future, but rather a codification of what already exists. While public and media attention in the early 1980s was focused on Mrs Thatcher's campaign to get 'her money' back from the EC, on growing agricultural surpluses and on interminable meetings in Brussels that failed to resolve the member states' many economic differences, Lord Carrington, the then Foreign Secretary, was stating that 'British foreign policy must now be conducted essentially in a European framework'. At the same time his deputy Douglas Hurd was stating that since he joined the Foreign Office in 1952 'the biggest change of diplomatic method stems from European Political Co-operation. In 1952 it was broadly speaking with the Americans only that we shared information and assessments: policy-making was a national preserve. Now in some areas of diplomacy our policy is formed wholly within a European context; and in no area is the European influence completely absent' (1981). Academic studies of political co-operation reveal the rapid growth of a complex diplomatic network of direct contacts between the foreign offices of the EC member states, extending to co-operation between the embassies of member states in third countries (see Allen, 1978; Allen, Rummel and Wessels, 1982; Wallace, 1983).

Although not all aspects of foreign policy are covered by EPC (there remain a number of taboo subjects, including the situation in Northern Ireland), and although the Twelve still find it hard to move beyond consultations and common declarations to common action, political co-operation has chalked up a number of substantive as opposed to procedural successes. In particular as states like Britain and France have dropped their insistence on enforcing a rigid separation between EC and EPC business, the basis for the development of a European foreign policy is beginning to emerge. Yet it would be a mistake to view diplomatic developments at the European level as representing a major shift of authority from the national to the European level. As Hill has shown, while most member states show a degree of enthusiasm for political co-operation that contrasts significantly with their collective reluctance to enthuse about the EC itself, this is mainly because the process can be shown to be serving the purposes of, rather than challenging, national foreign policy-makers (1983b).

It is certainly the case that British foreign policy-makers now work extremely closely with their opposite numbers in Community countries. The network of consultations, backed up by a direct telex network known as COREUR, is extensive both inside the Community, in third countries and at international organizations like the United Nations. Britain has been in the forefront of those states who have sought to improve the political co-operation mechanism. In the London Report of 1981, one of the rare positive achievements of a British presidency, a crisis mechanism was established. The idea of discussing security in its broadest aspects was mooted and the 'troika' system of interlocking presidencies (which developed in the Single European Act into a formal secretariat) was established. Within political co-operation, Britain is quite clearly in a leadership role along with France, West Germany and occasionally Italy. Although it is hard to find any common positions adopted in political co-operation that do not accord broadly with British thinking, it has to be said that over issues such as relations with the USSR in the wake of Afghanistan and over the Middle East a shift in British thinking away from US positions can be detected.

The more that EPC develops, the more likely it is that an adversary relationship with the USA will accompany it, raising again for the British the problem of reconciling Atlantic and European interests. If this is a potential cost there also seem to be many benefits for Britain in the development of this form of co-operation. The most obvious is the fact that it presents a vehicle within which Britain can continue to participate in global rather than just European international affairs. The combined economic power of the European Communities represents a resource base for the exertion of political influence that is by definition greater than anything Britain might muster alone. But while Britain has always supported political co-operation, it has not always demonstrated an understanding of the nature of its power potential. The Callaghan notion (propounded in the late 1970s) that it might be possible to carry on with foreign policy co-operation even if Britain were to leave the EC, and by doing so almost certainly destroy it, demonstrates a failure to appreciate the fact that it is the existence of the EC as a cohesive bloc with the potential for maintaining and expanding common economic, financial and industrial policies that makes its member states collectively politically interesting to the outside world. To the extent that Britain is unwilling to participate in the consolidation of economic integration under the Treaty of Rome, it undermines its own clearly stated interest in benefiting from political co-operation; the two things are, in the long term, inseparable.

European Political Co-operation has undoubtedly revived and enhanced the morale and reputation of the British Diplomatic Service. As far as British interests are concerned, it represents an additional rather than an alternative framework both for their definition and for their advancement. On a number of occasions, political co-operation has served a useful 'cover' function for disguising shifts of policy that would have been difficult to make unilaterally, for explaining failures to respond to external demands in terms of the problems of carrying Britain's partners and for providing European support for essentially British positions. Furthermore, as West European co-operation has matured, the previously rigid insistence on trying to do everything within the Community framework has been relaxed. Thus, while Britain does discuss most aspects of its foreign policy within the political co-operation framework, this has not prevented the development of an extensive network of bilateral relations with West European countries of which the ongoing dialogues with France and West Germany are the most important (see Wallace, 1984).

Conclusion

Membership of the EC and participation in political co-operation have therefore brought about a clear 'Europeanization' of both the procedures and the substance of British foreign policy, but this is reflected less in the transfer of authority from the British to the European level than in changes at the national level. These changes are considerable and almost certainly irreversible, representing adjustments to the realities of interdependence, which in Western Europe is more advanced than anywhere else in the international system. However, the striking thing is that the adjustments have been almost exclusively at the governmental level and have been directed outwards. As noted earlier, there has been no parallel shift in the habits and procedures of domestic politics or in domestic perceptions of Western Europe. This failure to adjust politically or even to recognize publicly that such changes in the nature of British foreign policy have taken place means that there is no effective domestic base or consensus in Britain to underpin the new West European-orientated and based diplomacy.

This reluctance on the part of government to come clean about the realities and imperatives of interdependence is not an exclusively British problem, and is not explained simply by a fundamental British resistance to the notion of sharing common aspirations based on common values with the inhabitants of the European mainland. It is perhaps not surprising that successive British governments have shown little interest in rectifying the problems experienced by Parliament in exercising democratic control over all this new European activity. From summit meetings down to the deliberations of the most lowly officials, the 'Europeanization' process is not susceptible to effective national parliamentary scrutiny, nor is the British government interested in enhancing the powers of the European Parliament. The British executive thus has an interest in disguising the full extent of its complex intermeshing with other West European executives. Just as the territorial boundaries of the state may be undermined by the activities of multinational companies, so the possibility of national governments jointly conspiring in the mutual deception, or at least persuasion, of their electorates arises. It is possible to see this in relation to issues such as the deployment in 1982–3 of US medium-range missiles in Western Europe; here, a number of West European governments effectively stood together in the face of domestic opposition to their collective decision.

The situation, particularly pronounced in Britain, whereby the myth of national autonomy is perpetuated for domestic political consumption, merely postpones the day when the electorate will have to be acquainted with the realities of contemporary political life in Western Europe. Until the British public is properly informed about the way that interdependence has altered the objectives and procedures of British foreign policy, British political leaders will be inhibited about publicly expressing views on the directions that West European co-operation, of both a formal and an informal kind, should take. To date, those responsible for British foreign policy have relied on a policy of pragmatic and low key adjustment to the imposed requirements of a West European orientation. The danger is that by adopting this stance, Britain is unable to seize the 'European initiative', and British policy thus becomes condemned to perpetual adjustment to a West European system of managed interdependence. The shape of this system is being determined by those states who are not prevented by domestic inhibitions from thinking strategically rather than tactically and, on occasions, idealistically rather than practically.

9 Britain and North–South Relations

JOHN VOGLER

To undertake a comprehensive review of Britain's relations with the South or the Third World would be a daunting if not impossible task. Because of the sheer number of states that would fall within this category one would have to encompass the greater part of the United Kingdom's bilateral relations. Instead, 'North–South relations' are taken here to have a more specific meaning. They denote a complex of negotiations, conflicts and diplomatic activity conducted between the developed industrial northern states and the economically disadvantaged and often newly independent states of the southern hemisphere organized in the Group of 77. For a number of reasons, which will emerge in the subsequent discussion, this axis of global political activity achieved prominence during the 1970s – most notably with the adoption by the UN General Assembly in 1974 of a programme for a New International Economic Order (NIEO).

These proposals, sponsored by the Group of 77, outlined the principles of a new order designed to achieve equity in the global economy. They included an assertion of national economic sovereignty in terms of resources and economic activity, together with a right to nationalization allied to the regulation of transnational corporations. Most significantly, the resolution called for a new approach to the problem of the terms of trade between North and South with positive action to establish a more equitable relationship between Third World imports and exports. Finally world monetary reform was envisaged to relieve indebtedness and enhance the flow of resources to the South. Thus, the NIEO constituted an attempt at structural and managed solutions which appeared to be in direct confrontation with northern economic interests and the accepted nostrums of liberal economics.

The most important immediate response to this demand for a new economic order was an attempt to restructure world commodity trades through the creation of a Common Fund, an Integrated Programme for Commodities (IPC). This became the main agenda item at a special North–South conference, the Conference on International Economic Co-operation, held in Paris during 1975–6. Elsewhere the NIEO theme was played out in a bewildering variety of contexts and institutions as the Group of 77 flexed its organizational muscle. By the beginning of the 1980s, however, East–West conflict had returned to something approaching its old vigour and the North–South dialogue had, in circumstances of global recession and northern parsimony, become frozen into a routine deadlock. None the less, efforts were made to initiate a new global negotiation in New York and, under the stimulus of the Brandt Report, to reinvigorate the dialogue through the special Cancun summit held in 1981.[1]

While the focus here is on Britain's role in the dialogue as a developed state with a very substantial national interest in trade with Less Developed Countries (LDCs) and the evolution of the world trading and financial system, other aspects of Britain's relationship to the South cannot be ignored. These have a significant and, on occasion, dominant influence on southern attitudes towards the UK. The most critical of these other aspects relate to the legacy of empire. Britain still superintends some thirteen dependent overseas territories with a combined population of 5.2 million people (5 million of whom reside in Hong Kong) (Central Office of Information, 1983, p. 14). As was most graphically illustrated by the Falklands War of 1982, these remnants of empire still have the potential to cause problems and to stimulate accusations of colonialism. The large ethnic groups from the New Commonwealth living in Britain itself constitute a living link with a number of important Third World countries and a possible source of friction. This may come about over immigration policy or as in 1984–5 over the activities of particular communities, in this instance the Sikhs, in conflict with a foreign government. Without doubt the largest millstone around the neck of British policy has been Southern Africa. This is no place to enter into the long and difficult history of Britain's responsibilities and actions towards

Rhodesia/Zimbabwe, Namibia and sanctions against South Africa, except to say that the UK remains peculiarly vulnerable on issues that have the capacity to unite the whole of the Third World movement against it.

The question at the heart of this chapter concerns Britain's independent ability to exert influence in the North–South arena. In the rhetoric of British political debate there is to be found a persistent assumption particularly amongst those sympathetic to Third World aspirations that the UK, despite loss of empire and its evidently diminished world role, somehow retains a special and influential position as regards North–South relations. This is usually associated with the Commonwealth and expressed in terms of 'Britain's unique role as a bridge between these hemispheres' (Burton *et al.*, 1984). Has this view any substance? Is it little more than well-intentioned but essentially post-imperial nostalgia? Are not the constraints upon British action such as to prevent this? At a more fundamental level and in the light of widespread scepticism it is also worth considering the extent to which the North–South dialogue continues to matter in terms of UK interests and policy.

This chapter seeks to tackle these questions. It begins with a review of British policy as it has emerged since the early 1970s, paying particular attention to the idea that changes in government can make a difference (in this case through the transition from the more consensus-oriented governments of the 1970s to the Thatcher government of the 1980s). The subsequent part of the chapter concentrates on the question of the independence of Britain's role. This is discussed under two headings. The first covers Britain's place amongst the players and coalitions in the arena. The second and related heading concerns the determinants of power and influence in North–South negotiations, leading to an assessment of Britain's political and economic capabilities and the significance of the arena for British interests.

British Policy

The British commitment to an open world trading system dates back to the 1940s and helped to underpin the construction of the Bretton Woods institutions. 'Economic liberalism was the key to future prosperity, and prosperity the means to civil order and good international relations' (Jones, 1983, p. 6). In this the British, despite their tradition of imperial preference, followed or perhaps acquiesced in the then current American doctrine. The remarkable success of the postwar economic order in the two decades following Bretton Woods and the perhaps disproportionate British representation in its institutions gave British policy-makers a strong incentive to preserve the status quo. In the words of a government memorandum of 1980:

> The Government believes very strongly in the merits of the present world economic system with its wide reliance on open markets for trade and financial flows. The system has regularly and flexibly adapted to changing conditions and can be adapted further. This gives the best hope of overcoming present difficulties and providing a firm basis for future growth.
>
> (House of Commons, 1981, vol. II, p. 7).

This statement would not misrepresent the view of any postwar British government although the point might not always have been made in such robust terms. As the Foreign Affairs Committee noted in 1981, 'the UK economy is more dependent than that of any other industrialised country on the level of world trade because we export a higher proportion of our GNP (29 per cent)' (House of Commons, 1981, vol. I, p. viii). British policy must also be highly sensitive to any change in world financial and commodity trading structures given the historic and continuing role of the City of London.

The NIEO proposals represented a radical attack on the shortcomings of the existing economic regime and thus contained an explicit threat to well-established British conceptions of economic self-interest. Throughout the 1970s the British stance in North–South negotiations tended to reflect this. In 1974 at the UN General Assembly, Britain was one of six states voting against the Charter of Economic Rights and Duties of States. At the Sixth Special Session where the NIEO principles were adopted without a vote, the British representative did not join his American colleague in ignoring the proceedings. Instead he entered the reservation that:

> We have seen resolutions in which the interests of a minority whose cooperation may be essential for their implementation

have been brushed aside . . . we are deeply concerned at these
attempts to create an impression of unanimity where it does not
exist.

(Weintraub, 1977, p. 196)

The British position was not always one of hard–line rejection.
More typically, there was a pragmatic desire not to indulge in root
and branch opposition to structural change but to seek areas of
constructive compromise; 'to find the common interest and act on
it to a point where all can see that they gain as well as give'
(Richard, 1975, p. 71).

In the latter part of the 1970s the North–South dialogue focused
upon the Commodity Fund and IPC proposals and the Conference
on International Economic Co-operation (CIEC) negotiations in
Paris. Heavy British involvement in commodity markets as a
source not only of raw materials but also of very significant
invisible earnings gave these negotiations particular point. British
officials became convinced that the political pressures for such a
fund were probably irresistible, but were concerned to minimize
the damage to existing markets. Thus indexation was opposed,
along with the idea that commodity agreements should provide a
mechanism for resource transfers from rich to poor. The preferred
approach was, as elsewhere, to 'negotiate on a case by case basis on
any commodity where consumer-producer cooperation appeared
possible' (Goodwin and Mayall, 1977, p. 154).

As in so many other areas, the years 1979–80 may be regarded
as a watershed. The election of the first Thatcher government,
sharing a philosophy of radical economic liberalism with the new
Reagan administration, appeared to bring about a sharp change of
course and a significant break with a previous policy. This was
highlighted by the publication of the Brandt Commission Report
(1980) which, with its emphasis on North–South interdependence
as the basis for co-operation, seemed to espouse at least some of the
objectives towards which previous British governments had been
groping (Mr Heath was in fact a prominent member of the
commission). Brandt stimulated a level of domestic political debate
in Britain on North–South issues that was unprecedented. In one
year, the report sold 126,000 copies in Britain, more than in any
other country, stimulated a 10,000-strong lobby of Parliament and
evoked a critical review of British policy by the Foreign Affairs

Committee (House of Commons, 1981, vol. I, p. vii). The debate on Brandt and the apparent antipathy to it of the Thatcher government raises a particular instance of a perennial question in the study of foreign policy which is worth some examination. Does a change in governing party make any essential difference to policies which are often seen to exhibit a continuity based on relatively fixed national interests, impervious to alteration by moral or ideological concerns?

The Thatcher government's approach to North–South issues may justly be regarded as an extension of its domestic economic philosophy: monetarism, a distaste for public spending and economic management, allied to a belief in the efficacy of market forces. Thus, the debate in the early 1980s over the Brandt Commission's proposals ran parallel to domestic controversy over the appropriate economic policy to tackle recession, inflation and rising unemployment. The two were linked in a concrete way in so far as domestic austerity impacted on the government's aid and development programmes. The official response to Brandt in the form of a 25-page Foreign Office memorandum put the matter bluntly in terms of analysis and solutions. It was asserted that the 'record of the 1970s shows that durable growth can only be achieved if these countries [the developed states] adjust to the higher cost of oil and bring inflation under control. This must be the first priority.' Just as governmental stimulation of the domestic economy was rejected, the administration was 'convinced that massive extra injections of spending' in the North–South context 'would not work' (House of Commons, 1981, vol. II, p. 153). The British contribution must therefore be the essentially insular one of 'putting its own house in order'.

In policy terms, this entailed an initial rejection of the proposals for global negotiations, manifested in joint action with the United States and West Germany to block such proposals at the UN. Resistance to any attempt to tamper with the autonomy and terms of reference of the IMF and the World Bank was particularly strong. These actions, coupled with the brutal tenor of government statements on North–South issues, led to the very widespread impression that Britain, with the United States, had become the most unyielding and uncaring defender of the economic status quo. A group of ten countries moved during 1980 to circumvent the impasse on global negotiations, through the mechanism of a more select summit meeting based upon Brandt's proposals (which was to result in the 1981 Cancun meeting), but the UK was conspicuous by its absence. There was even a 'widely held suspicion that Britain was trying to sabotage the so called Brandt summit' (*The Times*, 27 October 1980).

However, in reaction to domestic criticism and the exigencies of keeping in step with Commonwealth and EC partners, the government's line softened noticeably during 1981. It signified its willingness to participate in the Cancun summit, although as Mervyn Westlake put it this may have meant little more than the recognition that 'there was only one thing worse for the British government than the proposed summit and that was that it should be held without them' (*The Times*, 2 October 1981). The October 1981 Cancun summit produced nothing of substance save an agreement to pursue talks at the UN about preparations for the long-awaited global negotiations, but this in itself represented some change of attitude by both the Reagan and Thatcher governments. There was also some change on specifics: for example, Britain announced itself a belated convert to the idea of a special energy affiliate to the World Bank (*The Times*, 23 October 1981). Such changes in official attitude as did occur were probably indicative of alterations in tone, tactics and detail rather than substance. At the 1983 Commonwealth Conference in Delhi, Mrs Thatcher was to be found in a minority of one opposing the document *Towards a New Bretton Woods*. She would have no truck with new economic institutions or fixed exchange rates; the real solutions, in her view, were to be found in domestic good housekeeping and the free flow of world trade and investment. Although it might be tempting to think that there ought to be 'some grand design, some magic formula which would transform world trade and satisfy the aspirations of those we represent . . . no such tidy solution exists either internationally or at home' (*The Times*, 24 November 1983).

Aid has always been the touchstone of domestic political debate on Third World issues, and inter-party arguments about aid totals reflect the way in which they are used as indicators of levels of concern and even moral rectitude. Although accepting in principle the UN target figure of 0.7 per cent of GNP for official development aid, British governments have never achieved it in practice. Under the Wilson and Callaghan governments, official aid expenditure rose from 0.37 to 0.43 per cent of GNP between 1974 and

1979 and was claimed to be the fastest-growing part of the government's spending programme (Labour Party, 1981, p. 70). The succeeding Conservative government was heavily criticized domestically and by OECD for cuts that appeared disproportionate relative to overall public expenditure reductions. At the same time Mrs Thatcher was indelicate enough to refer to aid expenditure as 'hand-outs' (*The Times*, 25 January 1981). Yet by 1982–3, the aid-to-GNP ratio was of the order of 0.4 per cent.[2]

More significant than arguments about the volume of official aid and its relationship to GNP were qualitative concerns about the direction of assistance and the fate of particular programmes – for example, the raising of overseas student fees and the ending of Labour's Development Education Project. The announced aim of the Thatcher government's aid policy did represent a change in that it was 'to give more weight to political, industrial and commercial considerations' (*The Times*, 6 February 1981). In organizational terms, this was reflected in the much-criticized decision of October 1979 to transform Labour's independent Ministry of Overseas Development into an Overseas Development Administration within the Foreign Office. However, the Government did not formally dissociate itself from the 'aid to the poorest' strategy and was able to claim in 1983 that 58 per cent of bilateral aid went to countries with a per capita income of less than $370 p.a. (Central Office of Information, 1983, p. 24). Spokesmen could also claim with some justice that the British aid performance, although somewhat diminished, still compared very well with that of other industrialized countries; the OECD average being 0.35 per cent of GNP in 1981. US performance was consistently under 0.3 per cent, and as the Foreign Secretary was not slow to point out in an aid debate in 1983, Soviet aid was at a 'miserly' level of 0.15 per cent (*The Times*, 19 April 1983). In common with a number of other areas, it is perhaps the psychological and symbolic effect of government pronouncements rather than the magnitude of concrete effects that have been most damaging to Britain's standing in the North–South arena.

It is understandable that critics of the government including Mr Heath, the opposition parties and members of the Foreign Affairs Committee, should wish to maximize the extent to which the Thatcher government represented a radical shift of UK policy on North–South issues. All were broadly in favour of Brandt, despite extensive academic criticism of the validity of the report's economic analysis (Strange, 1981). Yet the extent to which any future government would be in a position to implement a real and effective change of direction, except perhaps in the area of the aid programme, must remain in doubt. This is especially so when Conservative policy is examined in terms of the elements of continuity that existed with the policy and behaviour of previous governments. The rhetoric of both government and opposition often tended to obscure the extent of such continuity, but it was real enough. The Thatcher government was prepared to endorse the Common Fund for Commodities and a doubling of funds available to the World Bank. Equally, the alterations of course prior to the Cancun summit have already been charted. In an otherwise critical review, the Society for International Development conceded that 'despite the conflict of philosophies with Brandt HMG has surpassed several of its contemporaries in support for several of Brandt's propositions' (House of Commons, 1981, vol. II, p. 152). Support for an open world trading system and a concern to maintain the autonomy of world financial institutions are hardly the exclusive preserve of a right-wing Conservative government but are closely associated with what have long been regarded as central British economic interests.

A constant in the British approach has also been a distrust of general schemes and a preference for the case by case approach. In the Foreign Office view, individual countries 'are more interested in their individual problems than they are in this whole set of subjects [NIEO]' (House of Commons, 1981, vol. II, p. 9). Perhaps it was asking too much to expect that the government embrace the benefits of 'managed interdependence' as outlined by Brandt. Amongst the OECD countries, with the significant exception of France under its Socialist government, Britain's was hardly a lone sceptical and negative voice in preparations for Cancun, although there were 'nuances of difference' (House of Commons, 1981, vol. II, p. 5). However true this might have been, and successive OECD summits do indicate a consensus of view, it was probably the 'nuances' that were politically significant. The acerbic tone of the British government's comments on North–South issues coupled with the identification of the UK as the major stumbling block to the imposition of effective sanctions against the apartheid regime in South Africa and particular actions such as its exit from

UNESCO in 1985, clearly cast the United Kingdom in the role of a principal opponent of Third World causes. It is perhaps here that the most significant change has been evident.

Players and Coalitions

In very broad terms and in line with the group structure at the United Nations Conference on Trade and Development (UNCTAD), the main axis of confrontation in North–South negotiations is between the developed countries of OECD and the Third World coalition organized in the Group of 77. Britain may thus be identified as a prominent member of the northern developed camp. However, the reality is much more complex than this, with important sub-divisions on each side. Amongst the OECD grouping, specific alignments and divergent interests contribute to a pattern which is almost as complex as that within the Group of 77. Essentially, the UK must operate in the context of three important alignments: the European Community, the bilateral relationship with the United States and the Commonwealth. For the purposes of this chapter, the latter is of particular significance because its membership spans the North–South divide. All three might be regarded not only as relationships within which it may be possible to advance British interests but as rival poles of attraction that may also serve to constrain independent action.

The southern coalition is of great diversity and it is probable that only a stress on the broad principles of NIEO allied to issues such as opposition to the apartheid regime in South Africa allows it to hold together. The evolution of the coalition may be traced in terms of a dialogue between the radical Non-Aligned Movement which has its origins in the Bandung meeting of 1955 and the much broader and all-inclusive Group of 77, now numbering over 120 members, that was created to handle the specific tasks of negotiation at the first UNCTAD conference of 1964. According to Mortimer (1984), the general pattern has been for the Non-Aligned Movement to provide stimulus and initiatives and for the Group of 77, in a close – almost symbiotic – relationship with the UNCTAD secretariat, to develop detailed negotiating positions. The Group of 77 does not really constitute a coherent caucus except at the highest level of generality. It includes newly industrialized states and conservative oil sheikdoms alongside the poorest of the Fourth World. Political alignments range across the board from Moscow to Washington and regional conflicts are highly intrusive. Neither is the coalition underpinned by the kind of South–South economic ties that many would like to develop. The watchword for the leaders of the coalition has therefore been to champion issues where a common denominator of agreement may be found. In the heady days of the mid-1970s, led by states such as Algeria, the coalition managed to adopt a radical stance. Since then observers have discerned a new mood of realism and a willingness to negotiate partial solutions in the context of global recession, Third World debt and a revival of East–West antagonism.

Within the northern bloc the major economic and political entities of concern to Britain are the European Community and the United States. British membership of the Community entails a commitment to collective action in international economic negotiations. This is most evident when matters of commercial policy under the treaties are concerned or where special arrangements involving common representation have been devised as for the CIEC or Lomé.[3] The procedure with the widest relevance is also the weakest in terms of enforcing community solidarity. Political Co-operation on general foreign policy matters developed during the 1970s and emphasizes the achievement of a common position through intergovernmental co-operation; much North–South business comes under this heading and the Community has attempted to act as a caucus in its approach to issues at the UN General Assembly (although not within the Security Council where France and Britain guard their special status). In the mid-1970s, the hostile attitude of the United States towards NIEO gave the Community an opportunity to act in concert as the voice of northern moderation. Major efforts appear to have been made, with no less than 170 meetings in New York under the Political Co-operation procedures between September and December 1975 (Lindemann, 1976, p. 264). Yet the record of voting solidarity was patchy, leading one Third World delegate to exclaim that 'the EEC states vote together on unimportant questions and apart on important ones in contrast to the Third World's voting where the reverse is true' (Lindemann, 1976, p. 264).

Of course, the fundamental problem is that there is rarely anything resembling a common European foreign policy. Except

in special circumstances where the treaties compel a unified
approach or where European solidarity can be obtained at mini-
mum cost, varying national interests and philosophies tend to come
to the fore. Alliances with states external to the Community appear
to have been as important as, and perhaps more important than, its
internal ties. West Germany was consistently to be found voting
with the United States and Japan and taking a 'hard-nosed' liberal
stance. By contrast, France adopted a high profile in terms of
support and sponsorship of North–South negotiations and was the
developed state most likely to be found voting with the LDC
majority at the General Assembly and UNCTAD (Weintraub,
1977, p. 191). The Dutch also adopted a more positive stance
towards NIEO than many of their EC colleagues, as did the Danish
government which tended to align itself with its Nordic partners,
Norway and Sweden. During the 1970s British policy was neither
'hard-line' nor 'progressive', but is best expressed in terms of
ambivalent pragmatism. The advent of the Thatcher government
appeared to introduce a realignment towards the United States, in a
much more forthright anti-NIEO stance.

There is still evidence that Community membership does, on
occasion, exert considerable influence. It is significant that the
changes of course that occurred prior to Cancun took place at a
time when Britain held the responsibility of the presidency of the
council and thus of concerting a joint approach to the summit.
Policy changes on the global negotiations and on an energy affiliate
to the World Bank were in fact shifts towards a common EC
position. Community policy was prefaced by the view that, in
comparison to the United States, the EC was peculiarly vulnerable
to economic instability in the South and that it followed that the
'myopic' preoccupation of the US administration with East–West
issues had to be challenged. Britain was described as a reluctant
supporter of the EC position, but a supporter none the less (*The
Times*, 2 October 1981). According to Weiss, something rather
similar appears to have occurred during the 1981 UN Conference
on Least Developed Countries in Paris (1983, p. 662).

The historical relationship with the United States is one of close
co-operation on many dimensions. In the late 1970s, a very close
similarity of view developed between the Carter and Callaghan
administrations, while under Reagan and Thatcher the approach
and indeed the rhetoric – the 'magic of markets' and the primacy

of self-help – appeared at times to be virtually indistinguishable. British closeness to the United States was most graphically illustrated by their mutual exit from UNESCO. This incident also illustrates the tripolar forces at work on British policy, although in this case US influence predominated. Sharing American distaste for amongst other things the North–South tenor of UNESCO debates, Britain followed the USA in withdrawing from the organization at the end of 1985. This was in the face of extensive lobbying in favour of continued membership from EC partners and Commonwealth members (Hindell, 1986, p. 21).

As must be evident from discussion of the British position within the EC grouping, the UNESCO decision did not represent a completely uniform trend in British policy. In 1984 the USA made explicitly similar charges against UNCTAD and, while sharing some of the criticism, other Western countries including the UK refused to agree to US proposals for a restriction of the organization's mandate (*Keesing's*, 1984, p. 33068). Similarly, Commonwealth Secretary-General Shridath Ramphal referred approvingly to the 'positive role of Britain in seeking to minimise the damage done by the United States' to the seventh replenishment of International Development Association (IDA) funds, 'in accordance with its Commonwealth role and with its highest traditions of support for multilateralism' (1984, p. 385).

Nowhere is the contention that the UK has a special role to play more in evidence than in discussions of the Commonwealth connection. Yet the evidence is of a decline in British interest which has on occasion in recent years amounted to an almost gratuitous insensitivity. None the less the Commonwealth remains rooted in British political consciousness. A sceptical observer might compare the function of the organization to that of methadone for the drug addict; necessary to wean the British from a psychological dependence upon empire, but creating its own insidious problem of addiction.[4]

The period under consideration marks the transition of the Commonwealth to its modern form. As an international organization it is probably unique in the informality of its procedures and its capacity to survive the conflicts of race, ideology and economic inequality that divide its forty-nine members. At its apex, biennial heads of government meetings (CHOGMs) allow state to state discussions at the highest level but in a seminar-like atmosphere. At lower levels, a network of informal contacts and functional co-operation operates, including a development aid dimension in the Commonwealth Fund for Technical Co-operation.

Two critical questions arise in the context of this chapter. How far is the Commonwealth, for all its manifold virtues, a significant player in North–South relations, and to what extent does it facilitate or constrain British participation? According to its Secretary-General, 'the Commonwealth's track record of contributing creatively to the North–South dialogue has placed it in a position to exert considerable intellectual influence internationally on both the form and substance of the dialogue' (Ramphal, 1984, p. 380). The choice of words is significant. Despite some indication in the early 1960s that the Commonwealth might operate as a caucus at the United Nations, there has been no development in this direction and certainly nothing comparable to the co-ordination procedures in which the UK is involved as an EC member. Nevertheless, there are consultative Commonwealth meetings prior to the meetings of some UN agencies; finance ministers, for example, consult before the annual meetings of the IMF and World Bank.

In the straightforward sense of the word, the Commonwealth cannot be regarded as a cohesive actor in the North–South arena, but North–South issues have been a constant preoccupation for it. Since 1975, the organization's response has been to commission an extensive series of reports. It might be tempting to regard this sustained exercise in academic analysis as a substitute for action, or more precisely as a means of dealing with an external problem that threatened the survival of the organization by warding off the kind of confrontation that was occurring in other international fora. The reports themselves are of high quality and provide the basis for Ramphal's claim of Commonwealth intellectual leadership. In most instances, though, their specific influence is difficult to trace. The Secretary-General describes them as 'widely acclaimed', 'acknowledged as timely and valuable' and 'hailed as a major contribution towards perfecting the process of North–South dialogue'. More specific claims are made for the 1977 Campbell Report, which was the basis for discussions between Commonwealth trade ministers and which helped to produce agreement on the Common Fund (Ramphal, 1984, p. 379). At worst, it might be argued that all this amounted to little more than piling up even greater quantities of paper on top of the mountain already deposited by UNCTAD. At best, it could be seen as having a significant ancillary input to negotiations.

As to British involvement, it cannot be said that Britain has led vigorous initiatives within the organization. Rather it has been the leaders of other developed members – Canada, Australia and New Zealand – who have aspired to this role. Britain's quiescence is explicable in terms of a number of impediments, some inherent in its historical and economic circumstances and others which have a more self-imposed character. The maintenance of the Commonwealth in the 1970s was predicated on British acceptance of a reduced role. It was no longer the 'British' Commonwealth and a secretariat was created to carry out organizational functions previously the prerogative of the British. Similarly, the dismantling of Commonwealth preference and British accession to the EC indicated clearly that, whatever else the Commonwealth was, it was not a British–led trading bloc.

The legacy of empire, and the sensitivity of former colonies on this matter, would render an assertive policy extraordinarily difficult to execute in any event. As one commentator put it: 'The British have responsibility without leadership . . . blame without power . . . she dare not lead except with great timidity for fear of being accused of intolerable arrogance' (Taylor, 1984, p. 312). In fact, British policy in recent years has shown little propensity to lead and is more calculated to sustain a sense of grievance amongst southern members.

Power in the Arena

The North–South dialogue has been variously described as 'fading towards oblivion' (Ramsay, 1984, p. 338) and 'virtually moribund' (Rothstein, 1980, p. 1). Measured in terms of concrete achievements that have had more than a marginal effect on the poverty gap, such claims may be well justified. Yet it may be argued that such a conclusion confuses the rhetoric with the real aims of the Third World coalition. Liberal economists claim that the actual implementation of NIEO proposals such as the Integrated Programme for Commodities would have brought about counterproductive economic effects, and that in the absence of a New International

Economic Order the real growth rates of many Third World
countries have been impressive. 'If the Third World countries were
only concerned with improving their economic situation, these
figures suggest that they would have endorsed the present international economic order' (Krasner, 1983a, p. 239). The point for
Krasner and other commentators is, of course, that this is not their
sole concern. The objectives of the coalition should be viewed politically in terms of a longer-range strategy of 'meta-power' – seizing
control and altering the norms of international regimes – and in
terms of the assertion of national sovereignty. Assessed in this way,
the outcome of more than a decade of Third World activity
appears much more successful and indicates a significant degree
of power. Thus Krasner concludes that 'in general the institutional
structure has become much more responsive to the South' (1981,
p. 142).

The power and influence of the Third World coalition in relation
to the developed countries cannot be viewed in conventional
resource or military terms, since economic inequalities between
even leading southern states and their northern counterparts are too
gross. There is little doubt that it was the energy crisis of the early
1970s and the cartel power of one section of the South organized in
OPEC that served as a lever to force some northern attention, yet
the solidarity of OPEC and high oil prices appear in retrospect to
have been a transient phenomenon. Equally, the effects of the energy
crisis on poor oil-dependent countries were so devastating as to
bring into currency the new category of 'fourth world' country. The
possibility of further cartels amongst commodity producers appears
extremely remote.

Such power as the South does possess clearly derives from its
collective capacity to mobilize within organizations and to deliver
large voting majorities when a one-state one-vote rule operates.
This is the pattern which has been repeated in a large number of
organizations and reflected in the complaints of developed countries
about their politicization; UNESCO being only the most recent and
visible example. A strategy based upon mobilization within international organizations does, however, have significant limitations.
The most obvious limitation concerns the effectiveness of resolu-
tions such as those passed by the UN General Assembly. The real
determinants of economic change do not lie with international organizations. In one view, the United States, by the sheer

scale of its economy, still occupies an hegemonic position. In another, the emergence of a transnationally organized global economy increasingly places control beyond the reach of state governments and probably beyond the reach of the interstate organizations in which the campaign for NIEO has been waged.

The collective strategy of the Group of 77 may in itself militate against the negotiation of specific and effective agreements. It is well understood that the maintenance of solidarity is crucial, yet with extreme diversity and very evident variations of specific economic interest among the members of the coalition such solidarity can often only be maintained through the adoption of positions notable for their vagueness and generality. According to one disillusioned servant of UNCTAD, there is more to this than the problem of aggregating diverse interests; rather it demonstrates a failure of both northern and southern governments to show any real concern for world poverty and inequality. The real distinction is not between rich and poor countries but between rich and poor people:

> There is a strong community of interest between the rich people of the rich countries and the rich people of the poor countries. The governments of poor countries are virtually all controlled by rich people who have more in common with rich people who control . . . corporations than they have with their own poverty-stricken countrymen.
>
> (Ramsay, 1984, p. 393)

This is an interpretation not dissimilar from that of Galtung (1971), in which the North–South dialogue between governments may be represented as something of a charade maintaining a system of economic dependency.

Somewhere between the notion that North–South relations display the impotence of the South on anything other than a symbolic level and the structuralist interpretation with its radical perspective on the nature of interests and power, lies a third conclusion. This would emphasize that under certain circumstances control of voting in international organizations does have significant consequences, giving rise to a degree of northern vulnerability and thus a measure of southern influence and even power. The role of certain organizations and associated regimes cannot be lightly dismissed, as may be evidenced by the staunch northern defence of the Bretton Woods apparatus. Interference and abrupt change in certain organizations could in situations of high interdependence have disruptive effects, particularly for developed countries. This became evident within the International Telecommunications Union (ITU), charged with arranging the radio frequency spectrum such that it might be efficiently used by all. Here, the less developed countries were able to extract some concessions from the ' North by posing the implicit and rather negative threat of disruption (Vogler, 1984). That this is not universally the case may be demonstrated by reference to parallel campaigns within UNESCO, an organization which may be abandoned by two leading members without incurring the kind of significant costs that might be encountered by similar action elsewhere.

Conclusion

This chapter started by asking whether the United Kingdom could exercise significant independent influence within the North–South arena. In the light of the scant achievements of negotiations and the relative weakness of the Third World coalition, the relevance of the question may well be open to doubt. Do North–South relations matter as far as British interests are concerned?

The contention here is that the arena does continue to matter in a number of ways. Britain's position in the arena is significant because, whatever the status of global level negotiations, perceptions of its stance will inevitably impinge upon a host of bilateral economic and political relations with Third World countries, particularly within the Commonwealth. It is arguable that the Thatcher government's apparently harsh and negative approach after 1979 has already entailed costs in this area. At the same time, the significance of a number of international organizations which have had North–South issues thrust upon them cannot be discounted in any reckoning of British interests. It has been argued that it is in this organizational context that the Third World coalition has exercised some power in shaping agendas and norms of conduct. In terms of economic security, Britain has as much, if not more, to lose from the disruption of trade, financial and communications regimes as other developed countries. Thus, there must be some policy concern with shaping the outcome of North–South antagonism in these areas.

Conceptions of interest overlap with moral concerns, as is most graphically demonstrated by the issue of British policy towards South Africa. North–South issues are not a matter of total indifference in the domestic political system. The reaction to the Brandt report showed that there is a surprisingly large domestic constituency concerned with the direction of British policy on development aid and the broad issues of North–South inequality. Brandt's view of interdependence – that what is right just happens to be what is expedient as well – has been echoed in many quarters, not least among the opposition parties.

The brief review of British policy since the mid-1970s demonstrated that change in the direction of policy was indeed possible within certain constraints, evidenced by the degree of continuity of approach between the Callaghan and Thatcher administrations. However, some of the radical departures so characteristic of the Thatcher government were in the end modified by the requirement to keep in step with EC partners. Clearly the three 'poles of attraction' for British policy set out boundaries to independence, although it is almost impossible to predict which will prove the stronger in any particular instance. Over the question of 'global negotiations' and the World Bank energy affiliate the EC line predominated, whereas over UNESCO the UK aligned itself strongly with the USA.

The point has been made that the North–South negotiations do not of themselves produce structural change. Rather, one should look for causes in the national economic policies of major developed states, and even these appear to be reacting to forces which frequently appear to be beyond the boundaries of governmental control. On any of the usual measures, the British economy is no longer internationally in the first rank, and it cannot be expected that an independent policy would have any direct influence. If the United States is now ceasing to be a hegemonic power in economic terms, it is only experiencing a loss that was encountered by Britain well before the end of the last century.

In the light of this, the hope is frequently expressed that by co-ordination rather than by independent action the major northern economies can bring about economic expansion in a way which will also benefit the South. Recent developed-world economic summits and adherents of Brandt's approach have of course somewhat different interpretations of what such co-operation might entail. Yet it is only within this context that the concept of a particular rather than an independent role for Britain makes sense. This is hardly a consequence of the scale of British economic activity, but rather it rests upon the special links enjoyed by Britain, especially those embodied in the Commonwealth. Regrettably, experience in the 1980s has demonstrated the limitations of the view that the Commonwealth provides the basis for a British mediating role in North–South relations. It is to be stressed that this is not a temporary judgement based upon the insensitivity of the Thatcher government to Commonwealth concerns. It reflects instead the evolution of that organization, and the long-term imperial legacy which makes it more difficult for the British to assume a leading role than almost any other member.

In a strange way, it may be the very absence of an extensive Commonwealth-like attachment that has allowed France (despite some notable neo-colonial activity in Africa) to play out the kind of role to which many would aspire in Britain. French policy provides an instructive comparison. A state of comparable size to the United Kingdom, it has managed to establish a position of salience and influence in North–South relations. France sponsored the CIEC, frequently departed from the standard northern line on NIEO, was host to the 1981 UN Conference on the Least Developed Countries and has generally emphasized its concern and independence. It is just conceivable that Britain could do likewise, but the basis of much French activity was a willingness to embrace '*dirigiste*' solutions alien to British tradition and (much more important) to maintain a studied and critical distance from the United States. For Britain to follow such a course would entail a general reorientation that would go well beyond policies in the North–South arena alone.

Notes

1 For a concise yet full history of the North–South negotiations the reader may be referred to Jones, 1983.
2 Calculations as to the extent of cuts in aid expenditure are fraught with difficulties over the accounting methods employed. Official figures

produced in 1981 indicated a reduction over the period 1980–3 of 15 per cent as against an overall public expenditure cut of merely 1.7 per cent (House of Commons, 1981, vol. I, table II, p. xxi). At the same time, the OECD expressed serious concern over the 'disproportionate' nature of the cut relative to other expenditure and lamented the drop in the aid–to–GNP figure to 0.34 per cent (*The Times*, 6 February 1981 and 25 June 1981). A subsequent study by Sutton and Hewitt (1983) showed that for technical reasons the figure criticized by OECD was artificially low and the real aid–to–GNP ratio was of the order of 0.4 per cent. None the less, the authors concluded that aid expenditure in the 1980s remained well below the levels achieved in the late 1970s. As to the other UN target of 1 per cent of GNP for all development finance, both public and private, this figure has always been comfortably exceeded with the UK figure standing at 2 per cent in 1983 (Central Office of Information, 1983, p. 23).

3 This commitment is at its strongest when articles 113 and 116 of the Treaty of Rome apply, such that the commission will negotiate according to a council brief on matters within the purview of common commercial policy. Whereas this applies to GATT negotiations, it is by no means the end of the story, and the Community has evolved separate procedures for dealing with other economic and political negotiations; these give much wider scope for the exercise of national independence. Within the CIEC negotiations in the mid-1970s, the ground rules for participation allowed for a single Community seat. Despite the claims of the British for a separate seat, they had to be content with participation in an exhausting process whereby commission and national government representatives strove to concert a common position prior to each day's negotiating session. Procedures evolved for the handling of the Lomé negotiations had rather more permanence and developed along the same lines, giving rather more weight to the council and its presidency. Discussion of the relevant Community procedures is to be found in Taylor (1982).

4 I am indebted to Susan Strange for suggesting this analogy.

10 Britain and the Advanced Industrial Countries

MICHAEL SMITH

During the 1970s and 1980s, it appeared for much of the time that British foreign policy was about nothing but economic issues and that it was directed at targets almost exclusively within the advanced industrial world. To take an arbitrary and random sample, the issues of agriculture, steel, aerospace production, North Sea oil, monetary collaboration and the future of the British motor industry, all claimed the attention of policy-makers in the international arena during the mid-1980s. Often it seemed that the eruption of 'traditional' issues such as the Falklands War or arms control made only a ripple on the surface of a great sea of technical, multinational and institutional interactions with members of the European Community (EC) or the Organization for Economic Co-operation and Development (OECD).[1] Significantly, it also seemed that British policy-makers entered this arena from a position of fragility and uncertainty about their appropriate role. In this chapter, the aim is to explore the development of Britain's position in the advanced industrial arena and to evaluate the quality of responses produced by successive governments.

Foreign Policy in the Advanced Industrial Arena

Any analysis of British foreign policy within the advanced industrial arena must immediately confront the problem of change and transformation. During the 1970s, it was often argued by foreign policy analysts that the world of the advanced industrial countries (AICs) had been transformed by processes of modernization and by the growth of 'complex interdependence' between societies (Morse, 1970, 1976; Keohane and Nye, 1977). In the new world, the traditional politics of interstate relations was replaced by a multilayered process involving new participants and new issues. The 'high politics' of power, security and strategy was supplanted by an often intractable universe of multinational institutions and of linkages between the domestic and the international arenas. As argued earlier in this volume (Chapter 1), the 1980s saw a series of rebuffs to this transformationalist view of world politics, but none the less (and some would argue, especially among the AICs) there was evidence of substantial and cumulative change. Indeed, the coexistence of trends towards interdependence and multilateralism with a renewed emphasis on military and diplomatic assertiveness made the 1980s an intriguing and often disconcerting decade.

These developments in the advanced industrial arena have had important implications for the study and the practice of foreign policy. It can be persuasively argued that the nature of foreign policy in AICs has been transformed along with the nature of relations between AICs (Morse, 1970, 1976). This transformation has affected several key components of foreign policy. First, the agenda of policy – its substance and the goals towards which it is directed – has broadened and deepened. Many more economic and social, domestic and parochial needs are now expressed through and impressed on foreign policy-makers, and their objectives are less those of national security and prestige than those of efficiency, profit and loss. Second, the process of policy-making itself has been revolutionized: participation and influence are more diffuse and fragmented, both within and outside the governmental machine, and bureaucrats and pressure groups can wield influence at the expense of traditional foreign policy elites. Third, the implementation and control of policy have changed in character: there are more channels, both bilateral and multilateral, through which policy can be pursued, but the proliferation of 'targets' for policy and the sheer range of policy activities can render the outcomes of any given course of action much less predictable. In these conditions, Morse argues, many AICs have almost literally lost control of their foreign relations. It is not beyond the wit of policy-makers, though, to respond to these challenges, and other commentators have chosen to stress the range of possible responses which can be mustered by national authorities in an interdependent world.

According to Cooper and Hollick (1985) and as outlined by Roger Tooze in Chapter 6, four patterns of response can be identified: defensive, accommodative, aggressive and co-operative. Whilst no government's posture will fall neatly into any one of these categories, they provide a useful reminder of the options open to foreign policy-makers or their domestic counterparts in increasingly penetrated national societies. They also highlight the diversity of possible strategies in the 'after hegemony' or 'post-multilateral' era, which has arguably created more rather than less room for nationally distinctive policy orientations (Keohane, 1984a; Woolcock *et al.*, 1985).

From the point of view of foreign policy, therefore, it seems best to refer to a substantial but incomplete transformation brought about by the development of the advanced industrial arena. The traditional and the novel coexist, often uneasily and in a transitional condition. Perhaps most important of all, the coexistence finds expression in the minds, perceptions, words and deeds of policy-makers themselves. This predicament, according to one observer, reflects 'rapid and continuing changes in technology, communications and industrial and financial integration which have eroded national boundaries and the powers of governments but left the structure – and the rhetoric – of national policies in place' (Wallace, 1986b, p. 367.) The next task must be to explore the position, problems and responses of British foreign policy within this context.

Britain in the Advanced Industrial Arena

It has already been noted that the emergence of a distinctive 'advanced industrial arena' reflected the spread of industrialization and industrial societies in Europe, North America and Japan. Arguably, for much of the 'first wave' of industrialization in the nineteenth century, Britain was the only 'advanced industrial society', with decisive leads in manufacturing technology, in social structure and in the sphere of commerce. This leadership position was not simply a reflection of domestic economic and social accomplishments: it was built also on British dominance of important international structures and institutions. Economic, technological and commercial skills, allied to military and diplomatic sophistication, gave Britain an empire and the freedom of the seas. The pound sterling was the predominant medium of international exchange, and the majority of world trade consisted of British goods carried in British vessels. In a very real sense, the British ran the international system in both its economic and its strategic dimensions, bolstering their dominance through free trade, the gold standard and the Royal Navy.

As many writers have pointed out, the period 1900–50 saw a decisive transition in the position of Britain within both the world economy and the international political system. Although the British share in world trade remained at or over 25 per cent and much of total world trade was still invoiced and paid for in sterling, the effects of two world wars and the rise of powerful industrial competitors within and outside Europe brought about a relative decline in the British position. The British governments of the 1920s and 1930s remained committed to the totems of free trade, the gold standard and freedom of the seas, but it was far from clear that these were either attainable by or in the interests of an increasingly embattled empire. The hour of greatest national triumph in 1945 only served to accentuate Britain's tenuous hold on world influence, coinciding as it did with economic exhaustion and the first evidence of American dominance within the Western world. None the less, as Robert Lieber notes, Britain was 'one of the key international actors in hammering out the postwar rules and institutions which were to shape the future course of international political and economic life' (1984, p. 1). British policymakers were alive to the vital connections between the economic and the military security of the Western democracies, and through both the Bretton Woods system and the North Atlantic alliance their influence made itself felt in significant measure (Younger, 1964; Wallace 1986b).

Since 1950, though, Britain's place within the advanced industrial arena has changed dramatically. Although it is possible to argue that this shift was merely the consummation of trends which had become evident as early as the 1870s and that these in their turn reflected long-term trends in British social or economic structures (Gamble, 1985; Pinder, 1983; Hall, 1986), it is important from the point of view of current British foreign policy to examine the dimensions of the shift as it has expressed itself over the period since 1945 and particularly in the 1970s and 1980s. Three qualities appear to be central to the developing British predicament: first, substantial openness and internationalization; second, high and increasing levels of integration; third, uneven levels of perform-ance. Together, they furnish the context within which British policy problems and responses can be analysed.

It has already been noted that the emergence and maintenance of the British Empire and broader British dominance in the nineteenth century relied heavily on the internationalization of the British economy. Indeed, one critic has concluded that 'during its rise to world power the British state abandoned self-sufficiency and became dependent for its very survival on the wider world economy' (Gamble, 1985, p. 3). While this was a feasible and even profitable strategy during the years of British supremacy, such structural openness was to become a liability in less propitious times. One of the implications was a tendency on the part of British policy-makers to concentrate on external financial goals at the expense of domestic industrial objectives, a tendency which led during the 1920s and 1930s to damaging exchange rate policies based on the gold standard. Another result of this basic orientation was a marked propensity towards the export of capital rather than its investment in the UK itself. Although the Second World War disrupted the established pattern to some extent, one of the first instincts of British policy-makers in the postwar period – not without American encouragement – was to re-establish the basi-cally 'open' structure of the British economy. After a false start in 1947, the convertibility of sterling was resumed in 1958, while trade controls were progressively eliminated under the auspices of the General Agreement on Tariffs and Trade (GATT). Britain became one of the major 'host' countries for American multi-national corporations and other forms of overseas investment, while at the same time the UK itself was a major source of invest-ment in other countries (Stopford and Turner, 1985). The creation of the European Free Trade Association (EFTA) in the 1960s and entry into the European Community during the 1970s created different patterns of trade and financial activity (see below), but in general the British economy has remained one of the most open in the advanced industrial arena. Such a situation is not without its attendant costs and risks, however, as a Parliamentary Select Com-mittee recognized in the early 1980s: 'the UK is still the most open of the five large non-Communist economies. This makes us particularly vulnerable to variations in external demand, whether caused by fluctuations in the exchange rate or the world business cycle' (Treasury and Civil Service Committee, 1983, p. xx).

This judgement is especially significant in view of the progressive integration of the UK into the advanced industrial arena. Although the British economy has always been highly internationalized, this has gone alongside a shifting focus of international economic activity. For a long time the chief targets of British overseas economic activity – and the chief sources of imports or investment – were to be found in the empire and North America. Commonwealth countries still account for a significant proportion of Britain's overseas transactions, but the overwhelming focus of Britain's trade is now the North Atlantic area and Japan – in fact, the advanced industrial arena. This pattern is confirmed by evidence relating to outward and inward investment; here, the USA predominates, but the roles played by the EC and Japan are also significant.[2]

It is thus apparent that Britain has been subject to high and increasing levels of integration into the advanced industrial arena. Earlier, it was noted that the growth of international trade and exchange, and of the institutions associated with it, has been one of the most characteristic features of the advanced industrial world. A process and a condition of integration results, sometimes enshrined in formal institutions like the EC but equally often expressed in powerful informal constraints on the behaviour of those involved. As in other spheres, British policy-makers and commentators were not backward in recognizing at least some of the implications of these processes: in 1964, Kenneth Younger pointed out that 'for her [i.e. the UK] international interdependence is not so much an aim which she can choose as a condition of her existence' (1964, p. 13). Interestingly, though, Younger went on to give a very different gloss to the notion of 'interdependence' from that with which this chapter started:

> Economically, a technically advanced country such as Britain can probably earn an adequate living within any of the alternative frameworks of world trade which are likely to develop. What she has to decide is rather the way in which she can best make her influence felt in the great issues of war and peace, and in the problems of organising collective security and promoting

international stability in an age when the peace is no longer
kept by imperial powers.

(1964, p. 14)

This opinion points up a feature often noted in British foreign
policy during the 1950s and 1960s. Even though, objectively, the
level to which Britain was becoming integrated into the advanced
industrial arena was fast and accelerating, foreign policy-makers
were reluctant to draw conclusions from it for the broader direction
of Britain's international activity. This disinclination was reinforced by the lingering imperial and Commonwealth orientation of
much British trade and commerce, creating a powerful barrier to
rapid adaptation.

By the end of the 1960s, however, recognition of Britain's
inescapable entanglement in the advanced industrial world was
apparent even to the most nostalgic of policy-makers. Western
Europe had replaced the Commonwealth as the major focus of
British trade, entry into the EC was increasingly seen as a question
of 'when' rather than 'if', and political disillusionment with the
Commonwealth as a consequence of the Rhodesian question added
a final reinforcement. Ironically, but by no means coincidentally,
this decisive shift of orientation came at a time when the fragility of
Britain's position in the advanced industrial arena was beginning
painfully to make itself felt (Frankel, 1975, ch. II; Jones, 1974,
ch. 5). The combination of considerable openness in the British
economy with high levels of integration into the world of the AICs
has posed a series of questions during the 1970s and 1980s which
British policy-makers have found it remarkably difficult to answer.

Perhaps the major reason why these questions are both so in-
sistent and so difficult to cope with lies in the uneven performance
of the British economy, both over the postwar period as a whole
and during the period since 1970 in particular. The remainder of
this section will attempt to highlight some of the major features of
British economic performance, particularly in the 1970s and 1980s,
which can be seen as contributing to the policy problems Britain
has encountered within the advanced industrial arena. Four interconnected areas will be explored: trade and industry, monetary and
financial developments, energy and technology. Although other
issues could no doubt be included in the analysis, these four are seen
as 'diagnostic' for Britain's overall predicament.

During the nineteenth century it was conventional to refer to Britain as 'the workshop of the world', importing raw materials and food and exporting a large part of the world's manufactured goods. As already noted, this has contributed to a consistently high dependence on external trade and transactions in the British economy. This is still the case in the 1980s: Britain depends on trade (broadly defined) for over 20 per cent of its national wealth. This is comparable to the situations of France and West Germany, but represents a notably higher level of dependence than that of the USA or Japan. As industrialization has spread during the twentieth century, Britain's share of the world trade in manufactures has declined in relative terms, producing an overall picture of high levels of dependence, a declining relative share in world trade and (as noted earlier) an increasing concentration on the industrial world itself. Britain still trades a lot, but more and more with similar countries in similar products.

The difficulty, though, is that Britain trades increasingly less effectively and less profitably. Whereas other AICs focus on 'leading edge' products in their mutual trade, the UK exports a large proportion of relatively 'low-tech' items whilst importing 'high-tech'. The composition of trade is therefore unfavourable. This would be acceptable if the returns on trade were sufficient to keep the UK in credit, but the 1970s and 1980s have in fact seen the UK run its first-ever consistent deficits on trade in manufactures. According to one analysis, the UK was caught in a 'pincer movement': on the one side were the 'high-tech' forces of other AICs, whilst on the other were the battalions of the 'newly industrializing countries' (NICs) with their advantages in traditional heavy industries (Grant and Nath, 1984, p. 201).

As a House of Lords Committee pointed out, 'trade in manufactures and the output of manufacturing industry are indissolubly linked' (House of Lords, 1984–5, I, p. 5). For an AIC such as Britain, the implications of domestic economic stagnation are central to its ability to face up to the challenges of the international arena, and there have even been suggestions that the UK's position in the early 1980s made it a prime candidate as the first AIC to return to the ranks of less developed countries. The British share in world manufacturing production fell from 14.2 per cent in 1964 to 9.7 per cent in 1980 and then to 7.9 per cent in 1983 (House of Lords, 1984–5, I. p. 12). Indices of competitiveness in relation to other AICs painted an alarming picture of inferiority, in addition to the confirmed inability to compete with the NICs in areas such as steel and shipbuilding. The nature of the British response to this predicament will be examined later, but at this point the fragility of the British trading position should need no further emphasis.

It is impossible to deal with Britain's international trade performance without at some stage coming up against the intimate link between trade, financial and monetary factors. The expansion and dominance of the British economy in the nineteenth century were as much a reflection of its financial as its manufacturing power. Indeed, some writers have pointed to the external orientation of the British financial community as both a crucial foundation for British dominance and a central factor in Britain's later decline. (Gamble, 1985; Coates, 1984; Pollard, 1982; Hall, 1986). The UK's leadership in the international exchange of money and other financial instruments made London the financial capital of the world and despite the rise of other centres in the post-1945 period the City remains a formidable force. Such a situation undoubtedly has material benefits for the UK economy in the form of income from investments or the provision of services (an increasingly significant item for many AICs), but it also produces important areas of weakness and vulnerability. One such area connects with the previous discussion of trade and industry: in simple terms it is often argued that the 'external orientation' of British investors, and their preference for financial dealings rather than industrial activity, has proved a fundamental obstacle to the kind of economic adjustments that would have been necessary in order to take advantage of developing relations in the AIC arena (Gamble, 1985; Coates, 1984; Pollard, 1982). The British have been expert at exporting capital, but this has by definition deprived industry of the status and the resources it needs.

A particular and poignant manifestation of this problem is the changing role of sterling in the international monetary system. In a smoothly logical world, the dominance of sterling in the nineteenth century, and its use as a 'master currency' for international dealings, would have been replaced in the twentieth century by a status more in line with the relative decline of the British economy in general and Britain's political weight. Instead, as several telling analyses have pointed out (Strange, 1971; Blank, 1977), the maintenance of values for the pound which were unrelated to economic realities proved a long-standing and often crippling restraint on Britain's economic adjustment. In the 1920s, the return to the gold standard choked off growth and recovery, whilst in the 1950s and 1960s the maintenance of an unrealistically high parity made British policy the prisoner of international 'confidence' and its concomitant speculation.

It could be argued that in the case of sterling a financial 'maladjustment' went along with a political distortion of Britain's international position and that following the 'Europeanization' of British foreign policy and the floating of sterling along with other AIC currencies during the early 1970s, the situation would at least begin to conform to the underlying realities of Britain's place in the advanced industrial arena. The solution does not appear to have been so simple, though, and the central role of sterling in the 'British disease' has persisted into the 1980s. The predicament has changed, however: since 1976 and the notorious intervention of the International Monetary fund (IMF) which caused the Chancellor of the Exchequer to return from London Airport to wrestle with financial crisis, it has been the instability of the pound rather than its maintenance at an unrealistically high value which has caused the major problems. Among other factors, the impact of inflation, stagnation and North Sea oil (which gave the pound 'petro-currency' status in the 1980s) created a volatile and delicate situation. The result was a succession of crises, some of them caused by excessive rises in sterling's value (1978–82) and others caused by its precipitous decline (1983–5.) Uncertainty created by the underlying economic performance of Britain was magnified by enhanced mobility of capital and by the adoption of an ostentatious 'hands off' policy under the Thatcher government after 1979. Such problems were not unique to Britain: all major AIC currencies suffered uncertainties and volatility during the late 1970s and 1980s, but arguably the severity of the British predicament was distinctive, and it certainly aggravated the commercial and industrial weaknesses already noted.

One further point about the British position in the financial arena should be made – and again it is one that links financial with commercial and industrial questions. A central feature of the advanced industrial world during the postwar period has been the proliferation and expansion of multinational companies (MNCs). Although much has been made of their activities in the Third

World and their links to dependency or exploitation, it is in the AICs that most MNCs are based and carry on their activities. Among the AICs, Britain's position in relation to multinationals is quite distinctive – indeed, a recent study describes it as 'remarkable', since despite its relative economic decline Britain remains second only to the USA both as a 'target' or 'host' for MNC investment and as a source or 'home' of such investment overseas. Britain played host to about £35 billion of MNC assets in 1983, and at the same time British direct investment in plant and facilities overseas amounted to about £63 billion (Stopford and Turner, 1985, p. 2). It is an open question whether this situation is in itself a source of weakness or of strength for the British economy, but it clearly reinforces the integration and openness of the British economy in the advanced industrial arena. When combined with the other weaknesses already described, it is logical to suppose that MNC involvement, whether as 'host' or 'home', can interact potently with the delicate position occupied by Britain overall.

In addition to its position in the broad issue areas of trade, industry and finance within the advanced industrial arena, it is important to draw attention to Britain's status in two key sectors of political and economic activity: energy and technology. Reference has already been made to the ways in which these factors can affect trade or currency trends, and there is good cause to see them as significant considerations for all AIC foreign policies. For Britain, though, these factors have assumed consistent and central importance and have magnified or focused the overall characteristics of the policy predicament. During the 1970s and 1980s, it was certainly energy that captured the most persistent attention and created the greatest drama. Initially, and in keeping with historical experience stretching back through Suez to the 1930s, it was the threat to energy supplies during the 1973 October War that preoccupied British policy-makers. Like other AICs, Britain during the early 1970s was critically dependent on imported energy sources to sustain its economic performance. Since then, however, the trajectory of the British energy problem has followed a markedly different course from that of all other AICs. The world recession of the mid and late 1970s, triggered off by the 1973 crisis and reinvigorated by the 'second shock' of 1978–9 after the Iranian revolution, threw Britain's long-term economic weaknesses into sharp relief – earlier into the recession, with higher inflation, less growth and higher unemployment and later out of the trough when recovery began in the early 1980s. At the same time, however, Britain was in the course of establishing itself as the only substantial AIC with a surplus of indigenous energy resources. North Sea oil made Britain self-sufficient by the 1980s and a major exporter to such AICs as the USA and West Germany thereafter. But the impact of 'black gold' was profoundly paradoxical: 'petro-currency' status exaggerated the instability of sterling, deindus-trialization accompanied energy self-sufficiency, and the 'third shock' of 1984 and after exposed the folly of relying on oil revenues in a period of oil glut. Above all, it was estimated that self-sufficiency would be a thing of the past by the mid-1990s and this created further uncertainty about Britain's future economic prospects.

While Britain's energy problem was full of contradictions, there has generally been less room for argument about British prospects and achievements in the field of technology. From a situation after the Second World War in which some European governments were genuinely worried about being swamped by the technological might of the UK, it has become and remained apparent that Britain suffers from fundamental weaknesses in several spheres of tech-nological activity. Although there have been great achievements in some areas of high technology and pure science, these have been overshadowed by evidence of major defects in the fields of innovation, application, investment and marketing. In this sense, the problem of British technological backwardness reflects the underlying fragility of the British industrial and financial struc-tures. Whereas the British have been remarkably productive as inventors and scientists, it is the Japanese, the West Germans and the Americans who seem to have the ability to carry through to fruition enterprises central to advanced industrial life. In the field of manufacturing technology, it is taken for granted that the British worker will have less to work with in terms of investment in up-to-date plant and equipment, as a function of historically low rates of manufacturing investment in general. In 1983, the average rate of gross investment as a percentage of GDP was 19.7 for all OECD members; for the UK the rate was 16.7, whilst for Japan it was 28.5, for West Germany 20.8 and for the USA 16.9 (House of Lords, 1984–5, I, p. 23). The area of 'traditional' high technology (including aerospace, for example) has seen the UK increasingly

unable to fund or to exploit the developments which would be
fundamental to continuing prosperity in the 1990s. As in a number
of other areas, this is not a problem unique to Britain, but it has
gone along with a cultural propensity to downgrade technology
and industry which would demand vast resources and a concerted
national effort for its correction. Finally, in the critical area of
information technology and computing, it has become apparent
that the British suffer from a comparative disadvantage, along with
some other European AICs, when confronted with the American
and Japanese challenges. Although the fruits of British research and
development are still considerable, there is evidence that the stream
may be drying up because of historically low funding levels, and
that the communications revolution and other processes of the next
decade may be the point at which the 'underdevelopment' of
Britain finally becomes a reality. Nor is this simply a question of
economic and social damage. As William Wallace concluded in the
early 1970s, 'the way in which technological progress became
identified . . . with the symbols of national prestige and sovereignty has elevated technological policy, like defence, to the status
of high policy' (1976, p. 122) and the link between technology and
national security has been increasingly apparent.

This overall review of Britain's position in the advanced industrial arena leads to the inescapable conclusion that times have been
bad and may well be getting worse. Sidney Pollard has summed up
the situation in a suitably colourful metaphor:

> The picture . . . is that the world has passed Britain by – as if, in
> a convoy travelling together, all the other ships are sailing
> serenely on while Britain has gone aground, hopelessly watching
> the rest of the convoy disappearing over the horizon. The
> captains of the convoy still meet for regular consultation, but
> while the others represent vessels which are seaworthy and
> moving towards their destination, the British captain commands
> a vessel which is little more than a hulk.
>
> (1982, pp. 3–4)

In the remainder of this chapter, the analysis turns to two important questions for British foreign policy which flow from the above
discussion. First, it will assess the problems for the making of
foreign policy which are associated with Britain's place in the

advanced industrial arena. Second, it will evaluate the patterns of response which have emerged from British policy-makers' attempts to grapple with a relatively uncongenial set of circumstances, before returning to the general issues outlined at the beginning of the chapter.

Problems of Policy-Making

It was suggested earlier that the foreign policies of the AICs had experienced a substantial but incomplete transformation. The discussion of Britain's position in the advanced industrial arena indicates that at least in that respect, the impact of this transformation on the UK has been dramatic and even traumatic. There are very few ways in which the British position during the 1980s is not substantially less impressive and stable than that of the 1950s and 1960s. In terms which would be familiar to students of 'complex interdependence', British society had by the 1980s confirmed its entanglement in the advanced industrial arena, but at the same time it had demonstrated its vulnerability to the processes – both economic and political – emerging from the arena. This means that the problem of foreign policy-making itself has become inherently more problematical for British governments, and arguably that the problems are especially severe for a society in such a fragile position. Whilst some societies and governments can benefit from, adapt to or use their place in the advanced industrial arena, for Britain the challenge has had a rather more negative impact. Three areas of policy-making will be examined here: first, the challenge of adjustment to Britain's changing status within the arena; second, the changing agenda and substance of policy; third, participation and inputs to the policy process. This will provide a foundation from which an evaluation of policy outputs or responses can be carried out.

The advanced industrial arena since 1945 has been characterized by a number of powerful but often paradoxical developments. Perhaps the most obvious of these has been the simple growth of interconnectedness between the societies of the North Atlantic area (usually defined so as to include Japan and other non-Atlantic members of the OECD). This interconnectedness has, however, been uneven in its impact and has produced asymmetries of status and influence. For a long time – most people would say, until the early 1970s – it was assumed that the predominance of the USA in economic, political and strategic terms gave American policy-makers both the privileges and the responsibilities of leadership. During the 1970s, the relative fragility of the American economy combined with challenges from outside the AICs – for example, from OPEC oil producers – and the shift of economic power within the OECD area, to disrupt the relatively well-ordered processes of the 1950s and 1960s. The 'post-hegemonial' or 'post-multilateral' era saw a diffusion and redistribution of economic influence, but this was often combined with a reluctance on the part of the new power-centres to enter into full leadership responsibilities. At the same time, increasing American unilateralism and introspection under the Carter and Reagan administrations meant that the erstwhile leader itself often became a source of disruption and uncertainty (Keohane, 1984a; Woolcock *et al.* 1985; Calleo, 1982).

In these conditions, the position of Britain could perhaps best be described as eccentric. At the end of the Second World War, the UK had played a major if secondary role in the construction and maintenance of the 'rules' by which the Western economic system was run – the Bretton Woods system, the GATT, the OEEC and later the OECD. Increasingly, though, it became painfully clear that the UK was the invalid of the advanced industrial arena. Formal status and responsibility were combined with operational vulnerability and even powerlessness. Secondary powers within the international arena inevitably live with the limitations imposed by their lack of authority and control (Wallace, 1976; Hanrieder and Auton, 1980), but for Britain the ability to manoeuvre, to specialize and to take advantage of 'gaps' in the system has been restricted by a combination of historical and contemporary 'blinkers', some of them economic and some of them in the broader political domain.

For the making of policy, these contextual and structural 'facts of life' have had important and largely negative implications. Three such implications can be spelt out here. First, British policy-makers have confronted a situation in which their resource power has consistently declined: even the bounty of North Sea oil can be presented as a contribution to British weakness rather than British strength, and the underlying fragility of the economy has acted as a continual constraint on policy. Second, although not at the same pace, the British have experienced a substantial diminution of their structural power within the advanced industrial arena. Here again, factors which in some contexts might be presented as strengths or privileges – such as the international role of sterling – have progressively come to be seen as limitations. It must be re-emphasized, though, that the formal abandonment of such commitments has at times been well out of line with developments in the 'real' economic position of the UK. Finally, it has become apparent that the UK as a national society is increasingly and irreversibly penetrated by events in the outside world, to the extent that domestic and international processes are often effectively fused. As Peter Katzenstein has argued, the management of interdependence starts at home (1978). When the home base is impoverished to the extent that it can be described as a 'black hole' (Stopford and Turner, 1985) or that British society in general can be seen as the culprit for the UK's international vulnerability (Henderson, 1979), then the constraints on policy-makers are severe.

A second feature of the British policy-making setting, and one which has a generalized impact on the AICs, is the changing agenda and substance of policy. For some writers (e.g. Wallace, 1976), the crucial shift is in the policy domain – the relative decline of 'high policy' issues with their connotations of national security and elitism. Others (Morse, 1976) have noted the shift in policy goals, from the 'transcendental' or symbolic to the 'instrumental'. Along with this has gone an increasing awareness that for the purposes of analysis and policy-making alike the crucial fact is that of linkage (whether intended or unintended) between areas of policy previously thought to exist in separate domains (see Keohane and Nye, 1977). These elements are interrelated, of course, and AIC policy-makers can generally be seen as confronting an expanded and more fluid set of issues and objectives. Again, for Britain the problem has assumed a distinctive form and has distinctive impacts. At the broadest – or most elevated – level, it is clear that for a substantial part of the postwar era British policy-makers were at the centre of the 'agenda-setting' process for the advanced industrial arena, through their presence at the 'top table' of international conferences and institutions. Even at the earliest stage, however, it was clear that this agenda-setting role could restrict Britain's ability to control its own agenda for national action, and economic weakness has played a decisive part since in constraining policy-makers' ability to allocate time, attention or resources to specific agenda items.

A number of specific manifestations of this problem have been apparent during the late 1970s and 1980s. In the first place, British foreign policy-makers have often found it difficult if not impossible to choose between domestic and foreign policy goals. Indeed, it has become increasingly difficult to know what is or is not a foreign policy goal, in an era when national economic regeneration is seen as inseparable from foreign policy influence. Where choices have been made, it has been argued, they have often placed traditional symbols of foreign policy ahead of the more instrumental needs of national welfare, and thus carried unacceptable or unbearable costs (Blank, 1977). Foreign policy-makers and their domestic colleagues have tended to play down the inescapable linkages between different agenda items and have thus placed themselves at a disadvantage in the agenda-setting process. As a consequence, when this lack of sensitivity is combined with lack of resource or structural power, the agenda of British foreign and domestic policy has often been set by outside forces, through overt intervention or less formal penetration of British society (for example, the IMF intervention of 1976 or the increasing interpenetration of multinational enterprises in the automobile industry). A final manifestation of the problem has been a declining ability to influence the ways in which issues within the advanced industrial arena are politicized – that is, the ways in which they are linked to strategic or security concerns to create both economic and political costs for those involved. Perhaps the most spectacular examples here are furnished by the several attempts during the 1980s to impose economic sanctions on various international wrongdoers. American actions against the USSR and Iran, for example, imposed costs on the British industrial and financial communities which were arguably beyond the control of them or their government.

The final feature of British policy-making which can be seen as reflecting the impact of progressive engagement in the advanced industrial arena is the policy process itself. For the purposes of this chapter, two particular components of the process are most significant: first, the range of participants in the process, their orientations and interests; second, the kinds of inputs into the process they provide. Earlier it was noted that participation and influence in

AICs' foreign policies had become more diffuse and fragmented and that a number of bureaucratic, sectional or other groupings could wield influence at the expense of 'traditional' foreign policy elites. Such a set of trends clearly reflects the changing nature of the advanced industrial arena and of the policy agendas it generates for its members. The picture, however, is unlikely either to be uniform across all AICs or to be unaffected by variations in the issue(s) under consideration. For most countries, the transformation is incomplete and far from unproblematic. In the British case, it seems logical on *a priori* grounds to suppose that the high levels of openness and integration into the advanced industrial arena that characterize its economic and social structures, combined with a relatively pluralistic political system, would increase the impact of a transformed international environment on the policy-making process.

The reality, though, appears to be a situation of considerable tension and ambivalence both in the area of participation and that of policy inputs. In the first place, although there has been a proliferation of participants in the foreign policy process, both within and outside government, the long-established habits and processes of elite policy-making persist. The Prime Minister and the Foreign Secretary have been joined on the stage by a variety of bit-part players and supporting actors, but they retain top billing for many purposes. While departmental interests and a variety of sectional private pressures can make themselves felt, the process of policy co-ordination at both the formal and the informal levels is still an integral part of the practice of British government, both at home and abroad. The combination of these elements of continuity with the transformation of the policy arena is the key to the tensions that emerge. A pertinent example is that of monetary policy, and particularly the sterling exchange rate. Although it could be argued that no British government has the power to determine the external value of the pound, successive administrations of the 1970s and 1980s none the less treated it as a matter of central symbolic interest and thus as a concern for elite policy-making. This did not alter the fact that a wide range of other actors was wont to appear on the monetary stage, either to complain about the level of the currency, to advise on appropriate measures, or to subvert government policies.

Alongside the tension between habits of co-ordination and the reality of diffusion which characterizes participation in the policy process, there exists a similar contradiction between the fragmentation of inputs and the inbuilt desire for unity of policy. It is inevitable, given the multinationalization of the advanced industrial arena, that the 'raw material' of policy will be disjointed over time and between issues. The fact that policy sectors can engage many parts and levels of government and society constitutes a formidable constraint on the building of coalitions and alignments within government and between government and society. In British government, though, there have been contradictory tendencies: on the one side, there have been moves (based precisely on the demands posed by multinational policy-making) to centralize strategic decisions in the Cabinet Office or other such bodies; on the other side, it is apparent that policies, as opposed to policy on the strategic level, are increasingly fragmented and diffuse. In the fields of energy and technology, for example, there were many attempts during the 1970s and 1980s to formulate national strategies for the multinational arena. The formidable difficulties of synthesizing a wide and diverse range of inputs, extending from the requirements of multilateral institutions to the demands of private interests and the positions of government departments themselves, meant that such strategies were often stillborn or superseded by the development of international conditions.[3]

The combination of a rapidly changing and unpredictable setting with a policy process which emphasizes co-ordination and reflects a wide range of interests has often been seen as fundamental to the British predicament within the advanced industrial arena. As Stephen Blank has noted, this phenomenon of 'pluralistic stagnation' can be used to compare British adaptability with the supposedly superior capacities of other AICs (1977). In 1985, the House of Lords Committee set up to assess Britain's trade performance pointed to a series of factors which might account for Britain's failings, among them the ways in which policy was formulated, and contrasted them with those practised in other countries (House of Lords, 1984–5). Although it would be misleading to draw too stark a contrast between British adjustment to the demands of life among the AICs and the policies pursued elsewhere, it appears more than likely that the make-up of the policy process itself constitutes a significant factor both in the way the arena impinges on Britain and in the policy responses which are generated. It is these responses that form the focus of the final evaluation here.

Policy Responses

Integral to the making of foreign policy in AICs is the question of policy responses. Given the complexity of the policy arena and the proliferation of both actors and issues, it is unclear whether responses framed on a purely national basis or utilizing purely national resources can be effective. Three central areas of debate have emerged here: first, the adequacy and variety of policy instruments; second, the ability to pay the costs and bear the burdens of interdependence; and third, the possibilty of 'learning' and adaptation by policy-makers in conditions of complexity and uncertainty.

Edward Morse has argued that in certain key respects, AICs have lost control of their external relations (1970, 1976). Partly, this reflects the 'spread' of intersocietal links to encompass transnational processes outside the awareness of governments. In addition to this problem of knowledge, however, there is another dimension to the question of control: that of the adequacy of policy instruments to the novel tasks they are called upon to perform. There appears to be a 'law of requisite variety' for AIC foreign policies, which demands that the range and diversity of instruments should match the challenges of the arena. According to Morse, such demands are only rarely satisfied even by the most powerful and resourceful of governmental machines. Simple possession and use of instruments does not guarantee control of outcomes, since the ramifications of policy undertakings reach far into the domestic life of other societies and may conjure up unsuspected resistance or limitations. Alongside this problem of control and instrumentalities goes another: that of estimating and bearing the costs of involvement in the advanced industrial arena. Quite often these costs are financial – gains or losses of markets, of industrial production, of purchasing power. But there are also human costs brought about by changes in employment, in cultural penetration of societies and in welfare broadly defined. Finally, there can be psychological or political costs attached to the perception of dependence, the erosion of legitimacy and the ineffectiveness of established institutions. Foreign policy in the light of these circumstances can be presented as the struggle to make others bear the costs and the policy-makers are faced with the task of identifying those costs they are able and prepared to pay (Keohane, 1979). This brings in the third area of debate: the possibility of learning and creative adaptation by the policy-makers. Several writers have pointed to the role played in foreign policy by habit, convention, or routines, but the advanced industrial arena demands that these be augmented by a good deal of innovation and adaptation (Steinbruner, 1974; Lovell, 1973). Self-interest and the need to avoid damaging outcomes for the system in general place a substantial premium on the search for creative solutions.

These general points can be applied to the case of British foreign policy by focusing on the broad patterns of responses mustered by the policy-makers, in the light of the pressures generated by engagement in the advanced industrial arena. Cooper and Hollick (1985) have suggested that a spectrum of responses is available to governments in the arena: defensive, accommodative, aggressive and co-operative. A defensive response implies the attempt to reduce the openness of the economy and society, to control the extent of their integration into the arena and to limit the costs entailed in external relations; various types of protectionism fall into this category. An accommodative response entails not resistance to the tide of interdependence but an adaptation to changing circumstances, a search for new policy instruments and flexibility in the allocation of costs or benefits. Deregulation or the encouragement of joint ventures would be typical here. Aggressive responses, on the other hand, indicate active attempts to extend the reach of national government and regulation – outside national boundaries if necessary – to turn back the tide, make others pay the costs and enhance the impact of government instruments. Extraterritorial application of domestic law, or various forms of sanctions, would be salient here. Finally, a co-operative posture sets out to enlarge the area covered by international agreements, regimes, or institutions, and by so doing to share the costs of interdependence, manage the arena and promote the common along with the national good. Given the British position in the advanced industrial world – open, integrated and vulnerable – it is clearly important to apply such criteria as these to an assessment of the overall effectiveness of foreign policy. By doing so, the argument here deals at the national level with the broader problems identified by Roger Tooze in Chapter 6.

Although some areas of British society have traditionally been well defended against the outside world (agriculture is a notable example), it is true to say that British foreign policy-makers have generally eschewed defensive measures within the advanced industrial arena. The internationalization of the British political economy has meant that the fear of retaliation against protective moves has been a powerful constraint and financial circles led by the Treasury have had a powerful voice in the determination of foreign economic policy. Industrial interests have indicated some support for protection, but have also had to take into account the frailty of their base in the domestic market and their need to export. This is not to say that there have not been voices in the UK calling for defensive measures: perhaps the most ambitious scheme of this kind put forward in recent years has been the 'alternative economic strategy' favoured by certain parts of the trade union movement and the Labour Party. This call for quota protection and a reimposition of exchange controls gathered relatively little support even within the party itself, however, and would require a major reorientation of domestic opinion as well as a fundamental shift in the way Britain relates to the advanced industrial arena. British policy-makers have also consistently supported action in the GATT against overtly defensive measures, and it could be argued that the accumulation of decades of 'openness' to trade and capital flows in itself constitutes a formidable obstacle to any shift in perceptions or attitudes. Although entry into the EC could be seen in part as a grand defensive measure, British policy in Brussels has generally been aimed at the liberalization of trade and capital movements.

Far more of British policy can be seen as falling within the accommodative part of the spectrum, but with some crucial qualifications. The British have encouraged MNCs to set up shop in the UK, they have liberalized capital movements and they have – especially under the Thatcher governments of 1979 and after – pursued deregulation both at the national and the international level. At times, it has almost been argued that the very openness of the British economy gives a potential lever against those who pursue unfair or restrictive trading practices elsewhere in the international system (such as the Japanese). There has thus arguably been a quasi-ideological component to British responses in the accommodative vein, which undoubtedly reflects the strength of tradition and experience as well as perceptions of the UK's role in the world economy. But such a stance carries with it substantial costs, especially where the adaptive capacity of the national economy and society are relatively limited. Britain may have been determinedly accommodative, but this line of policy has been followed within the context of poor performance and consequent vulnerability described earlier in the chapter. As a result, it could be argued that Britain has gained somewhat but others have gained markedly from their ability to penetrate the UK and that the propensity of the British to export capital has further undermined their ability to control the environment into which they are implanted.

There has been relatively little in British policy that parallels the American tendency to take aggressive measures against actors in the advanced industrial arena. Indeed, the preceding discussion has indicated that this is the least likely pattern to manifest itself in British policies. The British have for a variety of reasons shown themselves unwilling to contemplate the use of economic sanctions against other societies and have little in the way of extraterritorial legal weapons. At several points in the 1980s they found themselves resisting the blandishments or threats of their major ally, the USA, as its leaders pressed for the imposition of sanctions or the application of extraterritorial legislation on such products as computers. As time has passed and others have failed to respond positively to British openness, there have been heard voices advocating reciprocity in trade measures, and indeed a number of 'voluntary export restraint' agreements have been reached with Japan through the agency of the EC. Once again, the brutal fact appears to be that the British cannot afford to risk the consequences of aggression and that they thus resign themselves to the substantial and continuing costs of accommodation or acquiescence.

One way of defraying or diluting these costs is undoubtedly international co-operation. The British have shown themselves eager to participate in the management of interdependence and are assiduous in their support for international economic co-ordination. This very much supports the arguments of those who suggest that the uncertainties of the 'post-hegemonial' or 'post-multilateral' era will generate a persistent demand for mechanisms of international co-operation. In order to maximize their information about developments in the world economy and to reduce the uncertainties attending their position in the advanced industrial arena, the British subscribe to a multitude of arrangements in the field of trade, currencies, industry, energy and so on. Western

Economic Summits, the Group of Five, the Group of Ten, OECD, the International Energy Agency: the list is extensive and growing. It is painfully true, however, that the proceedings of these group-ings have a tendency to reflect the economic vitality and muscle of their members and that often the relatively dependent position of the British is magnified by the attempt to co-operate.[4] None the less, it is implicit in the argument here that the attempt to co-operate, however painful it may be, is essential to any hope the British have of surviving in the advanced industrial arena.

The pattern of British responses to their predicament therefore appears to reflect the 'accommodative-cooperative' part of the spectrum rather than the 'defensive-aggressive' area. Given the openness, integration and vulnerability of the UK as a member of the advanced industrial world, such a conclusion might have been predicted, mirroring as it undoubtedly does the intractability of the circumstances faced by the policy-makers. It also underlines the fact that the problems of knowledge, control, costs and adaptation are strongly influenced for any society by the way in which it experiences the demands of interdependence. The question now is, what do such judgements enable us to conclude about Britain's role in the advanced industrial arena?

Conclusions

This chapter has presented a picture of British policies within the advanced industrial arena using three central dimensions: first, the changing British position within the arena; second, the problems this creates for policy-making; third, the characteristics of the policy responses produced by British governments. It is clear from the evidence examined that Britain's position in the advanced industrial world has shown three major features. In the first place, the UK has remained one of the most 'open' of the industrial countries, committed to multilateralism and to the free movement of goods and capital. This openness has been accompanied by two other features which are the source of some important constraints and problems: on the one hand, the progressive integration of the UK into the advanced industrial world, speeded by the end of empire and the advent of EC membership and, on the other, the persistent fragility and vulnerability of the British economy. When it comes to policy-making, British governments have faced the need to adjust to their changing position, but have experienced considerable restrictions on their ability either to influence the changing agenda or to co-ordinate policies effectively. The policy responses that have emerged fall broadly into a pattern of accommodation or co-operation, but it is important to remember that these responses have been produced from a position of relative weakness and vulnerability rather than one of strength and resilience. From such conclusions as these, two important questions flow: first, how much choice or freedom of manoeuvre do British governments have in their dealings with the industrial world; second, what role is desirable or achievable for Britain in the advanced industrial arena of the 1980s and 1990s?

Not surprisingly, there are no clear-cut or decisive answers to these questions. It is clear, though, that the range of choice available to British governments has depended and will depend on Britain's collective ability to generate resource power and on the policy-makers' capacity to use interdependence rather than being constrained by it. If the performance and resilience of the economy can be improved, then the basis for greater freedom of manoeuvre will be laid. The question of role is connected to the issue of choice, but is in many ways more intangible; policy-makers' conceptions of the achievable or the desirable are influenced both by objective forces and constraints and by their experience or their capacity to adapt.

Pursuing this line of argument, it is possible to discern three 'alternative futures' for Britain in the advanced industrial arena. The first – and the most optimistic – is that of 'hero': the pain and sacrifice of maintaining a commitment to multilateralism would be repaid by a resurgence of British economic vitality and thus of influence within the industrial world. A second future is less sanguine, seeing Britain as 'villain': here, the incorrigible nostalgia of the British policy-making elite and the pernicious influence of class and financial interests would combine to perpetuate and worsen the dependence of the UK on external forces, at the expense both of economic development and of political autonomy. Finally, it is possible to see a future for Britain as 'victim': in common with other AICs, the UK would continue to be penetrated by forces beyond the control of any one government which would restrict the domain of choice implicit in the roles both of 'hero' and 'villain' and which would allow only the disjointed and incremental policy responses that are characteristic of those trapped in webs of complex interdependence.

The reality of the late 1980s and the 1990s will inevitably be an amalgam of forces, choices and roles for Britain. It is plain that the UK's role in the industrial world is an untidy blend of long experience, historic transformations and elemental social forces as well as the turbulence of the contemporary era. Whilst these coexisting elements can also be discerned in other arenas of policy, it is at least arguable that the advanced industrial arena brings them more forcefully to the notice of policy-makers than any other sphere of activity.

Notes

1 The membership of OECD in 1987 was: Australia, Austria, Belgium, Canada, Denmark, Finland, France, West Germany, Greece, Iceland, Ireland, Italy, Japan, Luxembourg, Netherlands, New Zealand, Norway, Portugal, Spain, Sweden, Switzerland, Turkey, United Kingdom, USA. Since this includes all members of the European Community, it serves as a convenient definition of the 'advanced industrial arena'.

2 The tables on the following two pages indicate on the one hand the changing direction and concentation of Britain's external trade and on the other the major focuses of outward and inward direct investment involving Britain.

3 A good example of this phenomenon is provided by the field of information technology, where the Thatcher government initiated the so-called 'Alvey programme' in an attempt to bring together the resources of government, industry and research establishments. Delays and inadequacies in funding, coupled to the absence of a coherent and well-defined overall strategy, meant that the programme was severely handicapped in relation to its foreign competitors.

4 There are numerous examples of this problem. In the EC context, the persistent difficulties over British budget contributions and the ambivalence of Britain's position in relation to the European Monetary System (EMS) are perhaps the most notable. Another interesting range of examples is furnished by collaboration in the fields of aerospace and 'big science': here, the financial limitations on Britain's ability to play a full and consistent role can be observed in projects as diverse as the European Airbus, the Ariane space launcher and the nuclear research programme at CERN in Geneva.

Table 10.1　*Area Composition of UK Merchandise Trade, 1955–85*
(percentages)

	imports c.i.f.				exports f.o.b.			
	1955	1970	1980	1985	1955	1970	1980	1985
Western Europe	25.7	41.5	55.9	63.1	28.9	46.2	57.6	58.3
EEC[1]	12.6	27.1	41.3	46.0	15.0	29.4	43.4	46.3
North America	19.5	20.5	15.0	13.8	12.0	15.2	11.2	17.0
USA	10.9	12.9	12.1	11.7	7.1	11.6	9.6	14.7
Other developed[2]	14.2	9.4	6.8	7.5	21.1	11.8	5.6	4.8
Japan	0.6	1.5	3.4	4.9	0.6	1.8	1.3	1.3
Total developed countries	59.4	71.4	77.7	84.3	62.0	73.2	74.5	80.0
Centrally planned economies	2.7	4.2	2.1	2.2	1.7	3.8	2.8	2.0
Oil-exporting countries	9.2	9.1	8.6	3.3	5.1	5.8	10.1	7.6
Other developing countries[3]	28.7	15.3	11.3	10.0	31.2	17.2	12.4	10.1
Total	100.0	100.0	100.0	100.0	100.0	100.0	100.0	100.0

Notes:　1　excluding Greece
　　　　　2　Japan, plus Australia, New Zealand and South Africa
　　　　　3　subject to minor changes in classification over time.
Source:　Green and Metcalfe, 1986, p. 146.

Table 10.2　*Investors in the UK, 1962–83*

	Percentage of stock of investments from[1]			
	USA	EEC	Japan	Other
1962	64	10	0	26
1971	64	13	0	23
1974	56	17	0	27
1978	58	18	0	24
1981	56	15	2	27
1982–3[2]	49	20	4	27

Notes:　1　Excludes oil, insurance, and banking
　　　　　2　Flows of inward direct investments, excludes oil
Source:　Stopford and Turner, 1985, p. 5.

Table 10.3   *Top Ten Investment Territories for the UK 1962–81*

1962	1968	1972	1978	1981
1 Australia	Australia	Australia	USA	USA
2 Canada	Canada	USA	Australia	Australia
3 USA	South Africa	Canada	South Africa	South Africa
4 South Africa	USA	South Africa	Germany	Germany
5 India	India	Germany	Canada	Canada
6 Malaysia	France	France	France	France
7 New Zealand	Germany	India	Benelux	Netherlands
8 Rhodesia	Malaysia	Malaysia	Brazil	Hong Kong
9 Nigeria	New Zealand	Netherlands	Switzerland	Irish Republic
10 France	Irish Republic	Irish Republic	Irish Republic	Nigeria

Note: Excludes oil, banking, and insurance; measured by book values of accumulated investments.

Source: Stopford and Turner, 1985, p. 81.

PART IV

Conclusion

11 The Study of British Foreign Policy

RICHARD LITTLE

The aim of this book has been to provide a general introduction to British foreign policy. Although it was never intended to offer a comprehensive or complete picture, the various authors have tried, nevertheless, to cover a good deal of ground in each chapter and they have relied, as a consequence, upon broad brush strokes rather than detailed filigree. Britain emerges from the analysis as a country which is having to manage two complex sets of foreign policy problems: one associated with its decline in the international hierarchy of states and the other associated with the need to adapt to an increasingly interdependent international system. The contributors broadly agree, first, that the British response has been complicated and contradictory and, second, that there has been growing disaffection with the British response. The domestic consensus which enveloped British foreign policy at the end of the Second World War has been largely dissipated. Almost every aspect of British foreign policy can now engender political controversy.

The purpose of this final chapter is not to pull together the specific findings that have emerged about British foreign policy or to provide an overarching summary. Instead, there is a return to the more general themes introduced at the beginning of the book. Smith and Smith suggest in Chapter 1 that foreign policy analysis has revolved around two central disputes. I want to show that although the intervening chapters do not address either of these debates directly, they do still shed considerable light on them.

The first debate centres on the role of theory in foreign policy analysis. At one extreme, the foreign policy analyst is depicted as an empirical historian who eschews theory and uses the facts to provide a coherent narrative of international events. At the other extreme, the analyst is seen as a scientist who develops theories to explain the foreign behaviour of states. The second debate concerns two divergent theoretical views about the international context in which foreign policy takes place. According to the traditionalist school of thought, foreign policy continues to be conducted in a world made up of autonomous nation states which still rely, in the final analysis, on military force to defend their interests. States, it is argued, have enduring interests which foreign policy-makers have a responsibility to foster and defend. The traditionalists, however, have come under fierce attack from a transformationalist school of thought which argues that the nature of international relations has undergone dramatic changes since 1945. The development of nuclear weapons has meant that the two superpowers can no longer consider that it is rational for them to engage in violent conflict. At the same time, the economic interests of all states have become tightly enmeshed and states have no alternative but to co-ordinate their domestic and international economic policies. The distinction between domestic and foreign policy has broken down and bilateral diplomacy, underpinned in the past by the potential to employ force, has given way to bureaucratic, multilateral bargaining where the threat of force has become an anachronism.

Expressed so bluntly, both debates are being caricatured or stereotyped to a certain extent. Yet there is no doubt that these debates exist, that academics have been influenced by them and that there have been some attempts to reconcile the competing positions. Knorr and Rosenau (1969), for example, have suggested that the divergent epistemological positions represented in the first debate are essentially compatible and that co-operation rather than conflict between analysts should be encouraged. Knorr has also endeavoured to close the gap between the traditionalist and the transformationalist assessment of force in the contemporary world. Having initially stressed the growing irrelevance of force, Knorr felt it necessary later to qualify his position and point to areas where the significance of force in international politics continues (1966, 1977).

The analysis in this book, however, does not reflect such a compromise; instead, it can be shown to transcend the divergent arguments made in the two debates. In the first place, it is made apparent that the concern with theory is not a purely academic phenomenon. Practitioners are also shown to rely upon a theoretical perspective. In the second place, practitioners are shown to subscribe to both traditionalist and transformationalist perspectives, with the result that British foreign policy is characterized by a high degree of ambiguity and contradiction.

The first section of this chapter suggests that the epistemological base to this book can best be described in hermeneutic terms. A hermeneutic approach is shown to cut across the established epistemological debate. The second section illustrates how previous chapters demonstrate that British practitioners are wedded to both a traditionalist and a transformationalist perspective. The third section concentrates on the contradictions and ambiguities in British foreign policy revealed in earlier chapters. It is concluded, therefore, that the analysis in this book not only helps to illuminate the nature of British foreign policy, but also exposes the strengths of a hermeneutic approach.

Theory in Foreign Policy Analysis

The original intention behind this book was to use a scientific approach to lay bare the nature of British foreign policy. It was hoped to show how a more theoretical approach to foreign policy analysis could yield new insights into the character of the foreign policy process in Britain. In this way, it was intended to kill two birds with one stone – providing an improved understanding of British foreign policy while demonstrating the virtues of a scientific approach to foreign policy analysis. In the event, none of the preceding chapters has made any self-conscious reference to the techniques and terminology normally associated with the scientific school. There are, for example, no allusions to the abstract theoretical frameworks or elaborate typologies which so often characterize this literature. Nevertheless, I want to argue that the original commitment to the virtues of a theoretical approach to foreign policy analysis has not been abandoned. There has been no sudden conversion to the cause of barefoot empiricism. Instead, I hope to show that the contributors have relied upon a hermeneutic rather than a positivist view of science and theory.

The positivist believes that there is no distinction to be drawn between studying nature and society. For the positivist, theory is designed to give a disinterested explanation of behaviour. In the social sciences, theory is generally couched in language which is quite alien to the actors whose actions are being theorized about, because the theory is external to their beliefs. The analyst is seen to be an outside investigator endeavouring to make sense of observed behaviour. There is a presumption made by the positivist that social actors cannot themselves provide adequate explanations of their own behaviour. And it is also presumed that there is no difference in principle between explanations of natural and social phenomena.

By contrast, the hermeneutist draws a sharp contrast between natural and social science. Hermeneutics was originally identified with the analysis of religious and literary texts, but it is now widely recognized that the approach has important lessons for the study of social action (Warnke, 1985; Hekman, 1986). Indeed, the text has even been regarded as a metaphor for social action (Ricoeur, 1981). The original protagonists argued that hermeneutics opened up the way for a scientific analysis of texts and, by the same token, it is now accepted that hermeneutics represents a scientific approach to the analysis of society but one which breaks with the natural science tradition associated with positivism.

The hermeneutist, therefore, makes no attempt to dispense with the idea of theory. On the contrary, the hermeneutist presupposes that it is necessary to acknowledge and to think about social theory on two dimensions. On the first dimension, theory is associated with the beliefs of the social actor. It is assumed that everyone has a theory of the world and that it is possible to describe and account for social behaviour through the medium of this theory. To understand social behaviour, therefore, it is necessary to step inside a circle described by the social actor. Within the circle lies the social actor's belief system or theory and once the theory is understood, it becomes possible to provide the actor's own explanation of social behaviour. The analyst must learn how to enter and move around the hermeneutic circle and view the world in the same terms as the social actors. Giddens has stressed the importance of this dimension of analysis and argues that by neglecting it, social scientists have underestimated the abilities of social actors. The persistence of any society needs to be understood in terms of the 'skilled accomplishment of active human subjects' (1976, p. 154). Giddens argues that this accomplishment involves 'practical theorizing' (p. 52) on the one hand, and 'ongoing reflexive monitoring' (p. 156) of behaviour on the other. In other words, social actors have an evolving and sophisticated theory of social reality, which is directly comparable to the conception of theory employed by social scientists.

But the hermeneutist also accepts that there is a second dimension to theory which must be established by anyone who wishes to develop a critical understanding of social reality. The second dimension requires the analyst to step back out of the circle described by the social actor and reassess the theories contained within it. Once this is done, it becomes possible to see that the theories may be inaccurate and lead to consequences undesired by those who hold them. The second dimension, as a consequence, opens up the possibility of raising questions about the potential for alternative courses of action. An analyst can postulate that the nature of reality would change if the social actors adhered to a different theory of reality. On this basis, it becomes possible to criticize the actions of social actors. The criticism rests on the assumption that with a different theory, social actors could operate more successfully. The hermeneutic approach is, therefore, profoundly concerned about alternative outcomes for social situations. It is not only interested in reality, but also in counter-factual realities – realities which do not exist but which potentially could emerge.

The analysis in this book, it seems to me, eschews the coldly clinical and disinterested view of theory propounded by the positivists and adopts a reflexive, involving, hermeneutic conception of theory. The analysts can be observed constantly moving in and out of the hermeneutic circle, seeking on the one hand to identify the theoretical orientation of the foreign policy-makers, and on the other to offer a critical assessment of this situation.

It is tempting to think that the hermeneutic approach to theory not only transcends the debate, amongst foreign policy analysts, about epistemology but can also be related to the debate between the traditionalists and transformationalists. There are, in fact, some grounds for thinking that the views of the traditionalist have been derived from the practitioner, operating within the hermeneutic circle, whereas the transformationalist, by contrast, can be seen to stand outside the circle, criticizing the views of the traditionalist.

Rothstein, for example, is a transformationalist who believes that statesmen have habitually been attracted to a traditional or, as he puts it, realist perspective (1972). He is highly sceptical, however, of the power-political, state-centric view propagated by the traditional realist. Nevertheless, it would appear that the realist, while denying the validity of the transformationalist position, is happy to acknowledge the link with the practitioner's view of the world. Morgenthau, for example, notes that it is necessary for the realist to look over the statesman's shoulder and to 'read and anticipate his very thoughts' (1973, p. 5). The same point is made, on the opposite side of the coin, by Brown who asserts that although few high officials have formally studied Morgenthau, his ideas, nevertheless, could well serve as a 'codification of the model of international relations implicit in most United States foreign policy decisions' (1984, p. 208). So, at first sight, it does not seem unreasonable to associate the traditionalist perspective with a view established within the hermeneutic circle and the transformationalist perspective with a view established beyond the circumference of the circle.

Unfortunately, however, although intuitively attractive and despite being endorsed by analysts like Brown and Rothstein, this attempt to relate the debate between traditionalists and transformationalists to the different dimensions of hermeneutic analysis is invalid. In practice, policy-makers do not subscribe exclusively to the traditionalist perspective. The diversity of perspectives adopted by policy-makers is very evident, for example, in the dispute between Acheson and Macmillan about Britain's foreign policy posture at the beginning of the 1960s. In the well-known speech to the US Military Academy at West Point in 1962, already alluded to in earlier chapters, Dean Acheson asserted that

> Great Britain has lost an empire and has not yet found a role. The attempt to play a separate power role – that is, a role apart from Europe, a role based on a 'special relationship' with the United States, a role based on being the head of a 'Commonwealth' which has no political structure, unity or strength and enjoys a fragile and precarious economic relationship by means of the sterling area and preferences in the British market – this role is about played out! (*Keesing's*, 1963–4, p. 19181)

It is hard to imagine a clearer expression of the traditionalist's position. Acheson was indicating that Britain's status as a great power had finally collapsed and that the various mechanisms being used by the British policy-makers to maintain Britain's power position were self-evidently ineffective. His advice was clear: Britain had no alternative but to accept a new position lower down on the power hierarchy.

The reply by Macmillan, who was Prime Minister at the time, is instructive. He did not attempt to defend Britain's posture in terms of the traditionalist frame of reference employed by Acheson. Instead, he shifted the ground of the argument and used a transformationalist's perspective to attack the traditionalist assumptions underpinning the argument made by Acheson. Macmillan insisted that he could accept Acheson's claim that Britain could no longer play a separate power role only if the assertion was extended to the United States and every other country in the free world. The activity of all these states, he suggested, was constrained by the doctrine of interdependence which precludes the possibility of any state's using power to serve its interests. Ironically, most academics at this time still viewed the international arena from a traditionalist perspective. By contrast, the interest in a transformationalist perspective was, from a very early stage, an active concern of the policy-maker. As Keohane and Nye have argued, by the beginning of the 1970s interdependence had begun to rival national security as the 'prime symbol' of the foreign policy-maker (1977, p. 7). It follows, therefore, that there is no easy way of relating traditionalist and transformationalist perspectives to the views which prevail inside and outside the hermeneutic circle. A review of the analysis of British foreign policy offered in this book reveals the influence of the two perspectives on both sides of the circle.

Traditionalism, Transformationalism and the Policy-Maker

There is no doubt that the traditionalist perspective continues to play an important role in British policy-making, with the international arena being conceived in essentially power terms and force being considered to play a vital role in the transactions between states. For British policy-makers, therefore, a key defining characteristic of the contemporary international arena is the bipolar struggle between the United States and the Soviet Union. A good deal of British policy can be identified in the context of this struggle. In particular, British policy-makers, well aware of the dynamic character of power, have become acutely conscious of the extent to which British power, relative to the power of other states, has been on the wane during the course of the twentieth century. Ever since the end of the Second World War, as a consequence, there have been persistent attempts to limit the effects of this decline.

At the heart of these efforts has been the determination to maintain an independent nuclear deterrent. In a world where military power counts, and where the possession of nuclear weapons represents a necessary feature of any state with front-rank pretensions, it has appeared incontrovertible to British policy-makers that they must make every effort to maintain a nuclear deterrent. The difficulties attached to maintaining an independent nuclear deterrent have been evident ever since 1962, when the British had to seek assistance from the Americans at Nassau. Yet each successive administration has sought to prolong the life of the deterrent.

The desire to possess a nuclear deterrent reflects a belief in the continuing importance of military power. It follows, therefore, as Tooze shows in Chapter 6, that security continues to be defined in military rather than economic terms. Decision-makers in Britain are still willing to devote scarce resources to the military in preference to public services because they believe that, in the final analysis, guns must come before butter. In an adversarial international political system, a state has no alternative but to give priority to the means of defending itself.

Another indicator of the importance attributed to the traditionalist perspective by British policy-makers is the significance accorded to the 'special relationship' between Britain and the United States. Because of Britain's former worldwide ties and the dispersal of British people around the world, it would be possible for the British to identify and cultivate special relationships with many countries around the world. But for British policy-makers, there is only one special relationship which matters. The relationship with the United States is given constant care and attention not because of historical ties and cultural links, but because the United States is the most powerful country in the world. By nurturing this relationship the British policy-makers hope that in a world where power counts above all, it will be possible to offset some of the effects of their own loss of power. Paradoxically, therefore, there is a positive advantage to requiring American assistance to maintain an independent nuclear deterrent, because it has the effect of highlighting and reinforcing the existence of the special relationship.

From the traditionalist perspective, any state which gives priority to its military capabilities will be able to exert influence in the international arena out of proportion to its inherent power capabilities. The British belief in the traditionalist perspective has encouraged them to pursue this strategy. As White indicates in Chapter 7, British policy-makers continue to believe that despite their decline in power they still possess the capacity to play a global role and this belief is reflected in various attempts to operate as mediator in the conflict between the United States and the Soviet Union. Indeed, Hill, in Chapter 2, discusses the view that not only have British policy-makers clung tenaciously to a traditionalist perspective but that, under the potent influence of nostalgia, like old men who refuse to acknowledge the loss of youth, British decision-makers continue to operate as if they were still in charge of a great power. But, as Hill demonstrates, it would be a mistake to overemphasize this illusion. In general, policy-makers, conscious of Britain's dwindling power, have looked around for means of slowing down the process and alleviating the consequences. It is in this context, for example, that the Zircon plan to develop an expensive, high-technology British system of military intelligence-gathering by satellite makes sense. As McGrew indicates in Chapter 5, the decision-makers have managed to maintain an artificially high military profile for Britain, given its overall power resources. This profile can be defended by the traditionalist but from the standpoint of the transformationalist it can only be described, in McGrew's terms, as 'eccentric'.

Before turning to the influence of a transformationalist perspective on foreign policy, however, it is worth reiterating how deeply the traditionalist perspective remains embedded in the British approach to foreign policy. On the institutional front, Clarke observes, in Chapter 4, how the administration of foreign policy continues to be highly centralized and McGrew notes that many key decisions in the foreign policy arena have been made without reference even to the Cabinet. Despite the emergence of the committee system, the influence of Parliament remains effectively marginalized. Moreover, policy-makers assume that the general public endorses the traditionalist's image of international politics. As Allen demonstrates in Chapter 8, despite the involvement of Britain in collective decision-making in Europe, there has never been any attempt to suggest to the British people that these actions directly impinge upon Britain's capacity to operate as an independent international actor. There has been a failure to grasp this nettle not because it is unseen but because it is believed that the average citizen finds the traditionalist's perspective persuasive and attractive.

Although public opinion in Britain may, in general, remain wedded to the traditionalist's theory of foreign policy, it has certainly been challenged in practice by the policy-makers. There has been a very widespread recognition that major transformations have been taking place in every dimension of foreign policy-making. In the first place, it has been recognized that power is no longer a fungible commodity. So, although Britain is still a very powerful state, relative to other states in the Commonwealth, Vogler shows in Chapter 9 that the survival of this institution has depended upon the willingness of the British not to make any attempt to sit in the driving seat. Britain's officials remain anxious to preserve the Commonwealth. But they have recognized and accepted that this can only happen if they are prepared to acknowledge and respond to the sensitivities of other Commonwealth members.

It has also been recognized that there are now almost no areas touching upon Britain's core interests where policy-makers have been left with independent or autonomous powers of decision-making. Instead, policy emerges on the basis of co-ordination with other states. McGrew, for example, notes how much of Britain's defence policy is now made through transgovernmental networks of civilian and military elites. Many decisions about strategic doctrine, intelligence, the procurement and deployment of weapons, and almost every other aspect of defence decision-making have been internationalized. The decisions are made in the committees of institutions which lie beyond the autonomy of the state. This development is an inevitable consequence of interdependent defence arrangements associated with the establishment of NATO. British decision-makers, like the other members of NATO, have had to accept that they are part of a co-ordinated alliance system which considerably constrains the freedom of manoeuvre for the partners.

For very different reasons, a similar phenomenon has occurred in the economic arena. As Smith reveals in Chapter 10, in the context of the advanced industrial countries, external economic relations, in certain key respects, are no longer within the control of the state. Britain has done as much as any country to promote a liberal or open world economy and the consequence is that many key decisions which can have a vital effect on the British economy are made by actors, inside and outside Britain, over whom the government has no immediate or direct control. Having encouraged the growth of an interdependent and transnational world economy, successive British governments have felt constrained to live with the consequences, rather than to adopt a defensive strategy which would aim to reduce the openness of Britain to the outside world or an aggressive strategy which would endeavour to make others pay the costs of the open economy. Instead, the British policy-makers have remained firmly committed to a strategy of accommodation and co-ordination, whereby governments agree to policies which will regulate their economies on a collaborative basis. It is argued that attempts to regulate the British economy on a national or even a regional basis are counterproductive and there is a commitment to identify solutions on an international level.

The greatest transformation in the attitude of British policy-makers, however, can be observed in the European context where, as Allen shows, there are now few areas of national governmental activity which do not have some kind of input from the European Community. Intervention within the community takes place at every level of government and the growth of transgovernmental politics has meant that all the European governments are finding it difficult to maintain a coherent posture. Allen cites the example of heads of government calling for a reduction in agricultural spending, while the agriculture ministers were calling for an increase in expenditure. Allen indicates how the British have been in the forefront of attempts to develop mechanisms which will permit the smooth co-ordination of policy within the Community. In the same vein, Clarke identifies an inexorable shift towards more horizontal bureaucratic structures between ministries and departments within Britain and across national boundaries. There has, in other words, been a substantial institutional response by British policy-makers who have recognized the need to accommodate the growth of interdependence and transnationalism.

Traditionalism, Transformationalism and the Analyst

There is no doubt that both traditional and transformational perspectives have a powerful hold on contemporary British policy-makers in the foreign policy arena. Once the analysts step out of the hermeneutic circle, however, it becomes necessary for them to explore in more detail the tension between these two perspectives and to identify the consequences of pushing, simultaneously, for the autonomy and the interdependence of Britain in the international community.

There is, in the first place, an obvious tension between the desire by British policy-makers to preserve Britain's status in the international power hierarchy of states and the desire to develop Britain as a successful modern society integrated into an interdependent international community. As Tooze argues, the emphasis on military security occurs at the expense of economic security. In the same vein, non-military factors which are designed to promote the image of Britain as a great power, such as the emphasis on advanced military technology and the perceived need to retain the capacity to regulate the value of the pound, are depicted as virility symbols which cannot be afforded by a state with an ailing economy.

The infrastructure of Britain, therefore, is seen to have suffered, in part, because of the attempts to preserve Britain's power status. In Chapter 3, Farrands argues that these attempts are counterproductive because they conflict with the image of urban decay and inner-city violence in Britain projected by the world's media. The reality is that Britain cannot hope to compete militarily with the two superpowers and, ironically, when comparisons are made with other states further down the power hierarchy, the indicators used are invariably economic and social rather than military. The British, therefore, have fallen between two stools. It turns out that they cannot compete successfully with either of the superpowers in military terms or with the middle-ranking powers in socio-economic terms.

A second area of tension exists between the attempt to maintain

British autonomy and the desire to promote co-ordinated international policies. As Allen argues, the tension has caused particular irritation in Britain's relations with Europe, where the interest in co-ordination has all too often been overshadowed by the running battle over Britain's budgetary contribution which has been taken as a symbol of the fact that Britain's commitment to Europe is less whole-hearted than that of the other European partners. Instead, Britain is seen to hanker after a global role. Attention is drawn to the British desire to play the part of international mediator or go-between in order to boost its otherwise impoverished position.

The major consequence of the tension between the traditional and transformational postures has been the growth of disaffection with British foreign policy. The disaffection is most evident in the context of defence where there are growing divides within and between the various political parties. The consensus surrounding Britain's independent deterrent and its role in NATO has been steadily eroded and has now virtually disappeared. But it is not only in defence where the differences lie. There are major disagreements in the economic sphere about whether Britain should continue to defend the liberal, open economy or should adopt a more closed and defensive stance. There are disagreements about the role of sanctions against South Africa, about Britain's relationship with the Commonwealth and with institutions like UNESCO. To a very large extent, these disagreements can be traced to the tension between the traditionalist and transformationalist perspectives on foreign policy.

Conclusion

The debate between traditionalists and transformationalists has conventionally been depicted as academic in character, representing a theoretical dispute between two competing schools of thought in foreign policy analysis. It has been suggested in this chapter, however, that such an assessment fails to appreciate that both perspectives can be observed in operation amongst policy-makers. It is not, in essence, an academic dispute, but a feature of foreign policy itself. There is, it has been argued here, an inherent tension in British foreign policy. On the one hand, there is a set of policies which are designed to maintain the position of Britain as a powerful and autonomous state. On the other hand, there is, at the same time, another set of policies which are endeavouring to accommodate British foreign policy to operating in an interdependent and transnational environment. Like Janus, British policy-makers appear to be looking in opposite directions at the same time. There is, therefore, an underlying inconsistency or ambivalence to British foreign policy which precipitates ambiguity. Policies are being implemented which pull in different directions.

What this book reveals, therefore, is that the academic debate between the traditionalists and the transformationalists is more complex than is often supposed. There has been a tendency for the debate to be assessed in positivist terms, with academics being drawn to either the transformational or the traditional camp on the grounds that one or the other provides the most effective theoretical framework for understanding contemporary foreign policy. The pervasive influence of positivism, therefore, has tended to mask the fact that British policy-makers have been influenced by both perspectives. It is not possible as a consequence to understand British foreign policy without drawing attention to traditionalism and transformationalism. Once it is acknowledged that policy-makers are influenced by both perspectives, however, it follows that when academics enter the debate, they are inevitably becoming involved in a discourse about foreign policy practice. The hermeneutists have no difficulty acknowledging the inevitability of this position; they have always recognized that there is no clear-cut divide to be drawn between standing inside and outside of the hermeneutic circles. The boundary is permeable and ideas can filter from one side to the other. There is, as a result, a recursive relationship between analysts and practitioners.

Standing outside the hermeneutic circle, the analysts in this book have identified a tension between policies based on the traditional and the transformational perspectives. There seems, moreover, to be a broad consensus that British policy-makers must move beyond the logic of the traditional perspective and accept the logic of the transformational perspective. It is clear that such a consensus does not exist in the political arena where there are growing divisions about the direction which British foreign policy should take in the future. The arguments developed in this book, therefore, are not purely academic. The analysis is not simply designed to improve our understanding of foreign policy, but aims also to change its direction and the way in which it is formulated. In particular, it has been argued that the continuing attempt to preserve Britain's status as an independent military power conflicts with a realistic assessment of Britain's power potential and with the efforts to co-ordinate and harmonize its economic and social policies with other states. The nuclear policy, the special relationship with the United States and the panoply of policies designed to enhance Britain's status as an autonomous and influential state, inevitably conflict with the attempts by Britain to integrate with other states. The dissonance between these two policy perspectives has been exacerbated by the persistent attempts to shroud Britain's military posture with secrecy. Repeated attempts by British governments to restrict the public scrutiny of military policy inevitably raise questions about the openness of its policies in other areas. There is, therefore, a polemical edge to the discourse developed in this book. It follows that the essays are not only endeavouring to provide an account of the past and the present, but are, more ambitiously, hoping to bear the weight of policies in the future.

Bibliography

Aaronovitch, S., Smith, R. *et al.* (1981), *The Political Economy of British Capitalism: A Marxist Analysis* (London: McGraw-Hill).

Adler-Karlsson, G. (1982), 'Instruments of economic coercion and their use', in F. Alting Von Geusau and J. Pelkmans (eds), *National Economic Security: Perceptions, Threats and Policies* (Tilburg: J. F. Kennedy Institute), pp. 160–205.

Allen, D. (1978), 'Foreign policy at the European level: beyond the nation-state?' in W. Wallace and W. E. Paterson (eds), *Foreign Policy Making in Western Europe* (Farnborough: Saxon House), pp. 135–54.

Allen, D. and Pijpers, A. (eds) (1985), *European Foreign Policy Making and the Arab-Israeli Conflict* (The Hague: Nijhoff).

Allen, D., Rummel, R. and Wessels, W. (eds) (1982), *European Political Co-operation* (London: Butterworth).

Allison, G. T. (1971), *Essence of Decision: Explaining the Cuban Missile Crisis* (Boston, Mass.: Little, Brown).

Alt, J. E. (1979), *The Politics of Economic Decline* (Cambridge: Cambridge University Press).

Alting Von Geusau, F. and Pelkmans, J. (eds) (1982), *National Economic Security: Perceptions, Threats and Policies* (Tilburg: J. F. Kennedy Institute).

Anell, L. (1981), *Recession, the Western Economies and the Changing World Order* (London: Pinter).

Arkin, W. and Fieldhouse, R. W. (1985), *Nuclear Battlefields: Global Links in the Arms Race* (Cambridge, Mass.: Ballinger).

Arnaud, D. (1986), 'What is Eureka?', *NATO Review*, vol. 34, no. 3, pp. 12–15.

Artis, M. and Ostry, S. (1986), *International Economic Policy Coordination* (London: Routledge & Kegan Paul).

Austin, D. (1986), 'A South African policy: six precepts in search of a diplomacy?', *International Affairs*, vol. 62, no. 3, pp. 391–403.

Axelrod, R. (1976), *The Structure of Decision* (Princeton, NJ.: Princeton University Press).

Barber, J. (1975), 'British foreign policy: a review of some recent literature', *British Journal of International Studies*, vol. 1, no. 3, pp. 272–82.

Barber, J. (1976), *Who Makes British Foreign Policy?* (Milton Keynes: Open University).

Barber, J. (1978), 'The study of British foreign policy: a reply to Brian White', *British Journal of International Studies*, vol. 4, no. 3, pp. 266–9.

Barker, E. (1983), *The British between the Superpowers 1945–50* (London: Macmillan).

Barnaby, F. and Thomas, G. (eds) (1982), *The Nuclear Arms Race: Control or Catastrophe* (London: Pinter).

Barnett, A. (1982), *Iron Britannia: Why Parliament Waged its Falklands War* (London: Allison & Busby).

Bartlett, C. J. (1977), 'The military instrument in British foreign policy', in J. Baylis (ed.), *British Defence Policy in a Changing World* (London: Croom Helm), pp. 30–51.

Baylis, J. (ed.) (1977), *British Defence Policy in a Changing World* (London: Croom Helm).

Baylis, J. (ed.) (1983), *Alternative Approaches to British Defence Policy* (London: Macmillan).

Baylis, J. (1984), *Anglo-American Defence Relations 1939–84*, 2nd edn (London: Macmillan).

Baylis, J. (1986), '"Greenwoodery" and British defence policy', *International Affairs*, vol. 62, no. 3, pp. 443–57.

Bell, C. (1962), *Negotiation From Strength* (London: Chatto & Windus).

Beloff, M. (1961), *New Dimensions in Foreign Policy*, (London: Allen & Unwin).

Berridge, G. (1980), 'The political theory and institutional history of states systems', *British Journal of International Studies*, vol. 6, no. 1, pp. 82–92.

Berridge, G. (1981), 'International relations', *Teaching Politics*, vol. 10, no. 1, pp. 78–84.

Berridge, G. (1982), 'International relations: reply to Smith', *Teaching Politics*, vol. 11, no. 1, pp. 30–2.

Blank S. (1977), 'Britain: the politics of foreign economic policy, the domestic economy, and the problem of pluralistic stagnation', *International Organization*, vol. 31, no. 4 (Autumn), pp. 673–721.

Boardman, R. (1976), *Britain and the People's Republic of China 1949–74* (London: Macmillan).

Boardman, R. and Groom, A. J. R. (eds) (1973), *The Management of Britain's External Relations* (London: Macmillan).

Brandon, H. (1970), *Anatomy of Error* (London: Deutsch).

Brandt Commission (1980), *North–South: A Programme for Survival* (London: Pan).

Brett, E. A. (1985), *The World Economy Since the War: The Politics of Uneven Development*. (London: Macmillan).

Brown, G. (1972), *In My Way* (Harmondsworth: Penguin).

Brown, R. G. S. (1971), *The Administrative Process in Britain* (London: Methuen).

Brown, S. (1984), *On the Front Burner: Issues in US Foreign Policy* (Boston, Mass.: Little, Brown).

Bull, H. (1977), *The Anarchical Society: A Study of Order in World Politics* (London: Macmillan).

Bullock, A. (1985), *Ernest Bevin: Foreign Secretary 1945–51* (Oxford: Oxford University Press).

Burton, J. *et al.* (1984), *Britain Between East and West: A Concerned Independence* (Aldershot: Gower).

Butler, D. (1979), 'Public opinion and Community membership', *Political Quarterly*, vol. 50, no. 2, pp. 151–6.

Butler, M. (1986), 'The Commonwealth: Britain can get along without it', *Financial Times*, 24 September.

Buzan, B. (1983), *People, States and Fear* (Brighton: Wheatsheaf).

Cable, J. (1981), 'The useful art of international relations', *International Affairs*, vol. 57, no. 2, pp. 301–14.

Cable, J. (1983), 'Interdependence: a drug or addiction?', *International Affairs*, vol. 59, no. 3, pp. 365–79.

Calder, A. (1971), *The People's War* (London: Panther).

Calleo, D. (1982), *The Imperious Economy* (Cambridge, Mass.: Harvard University Press).

Calvocoressi, P. (1978), *The British Experience 1945–75* (London: Bodley Head).

Capitanchik, D. (1982), *The Changing Attitude to Defence in Britain* (Centrepiece, Aberdeen: University of Aberdeen).

Carr, E. H. (1941), *The Twenty Years Crisis* (London: Macmillan).

Carrington, P. (1983), Alastair Buchan Memorial Lecture, *Survival*, vol. 25, no. 4, pp. 136–53.

Cawson, A. (ed.) (1985), *Organized Interests and the State* (London: Sage).

Ceadel, M. (1980), *Pacifism in Britain 1914–45* (Oxford: Clarendon Press).

Central Office of Information (1983), *Britain's Overseas Relations*, COI Reference Pamphlet no. 163 (London: HMSO).

Chalmers, M. (1985), *Paying for Defence: Military Spending and British Decline* (London: Pluto).

Charlton, M. (1981), 'How and why Britain lost the leadership of Europe', *Encounter*, vol. 58, no. 1, pp. 9–22.

Chichester, M. and Wilkinson, J. (1982), *The Uncertain Ally* (London: Gower).

Churchill, W. (1956–8), *The History of the English-Speaking Peoples*, 4 Vols (London: Cassell).

Clarke, M. (1978–9), 'The Foreign Office and its critics', *Millennium: Journal of International Studies*, vol. 7, no. 3, pp. 222–36.

Clarke, M. (1986), 'Foreign policy and comparative politics: a strange divide', *Politics*, vol. 6, no. 2, October 1986, pp. 3–9.

Clarke, M. (1987), 'The defence debate in Britain', in K. Kaiser and J. Roper (eds.), *British-German Defence Co-operation: European Partners within the Alliance* (London: Jane's), forthcoming.

Coates, D. (1984), *The Context of British Politics* (London: Hutchinson).

Cohen, B. J. (1977), *Organizing the World's Money* (London: Macmillan).

Colville, J. (1976), *Footprints in Time* (London: Collins).

Colville, J. (1981), *The Churchillians* (London: Weidenfeld & Nicolson).

Cooper, F. (1985), 'Affordable defence: in search of a strategy', *Royal United Services Institute Journal*, vol. 130, no. 5, pp. 1–6.

Cooper, R. (1968), *The Economics of Interdependence* (New York: McGraw-Hill).

Cooper, R. (1975), *Security and the Energy Crisis* (London: International Institute for Strategic Studies).

Cooper, R. N. (1985), 'Economic interdependence and co-ordination of economic policies', in R. W. Jones and P. B. Kenen (eds), *Handbook of International Economics*, vol. 2 (Oxford: North-Holland), pp. 1195–1234.

Cooper, R. and Hollick, A. L. (1985), 'International relations in a technologically advanced future', in A. G. Keatley (ed.), *Technological Frontiers and International Relations* (Washington DC: National Academy Press).

Cottam, R. (1977), *Foreign Policy Motivation: A General Theory and a Case Study* (Pittsburgh, PA: University of Pittsburgh Press), pp. 227–65.

Crewe, I. and Sarlvik, B. (1983), *Decade of Dealignment* (London: Cambridge University Press).

Dannenbring, F. (1985), 'Consultations: the political lifeblood of the Alliance', *NATO Review*, vol. 33, no. 6, pp. 5–11.

Darby, P. (1973), *British Defence Policy East of Suez 1947–68* (London: Oxford University Press).

Darby, P. (1977), 'East of Suez reassessed', in J. Baylis (ed.), *British Defence Policy in a Changing World* (London: Croom Helm), pp. 52–65.

Deutsch, K. (1978), *The Analysis of International Relations*, 2nd edn. (Englewood Cliffs, NJ: Prentice-Hall).

Documents on International Affairs 1959 (1963), (London: RIIA/Oxford University Press).

Documents on International Affairs 1960 (1964), (London: RIIA/Oxford University Press).

Dougherty, J. E. (1975), *British Perspectives on a Changing Global Balance* (London: Sage).

Eatwell, J. (1981), *Whatever Happened to Britain?* (London: Cambridge University Press).

Eden, A. (1960), *Memoirs: Full Circle* (London: Cassell).

Edwards, G. (1984), 'Europe and the Falkland Islands crisis 1982', *Journal of Common Market Studies*, vol. 22, no. 4, pp. 295–313.

Festinger, L. (1957), *A Theory of Cognitive Dissonance* (Evanston, Ill.: Row Peterson).

Frankel, J. (1975), *British Foreign Policy 1945–73* (London: Oxford University Press).

Frankel, J. (1981), 'Conventional and theorising diplomats: a critique', *International Affairs*, vol. 57, no. 4, pp. 537–48.

Freedman, L. (1980), *Britain and Nuclear Weapons* (London: Macmillan).

Freedman, L. (1983), 'British defence policy after the Falklands', in J. Baylis (ed.), *Alternative Approaches to British Defence Policy* (London: Macmillan), pp. 62–76.

Freedman, L. (1986), 'Defence policy after the next election', *Political Quarterly*, vol. 57, no. 4, pp. 364–81.

Fry, G. K. (1985) *The Changing Civil Service* (London: Allen & Unwin).

Fry, G. K. (1986), 'Inside Whitehall', in H. Drucker *et al.* (eds), *Developments in British Politics* (London: Mamillan), pp. 88–106.

Gaddis, J. L. (1982), *Strategies of Containment* (New York: Oxford University Press).

Galtung, J. (1971), 'A structural theory of imperialism', *Journal of Peace Research*, vol. 13, no. 2, pp. 81–94.

Galtung, J. (1978), *Peace and Social Structure: Essays in Peace Research*, Vol. 3, (Copenhagen: Christian Ejlers).

Gamble, A. (1985), *Britain in Decline*, 2nd edn (London: Macmillan).

Garnett, J. (1983), 'Some constraints on defence policy-makers', in A. G. McGrew and M. J. Wilson (eds) (1982), *Decision-Making: Approaches and Analysis* (Manchester: Manchester University Press/Open University), pp. 205–15.

Giddens, A. (1973), *The Class Structure of the Advanced Societies* (London: Hutchinson).

Giddens, A. (1976), *New Rules of Sociological Method: A Positive Critique of Interpretive Sociologies* (London: Hutchinson).

Gilbert, M. (1976), *Winston S. Churchill*, Vol. 5, *1922–39* (London: Heinemann).

Glasgow University Media Group (1985), *War and Peace News* (Milton Keynes: Open University Press).

Goldthorpe, J. (1980), *Social Mobility and Class Structure in Modern Britain* (Oxford: Clarendon Press).

Goodwin, G. and Mayall, J. (1977), 'The political dimension of the UNCTAD Integrated Commodity scheme', *Millennium: Journal of International Studies*, vol. 6, no. 2, pp. 146–61.

Gore-Booth, P. (1974), *With Great Truth and Respect* (London: Constable).

Grant, W. and Nath, S. (1984), *The Politics of Economic Policy-Making* (Oxford: Blackwell).

Green, S. J. and Metcalfe, J. S. (1986), 'Foreign trade and the balance of payments', in M. J. Artis (ed.), *The UK Economy: A Manual of Applied Economics*, 6th edn (London: Weidenfeld & Nicolson), pp. 130–202.

Greenwood, D. (1977), 'Defence and national priorities since 1945', in J. Baylis (ed.), *British Defence Policy in a Changing World* (London: Croom Helm), pp. 174–207.

Greenwood, D. (1985), 'Memorandum to the House of Commons Committee', in House of Commons Third Report from the Defence Committee, *Defence Commitments and Resources and the Defence Estimates 1985–86*, vol. 2, 23 May.

Gregory, F. (1982), 'The European Community and defence', *ADIU Report*, vol. 3, no. 2, pp. 5–9.

Hager, W. (1982), 'Perceptions of economic security', in F. Alting Von Geusau and J. Pelkmans (eds), *National Economic Security: Perceptions, Threats and Policies* (Tilburg: J. F. Kennedy Institute), pp. 19–46.

Hall, P. A. (1986), 'The state and economic decline', in B. Elbaum and W. Lazonick (eds), *The Decline of the British Economy* (Oxford: Clarendon Press), pp. 266–302.

Halsey, A. H. (1981), *Change in British Society* (London: Oxford University Press).

Hanrieder, W. F. and Auton, G. P. (1980), *The Foreign Policies of West Germany, France and Britain* (Englewood Cliffs, NJ: Prentice-Hall).

Harris, R. (1983), *Gotcha: The Media, the Government and the Falklands Crisis* (London: Faber).

Harrisson, T. (1976), *Living Through the Blitz* (London: Collins).

Hekman, S. J. (1986), *Hermeneutics and the Sociology of Knowledge* (Cambridge: Polity Press).

Held, D. (ed.) (1983), *States and Societies* (Oxford: Martin Robertson for Oxford University).

Henderson, N. (1979), 'Britain's decline: its causes and consequences', *The Economist*, 2 June, pp. 29–41.

Hennessy, P. (1985), 'Does the elderly Cabinet machine need oiling?', *The Listener*, 27 June, pp. 8–9.

Hennessy, P. (1986), 'How to control the secret state', *The Independent*, 3 December, p. 17.

Heseltine, M. (1984), 'The defence of Europe: Europe's interests, Europe's choices', *RUSI Journal*, vol. 129, no. 4, pp. 3–9.

Hill, C. (1974), 'The credentials of foreign policy analysis', *Millennium: Journal of International Studies*, vol. 3, no. 2, Autumn 1974, pp. 148–65.

Hill, C. (1979), 'Britain's elusive role in world politics', *British Journal of International Studies*, vol. 5, no. 3, pp. 248–59.

Hill, C. (1983a), 'Britain: a convenient schizophrenia', in C. Hill (ed.), *National Foreign Policies and European Political Co-operation* (London: Allen & Unwin), pp. 19–33.

Hill, C. (ed.) (1983b), *National Foreign Policies and European Political Cooperation* (London: Allen & Unwin).

Hill, C. and Wallace, W. (1979), 'Diplomatic trends in the European Community', *International Affairs*, vol. 55, no. 1, pp. 47–66.

Hindell, K. (1986), 'Britain leaves UNESCO', *World Today*, vol. 42, no. 2, p. 21.

HMSO (1967), *Supplementary Statement on Defence Policy 1967*, Cmnd 3357, July (London: HMSO).

HMSO (1968), *Supplementary Statement on Defence Policy 1968*, Cmnd 3701, July (London: HMSO).

HMSO (1969), *Review Committee on Overseas Representation*, Cmnd 4107, 'The Duncan Report' (London: HMSO).

HMSO (1977), *Miscellaneous No. 17: Selected Documents Relating to Problems of Security and Co-operation in Europe 1954–77*, Cmnd 6932 (London: HMSO).

HMSO (1977), *Review of Overseas Representation, Report by the Central Policy Review Staff*, 'The Berrill Report' (London: HMSO).

HMSO (1981a), *The United Kingdom's Defence Programme: The Way Forward*, Cmnd 8288 (London: HMSO).

HMSO (1981b), *Statement on the Defence Estimates, 1981*, pt 1, Cmnd 82121, pt 2, Cmnd 82122 (London: HMSO).

HMSO (1982), *The Falkland Campaign: the Lessons*, Cmnd 8758 (London: HMSO).

HMSO (1983), *Falklands Islands Review*, Cmnd 8787, 'The Franks Report' (London: HMSO).

HMSO (1984), *Statement on the Defence Estimates, 1984*, 1, Cmnd 9227–1 (London: HMSO).

HMSO (1986), *Statement on the Defence Estimates, 1986*, 1 Cmnd 9763–1 (London: HMSO).

Hocking, B. and Warhurst, J. (1986), 'Australia and Britain: drifting apart?', *The World Today*, vol. 42, no. 12, pp. 214–17.

Hoffmann, S. (1983), 'Reflections on the nation-state in Western Europe today', in L. Tsoukalis (ed.), *The European Community: Past, Present and Future* (Oxford: Blackwell), pp. 21–38.

House of Commons, Foreign Affairs Committee (1980), *Second Report from the House of Commons Foreign Affairs Committee, Session 1979–80, Foreign and Commonwealth Office Organisation*, HC 511 (London: HMSO).

House of Commons, Foreign Affairs Committee (1981), *Fifth Report from the House of Commons Foreign Affairs Committee, Session 1980–81, The Mexico Summit: The British Government's Role in the Light of the Brandt Report*, vols. I and II, HC 211–I, 211–II (London: HMSO).

House of Commons, Defence Committee (1982), *First Report, Session 1981–2, Allied Forces in Germany*, February (London: HMSO).

House of Commons, Defence Commitee (1985), *Third Report, Defence Commitments and Resources and the Defence Estimates 1985–86*, vol. 2, 23 May (London: HMSO).

House of Commons, Defence Commitee (1986), *Second Report, Statement on the Defence Estimates 1986*, 5 June (London: HMSO).

House of Lords (84–5), 238–I, *Report from the Select Committee on Overseas Trade*, vol. I (London: HMSO).

House of Lords (84–5), 238–II, *Report from the Select Committee on Overseas Trade*, vol. II, Oral Evidence (London: HMSO).

Hunt, J. and Owen, H. (1984), 'Taking stock of the seven-power summits: two views', *International Affairs*, vol. 60, no. 4, pp. 655–61.

Hurd, D. (1981), 'Political co-operation', *International Affairs*, vol. 57, no. 1, pp. 383–93.

International Institute for Strategic Studies (1986), *The Military Balance 1986–87* (London: IISS).

Janis, I. and Mann, L. (1977), *Decision-Making: A Psychological Analysis of Conflict, Choice and Commitment* (New York: Free Press).

Jenkins, R. (1983), 'Britain and Europe: ten years of Community membership', *International Affairs*, vol. 59, no. 2, pp. 147–53.

Jervis, R. (1976), *Perception and Misperception in International Politics* (Princeton, NJ: Princeton University Press).

Joll, J. (ed.) (1967), *Britain and Europe: Pitt to Churchill 1793–1940* (Oxford: Clarendon Press).

Jones, C. A. (1983), *The North–South Dialogue: A Brief History* (London: Pinter).

Jones, R. E. (1974), *The Changing Structure of British Foreign Policy* (London: Longman).

Jones, R. J. B. (1986), *Conflict and Control in the World Economy* (Brighton: Wheatsheaf).

Jones, R. B. J. and Willetts, P. (eds) (1984), *Interdependence on Trial* (London: Pinter).

Jowell, R. and Airey, C. (eds) (1984), *British Social Attitudes: The 1984 Report* (London: Longman).

Kaiser, K. and Morgan, R. (eds) (1971), *Britain and West Germany* (London: Oxford University Press).

Kaldor, M. (1982), *Baroque Arsenal* (London: Abacus).

Kaldor, M., Sharp, M. and Walker, W. (1986), 'Industrial competitiveness and Britain's defence', *Lloyds Bank Review*, no. 162 (October), pp. 31–49.

Katzenstein, P. J. (1978), 'Introduction: domestic and international forces and strategies of foreign economic policy', in P. J. Katzenstein (ed.), *Between Power and Plenty: Foreign Economic Policies of Advanced Industrial States* (Madison, Wis.: University of Wisconsin Press), pp. 3–22.

Keesing's Contemporary Archives (1963–64), Vol. 14, (Bristol: Keesing's Publications Ltd).

Kennedy, P. (1976), *The Rise and Fall of British Naval Mastery* (London: Macmillan).

Kennedy, P. (1981), *The Realities behind Diplomacy: Background Influences on British External Policy 1865–1980* (London: Fontana).

Keohane, R. O. (1979), 'US foreign economic policy toward other advanced capitalist states: the struggle to make others adjust', in K. Oye, R. Rothchild and R. J. Lieber (eds), *Eagle Entangled: US Foreign Policy in a Complex World* (New York: Longmans), pp. 91–122.

Keohane, R. O. (1984a), *After Hegemony* (Princeton, NJ: Princeton University Press).

Keohane, R. O. (1984b), 'The world political economy and the crisis of embedded liberalism', in J. H. Goldthorpe (ed.), *Order and Conflict in Contemporary Capitalism* (Oxford: Oxford University Press), pp. 15–38.

Keohane, R. O. (ed.) (1986), *NeoRealism and its Critics* (New York: Columbia University Press).

Keohane, R. O. and Nye, J. S. (eds) (1972), *Transnational Relations and World Politics* (Cambridge, Mass.: Harvard University Press).

Keohane, R. O. and Nye, J. S. (1977), *Power and Interdependence* (Boston, Mass.: Little, Brown).

Kirby, M. W. (1981), *The Decline of British Economic Power Since 1870* (London: Allen & Unwin).

Kirby, S. (1977), 'Britain, NATO and European Security', in J. Baylis (ed.), *British Defence Policy in a Changing World* (London: Croom Helm), pp. 95–119.

Kissinger, H. (1979), *White House Years* (Boston, Mass.: Little, Brown).

Kissinger, H. (1982), *Years of Upheaval* (Boston, Mass.: Little, Brown).

Kitzinger, U. (1973), *Diplomacy and Persuasion: How Britain Joined the Common Market* (London: Thames & Hudson).

Knorr, K. (1966), *On the Uses of Military Power in the Nuclear Age* (Princeton, NJ: Princeton University Press).

Knorr, K. (1973), *Power and Wealth: The Political Economy of International Power* (London: Macmillan).

Knorr, K. (1977), 'On the international uses of military power in the nuclear age', *Orbis*, vol. 21, no. 1, Spring, pp. 5–20.

Knorr, K. and Rosenau, J. N. (eds) (1969), *Contending Approaches to International Politics* (Princeton, NJ: Princeton University Press).

Knorr, K. and Trager, F. N. (eds) (1977), *Economic Issues and National Security* (Lawrence, Kans: University of Kansas Press).

Krasner, S. D. (1981), 'Transforming international regimes: what the Third World wants and why', *International Studies Quarterly*, vol, 25, no. 1, pp. 119–48.

Krasner, S. D. (1983a), 'Third World vulnerabilities and global negotiations', *Review of International Studies*, vol. 9, no. 4, pp. 235–50.

Krasner, S. D. (ed.) (1983b), *International Regimes* (London: Cornell University Press).

Labour Party (1981), *A Socialist Foreign Policy: A Labour Party Discussion Document* (London: Labour Party).

Leifer, M. (ed.) (1972), *Constraints and Adjustments in British Foreign Policy* (London: Allen & Unwin).

Leifer, M. (1983), 'Anglo-Malaysian alienation', *Round Table*, no. 285, January, pp. 56–63.

Leiber, R. J. (1984), 'British foreign policy: the limits of manoeuver', in R. C. Macridis (ed.), *Foreign Policy in World Politics*, 6th edn (Englewood Cliffs, NJ: Prentice-Hall), pp. 1–21.

Lindemann, B. (1976), 'Europe and the Third World: the Nine at the United Nations', *The World Today*, vol. 32, no. 7, pp. 260–9.

Lomax, D. F. and Gutmann, P. T. G. (1981), *The Euromarkets and International Financial Policies* (London: Macmillan).

Lovell, J. P. (1973), *Foreign Policy in Perspective: Strategy, Adaptation and Decision-Making* (New York: Harcourt Brace Jovanovitch).

Lukes, S. (ed.) (1986), *Power* (London: Oxford University Press).

Macmillan, H. (1971), *Riding the Storm 1956–59* (London: Macmillan).

Macmillan, H. (1972), *Pointing the Way 1959–61* (London: Macmillan).

Macmillan, H. (1973), *At the End of the Day 1961–63* (London: Macmillan).

Maier, C. (1984), 'Preconditions for corporatism', in J. Goldthorpe (ed.), *Order and Conflict in Contemporary Capitalism* (Oxford: Clarendon Press), pp. 39–59.

Mansbach, J., Ferguson, Y. and Lampert, D. (1976), *The Web of World Politics* (Englewood Cliffs, NJ: Prentice-Hall).

Mansbach, R., and Vasquez, J. (1981), *In Search of Theory* (New York: Columbia University Press).

Marwick, A. (1965), *The Deluge: British Society and the First World War* (London: Macmillan).

Marwick, A. (1982), *British Society Since 1945* (Harmondsworth: Penguin).

May, E. (1973), *'Lessons' of the Past: The Use and Misuse of History in American Foreign Policy* (New York: Oxford University Press).

McGeehan, R. (1985), 'European defence co-operation: a political perspective', *The World Today*, vol. 41, no. 6, pp. 116–19.

McKinlay, R. D. and Little, R. (1978), 'A foreign policy model of the allocation of British bilateral aid, 1960–70', *British Journal of Political Science*, vol. 8, no. 3, July, pp. 313–32.

McKinlay, R. D., and Little, R. (1986), *Global Problems and World Order* (London: Pinter).

McLean, S. (ed.) (1986), *How Nuclear Weapons Decisions Are Made* (London: Macmillan).

Medlicott, W. N. (1968), *British Foreign Policy Since Versailles 1919–63* (London: Methuen).

Miliband, R. (1973), *The State in Capitalist Society* (London: Quartet).

Minogue, K. (1978), 'Social contract and social breakdown', in P. Birnbaum, J. Lively and G. Parry (eds), *Democracy, Consensus and Social Contract* (London: Sage for the ECPR), pp. 127–52.

Mitchell, J. B. D. (1986), *International Cultural Relations* (London: Macmillan).

Moorhouse, G. (1977), *The Diplomats: The Foreign Office Today* (London: Cape).

Morgan, R. (1976), 'The foreign policies of Britain, France and West Germany', in J. N. Rosenau, K. W. Thompson and G. Boyd, (eds), *World Politics: An Introduction* (New York: Free Press), pp. 150–77.

Morgenthau, H. (1973), *Power Among Nations*, 5th edn (New York: Knopf).

Morse, E. L. (1970), 'The tranformation of foreign policies: modernisation, interdependence and externalisation', *World Politics*, vol. 22, no. 3, April, pp. 371–92.

Morse, E. L. (1976), *Modernisation and the Transformation of International Relations* (New York: Free Press).

Mortimer, R. A. (1984), *The Third World Coalition in International Politics*, 2nd edn (Boulder, Colo: Westview).

Murdock, C. (1977). 'Economic factors as objects of security: economics, security and vulnerability', in K. Knorr and F. N. Trager (eds), *Economic Issues and National Security* (Lawrence, Kans: University of Kansas Press), pp. 67–98.

Nairn, T. (1981), *The Break-Up of Britain* (London: Verso).

Newman, M. (1983), *Socialism and European Unity: The Dilemma of the Left in Britain and France* (London: Junction).

Northedge, F. S. (1970), 'Britain as a second-rate power', *International Affairs*, vol. 46, no. 1, pp. 37–47.

Northedge, F. S. (1974), *Descent From Power: British Foreign Policy 1945–73* (London: Allen & Unwin).

Northedge, F. S. and Wells, A. (1982), *Britain and Soviet Communism* (London: Macmillan).

Nunnerly, D. (1972), *President Kennedy and Britain* (London: Bodley Head).

Nye, J. S. (1974), 'Collective economic security', *International Affairs*, vol. 50, no. 4, pp. 584–98.

Nye, J. S. (1976), 'Independence and interdependence', *Foreign Policy*, no. 2 (Spring), pp. 130–61.

Ovendale, R. (ed.) (1984), *The Foreign Policy of the British Labour Governments 1945–51* (Leicester: Leicester University Press).

Panić, M. (1982), 'Monetarism in an open economy', *Lloyds Bank Review*, no. 145 (July), pp. 36–47.

Parsons, A. (1984–5), 'Vultures and philistines: British attitudes to culture and cultural diplomacy', *International Affairs*, vol. 61, no. 1, pp. 1–8.

Pierre, A. J. (ed.) (1986), *The Conventional Defence of Europe: New Technologies and New Strategies* (New York: Council on Foreign Relations).

Pinder, J. (1983), 'The "policies of the 1960s" and Britain's place in the world economy', *Policy Studies*, vol. 3, part 3, January, pp. 184–203.

Pollard, S. (1982), *The Wasting of the British Economy; British Economic Policy, 1945 to the Present* (London: Croom Helm).

Putnam, R. D. and Bayne, N. (1984), *Hanging Together: the Seven-Power Summits* (Aldershot: Gower).

Ramphal, S. (1984), 'Our and the world's advantage: the constructive Commonwealth', *International Affairs*, vol. 60, no. 3, pp. 371–91.

Ramsay, R. (1984), 'UNCTAD's failures: the rich get richer', *International Organization*, vol. 38, no. 2, pp. 387–97.

Reynolds, D. (1986), 'A "special relationship"? America, Britain and the international order since the Second World War', *International Affairs*, vol. 62, no. 1, pp. 1–20.

Richard, I. (1975), 'The United Nations and the new international economic order', *Millennium: Journal of International Studies*, vol. 4, no. 1, pp. 67–71.

Richards, P. (1967), *Parliament and Foreign Affairs* (London: Allen & Unwin).

Ricoeur, P. (1981), 'The model of the text: meaningful action considered as a text', in J. B. Thompson (ed.), *Paul Ricoeur: Hermeneutics and the Human Sciences: Essays on Language, Action and Interpretation* (Cambridge: Cambridge University Press), pp. 197–221.

Riddell, P. (1985), *The Thatcher Government*, rev. edn (Oxford: Blackwell).

Roberts, K. (1977), *The Fragmentary Class Structure* (London: Heinemann).

Rosenau, J. (1979), 'Muddling, meddling and modelling', *Millennium: Journal of International Studies*, vol. 8, no. 2, pp. 130–44.

Rothstein, R. L. (1972), 'On the costs of realism', *Political Science Quarterly*, vol. 87, no. 3, pp. 347–62.

Rothstein, R. L. (1980), 'The North–South dialogue: the political economy of immobility', *Journal of International Affairs*, vol. 34, no. 1, pp. 1–17.

Ruggie, J. G. (1986), 'Continuity and transformation in the world polity: towards a neorealist synthesis', in R. O. Keohane (ed.), *Neorealism and its critics* (New York: Columbia University Press), pp. 131–57.

Russett, B. (1985), 'The mysterious case of vanishing hegemony: or is Mark Twain really dead?', *International Organization*, vol. 39, no. 2, Spring, pp. 207–31.

Sargent, J. (1985), 'Corporatism and the European Community', in W. Grant (ed.), *The Political Economy of Corporatism* (London: Sage), pp. 229–54.

Schattschneider, E. (1960), *Semi-Sovereign People* (New York: Holt, Reinhart & Winston).

Schott, K. (1984), 'Investment, order and conflict in a simple dynamic model of capitalism', in J. Goldthorpe (ed.), *Order and Conflict in Contemporary Capitalism* (Oxford: Clarendon Press), pp. 81–97.

Seaborg, G. T. (1981), *Kennedy, Khruschev and the Test Ban* (Berkeley, Calif.: University of California Press).

Shaw, M. (ed.) (1984), *War, State and Society* (London: Macmillan).

Shlaim, A. (1978), *Britain and the Origins of European Unity 1945–51* (Reading: Reading University Press).

Shlaim, A. (1983–4), 'Britain, the Berlin blockade and the cold war', *International Affairs*, vol. 60, no.1, pp. 1–14.

Shlaim, A., Jones, P. and Sainsbury, K. (1977), *British Foreign Secretaries Since 1945* (Newton Abbot: David & Charles).

Shonfield, A. (1970), 'The Duncan Report and its critics', *International Affairs*, vol. 46, no. 2, pp. 247–68.

Smith, B. (1976), *Policy-Making in British Government: An Analysis of Power and Rationality* (London: Martin Robertson).

Smith, D. (1980), *The Defence of the Realm* (London: Croom Helm).

Smith, D. (1984), 'The political economy of British defence policy', in D. Shaw (ed.), *War, State and Society*, (London: Macmillan), pp. 195–216.

Smith, M., Little, R., and Shackleton, M. (eds) (1981), *Perspectives on World Politics* (London: Croom Helm).

Smith, S. (1982), 'Berridge on international relations', *Teaching Politics*, vol. 11, no. 1, pp. 23–9.

Smith, S. (1983), 'Foreign policy analysis: British and American orientations and methodologies', *Political Studies*, vol. 31, no. 4, December 1983, pp. 556–65.

Smith, S. (1984), 'Foreign policy analysis and interdependence', in R. J. B. Jones and P. Willetts (eds), *Interdependence on Trial* (London: Pinter), pp. 64–82.

Smith, S. (1986), 'Reasons of state', in D. Held and C. Pollitt (eds), *New Forms of Democracy* (London: Sage), pp. 192–217.

Sprout, H. and Sprout, M. (1968), 'The dilemma of rising demands and insufficient resources', *World Politics*, vol. 20, no. 4 (July), pp. 660–93.

Statler, J. (1979), 'British foreign policy to 1985 VIII: the European monetary system from conception to birth', *International Affairs*, vol. 55, no. 2, pp. 206–24.

Steiner, Z, (1969), *The Foreign Office and Foreign Policy 1898–1914* (Cambridge: Cambridge University Press).

Steinbruner, J. (1974), *The Cybernetic Theory of Decision: New Dimensions of Political Analysis* (Princeton, NJ: Princeton University Press).

Stockholm International Peace Research Institute (1985), *World Armaments and Disarmament Yearbook 1985* (London: Taylor & Francis).

Stopford, J. and Turner, L. (1985), *Britain and the Multinationals* (Chichester: Wiley).

Strange, S. (1971), *Sterling and British Policy* (London: Oxford University Press).

Strange, S. (1974), *The Financial Factor and the Balance of Power*, Open University, Course Unit D332, Block 3, parts 1–5.

Strange, S. (1981), 'Reactions to Brandt: popular acclaim and academic attack', *International Studies Quarterly*, vol. 25, no. 2, pp. 328–42.

Strange, S. (1986), *Casino Capitalism* (Oxford: Oxford University Press).

Sutton, M. and Hewitt, A. (1983), 'Taking stock: three years of Conservative aid policy', *ODI Review*, no. 1, pp. 20–37.

Taylor, P. (1982), 'The European Communities as an actor in international society', *Journal of European Integration*, vol. 6, no. 1, pp. 7–41.

Taylor, P. (1984), 'The Commonwealth in the 1980s: challenges and opportunities', in A. J. R. Groom and P. Taylor (eds), *The Commonwealth in the 1980s* (London: Macmillan), pp. 305–23.

Taylor, T. (1982), *Defence Technology and International Integration* (London: Pinter).

Taylor, T. (1984), *European Defence Co-operation* (London: RIIA).

Taylor, T. (1987), 'British attitudes to alternative patterns of institutional development for European security development', in K. Kaiser and J. Roper (eds), *British-German Defence Co-operation: European Partners within the Alliance* (London: Jane's), forthcoming.

Thompson, E. P. (1982), 'Deterrence and addiction', in F. Barnaby and G. Thomas (eds), *The Nuclear Arms Race: Control or Catastrophe?* (London: Pinter), pp. 49–72.

Thorne, C. (1972), *The limits of Foreign Power* (London: Hamilton).

Thorne, C. (1978), *Allies of a Kind* (London: Hamilton).

Tolstoy, N. (1986), *The Minister and the Massacre* (London: Century Hutchinson).

Townsend, P. (1979), *Poverty in the United Kingdom* (Harmondsworth: Penguin).

Treasury and Civil Service Committee (1983), *Second Special Report* (London: HMSO).

Ullman, R. H. (1983), 'Redefining security', *International Security*, vol. 8, no. 1, pp. 129–53.

Urban, G. R. (ed.) (1976), *Detente* (London: Temple Smith).

Vasquez, J. (1979), 'Colouring it Morgenthau: new evidence for an old thesis on quantitative international politics', *British Journal of International Studies*, vol. 5, no. 3, pp. 210–28.

Verrier, A. (1983), *Through the Looking Glass: British Foreign Policy in an Age of Illusions* (London: Cape).

Vital, D. (1968), *The Making of British Foreign Policy* (London: Allen & Unwin).

Vogler, J. (1984), 'Interdependence, power and the world administrative radio conference', in R. J. B. Jones and P. Willetts (eds), *Interdependence on Trial* (London: Pinter), pp. 200–25.

Wallace, H. (1986), 'The British presidency of the EC Council of Ministers: the opportunity to persuade', *International Affairs*, vol. 62, no. 4, pp. 583–99.

Wallace, W. (1974), 'The management of foreign economic policy in Britain', *International Affairs*, vol. 50, no. 2, pp. 251–67.

Wallace, W. (1976), *The Foreign Policy Process in Britain* (London: Allen & Unwin for the RIIA).

Wallace, W. (1978a), 'Old states and new circumstances: the international predicament of Britain, France and Germany', in W. Wallace and W. Paterson (eds), *Foreign Policy-Making in Western Europe: A Comparative Approach* (Farnborough: Saxon House), pp. 31–55.

Wallace, W. (1978b), 'After Berrill: Whitehall and the management of British diplomacy', *International Affairs*, vol. 54, no. 2, pp. 220–39.

Wallace, W. (1983), 'Political co-operation: integration through intergovernmentalism' in H. Wallace, W. Wallace and C. Webb (eds), *Policy-Making in the European Communities*, 2nd edn (London: Wiley), pp. 373–402.

Wallace, W. (1984), *Britain's Bilateral Links within Western Europe* (London: Routledge & Kegan Paul).

Wallace, W. (1986a), 'Foreign policy: the management of distinctive interests', in R. Morgan and C. Bray (eds), *Partners and Rivals in Western Europe: Britain, France and Germany* (London: Gower), pp. 205–23.

Wallace, W. (1986b), 'What price independence? Sovereignty and interdependence in British politics', *International Affairs*, vol. 62, no. 3, pp. 367–89.

Wallace, W. (1987), 'Public expenditure: the international dimension', in M. S. Levitt (ed.), *New Priorities in Public Spending*, Joint Studies in Public Policy, no. 13 (London; National Institute for Economic and Social Research), forthcoming.

Waltz, K. (1967), *Foreign Policy and Democratic Politics: The British and American Experience* (Boston, Mass.: Little, Brown).

Waltz, K. (1979), *Theory of International Politics* (Cambridge, Mass.: Addison-Wesley).

Ward, B. (1979), *The Ideal World of Economics* (New York: Basic Books).

Warnke, G. (1985), 'Hermeneutics and the social sciences: a Godamerian critique of Rorty'. *Inquiry*, vol. 28, no. 3, pp. 339–57.

Watt, D. C. (1965), *Personalities and Policies* (London: Longmans).

Weintraub, S. (1977), 'How the UN votes on economic issues', *International Affairs*, vol. 53, no. 2, pp. 649–76.

Weiss, T. G. (1983), 'The UN conference on the least developed countries: the relevance of conference diplomacy in Paris for international negotiation', *International Affairs*, vol. 59, no. 4, pp. 649–76.

White, B. P. (1977), 'The study of British foreign policy: a reply to Professor Barber', *British Journal of International Studies*, vol. 3, no. 3, pp. 340–8.

White, B. P. (1987), 'Britain and the rise of détente', in R. Crockatt and S. Smith (eds), *The Cold War Past and Present* (London: Allen & Unwin), pp. 91–109.

Wiener, M. J. (1981), *English Culture and the Decline of the Industrial Spirit 1850–1980* (London: Cambridge University Press).

Williams, P. (1986), 'Britain, detente and the Conference on Security and Co-operation in Europe', in K. Dyson (ed.), *European Detente* (London: Pinter), pp. 221–37.

Williamson, S. (1969), *The Politics of Grand Strategy* (Cambridge, Mass.: Harvard University Press).

Wilson, H. (1971), *The Labour Government 1964–70* (London: Weidenfeld & Nicolson/Michael Joseph).

Wilson, H. (1976), *The Governance of Britain* (London: Weidenfeld & Nicolson/Michael Joseph).

Wolfers, A. (1962), *Discord and Collaboration* (London: Johns Hopkins University Press).

Woolcock, S., Hart, J. and Van Der Veu, H. (1985), *Interdependence in the Post-Multilateral Era: Trends in US-European Trade Relations* (Harvard, Mass.: Center for International Affairs and University Press of America).

Wright, M. (1964), *Disarm and Verify* (New York: Praeger).

Wyllie, J. (1984), *Arms and British Influence* (London: Croom Helm).

Young, J. W. (1984), *Britain, France and the Unity of Europe* (Leicester: Leicester University Press).

Young, O. R. (1972), 'The actors in world politics', in J. N. Rosenau, V. Davis and M. East (eds), *The Analysis of International Politics* (New York: Free Press), pp. 125–44.

Younger, K. (1964), *Changing Perspectives in British Foreign Policy* (London: Oxford University Press).

Index